AF510167

Google Analytics Alternatives

Jason Packer

Google Analytics Alternatives
Copyright © 2026 Jason Packer. All rights reserved.

Published by Quantable, LLC
Edition 2.0 (2026-02-01)
Errata and updates available at: https://gaalternatives.guide/changelog

If you'd like to suggest a correction or clarification, please email your suggestion to jason@quantable.com.

Editors: Liz Wheeler (second edition), Rachel Andrea Go (first edition)
Cover art based upon work by Vince Smith (https://www.instagram.com/vincesmithart)

All copyrights, trademarks, brands, names, symbols, logos, and designs used within this book are the property of their respective owners. They are used for identification and reference purposes, and do not imply any endorsement of this book. All product evaluations represent the personal opinions of the author, and were not vendor compensated in any way.

While the author has made a good faith effort to ensure information in this book is accurate, he disclaims all responsibility for damages resulting from it. Information regarding legal compliance should not be acted upon without first seeking professional legal advice.

No part of this publication may be reproduced without the prior written permission of the author.

ISBN: 979-8-9871245-4-3

CONTENTS

Part One

Background

Chapter 1 - Introduction

It's always an interesting time to work in analytics. As web and digital analytics have matured and attracted more attention over the last decade, there have also been significant technological and regulatory changes.

Even after decades of development, analytics still feels like a new field, and remains ever-changing, evidenced by the lack of a consistently used name or definition within the field. What kind of analytics is it? Web? Digital? Product? Mobile app? I think of web analytics as an accidental industry, one that began as a generally ignored offshoot of IT that's grown to be an important part of marketing, product, and development.

If the first age of web analytics was the era of log file processing, which started in the 1990s, the advent of client-side JavaScript and Google Analytics (GA) in the 2000s marked a second era.

Google Analytics has been the predominant analytics tool since its launch in 2005 and is so entrenched that it's practically synonymous with the term "web analytics." Google has also helped move the field from its roots in IT towards marketing, integrating GA into its larger advertising technology stack and focusing functionality on marketing analytics.

On July 1, 2024, this second era came to an end, as Google Analytics Universal Analytics (UA) was shut down. This end to 19 years of contiguous data upset many people and brought into question Google's long-standing dominance in the field.

The table below lays out the three main eras of analytics, the predominant tools, and the technologies they employed.

Era	Predominant Tools	Technologies
1st:1995–2004	Webtrends, Analog, Webalizer, Omniture	Logfile analysis, hit counters
2nd:2005–2022	Google Analytics	JavaScript tags, third-party web data collection
3rd:2023–	Google Analytics 4 and ???	Hybrid client + server, first-party data, multi-platform data collection

In this guide, we'll look at some of the most popular alternatives to Google Analytics and create a decision-making framework to select a new solution. Instead of declaring a single best solution, it'll inform you of the available options and how to choose between them.

Even though this is a guide to GA alternatives, we will approach GA both as a baseline for comparison and as a potential solution itself. You may find Google Analytics 4 (GA4) is the right solution for you. My goal is to help you make that choice in an informed way.

I come at analytics from a technical perspective, so this guide will be oriented towards technical details more than business concerns.

You also won't find any big lists of feature comparisons. Instead, I look at the point of view that each tool comes from and its most appropriate use cases.

Giant feature comparison matrices are helpful, but they can also be misleading and cause choice paralysis. Just because a feature is available doesn't guarantee it'll be able to solve the particular issue you have. The vendor's idea of what checks that feature box may not align with how you envision that feature. Additionally, those comparison lists become outdated very quickly, with features and pricing changing even from week to week.

We'll go through a series of Google Analytics alternatives, review their pros and cons, and compare them to each other. I'll do my best to highlight features that I think are most representative, but we will not go deep into implementation details. While I have used all of these tools with real website data, I do not profess to be an expert in all of them. I don't think it is actually possible to be an expert on 15 different tools.

Despite the title of this book, I find the term "Google Analytics alternatives" to be problematic. It enshrines GA as the default choice and suggests that other options should be considered only *after* GA has been rejected. Yet the long and continued dominance of GA in the field also makes this term very practical.

Tool choice is only a small part of a successful analytics practice. Poor tool choice can make finding success difficult, but even an excellent choice is only a first step towards success.

No solution will meet your needs perfectly. It's all about finding the best fit and *then* putting in the time to learn, customize, and implement the tool. Much too commonly, companies abandon Tool A for Tool B because they think the former isn't right for them, but in reality, they simply failed to use it well.

The background context we will go over in Part One of this guide is not only to help with tool selection, but to provide a better understanding of the paradigm each tool works within. It's my belief that this deeper understanding will also help you to better utilize whichever tool you pick.

Chapter 2 - The Product Space

In this chapter, we'll cover what Google Analytics is, and our next step will be to discover the GA alternatives we want to evaluate. We're entering an age where no single tool will dominate the market, so it's important to identify all the possibilities, rather than blindly relying on one market leader.

This is a difficult task, because the analytics space is overflowing with tools all vying for your attention and a spot in your tag manager. GA is still by far the most popular solution, but there are a multitude of other options—so many, it's impossible for me to evaluate them all (sorry to disappoint if you were hoping for a 1,000-page book).

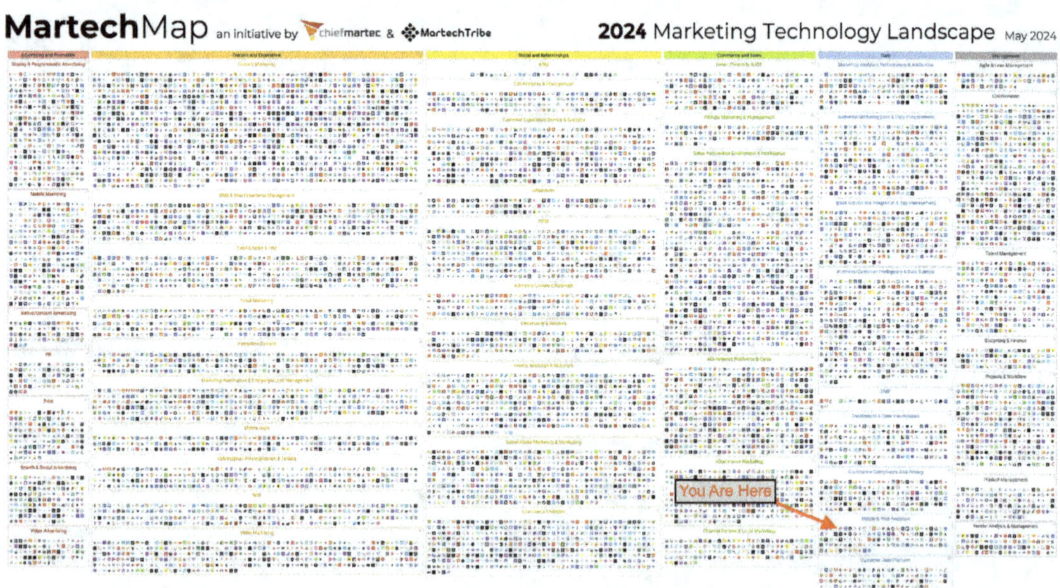

visit martechmap.com to search, sort & filter

The famous chiefmartec industry map (available at https://martechmap.com) now includes over 15,000 marketing technology (martech) tools. Once you find your electron microscope to read it, you'll see it lists 124 vendors in the "Mobile & Web Analytics" category (as of November 2025), but there are certainly more than that! Many popular but lesser-known options (Simple Analytics, Umami, Wide Angle

Analytics) are not included in the map at all. Additionally, many tools are in unexpected categories. For example, PostHog (reviewed later in this book) is listed under "Product Management" for some reason.

We're starting with well over 124 possible solutions. But with seemingly every article and product review site listing a different group of purported alternatives, how do we proceed?

I imagine the first thing many people would do is do a Google search for "Google Analytics Alternatives," implicitly trusting Google to give us an unbiased opinion on how to replace its own product. As is typical with this type of search, there are some good results, along with plenty of junk written solely for SEO. Tragically, the first edition of this book is only ranked 44th.

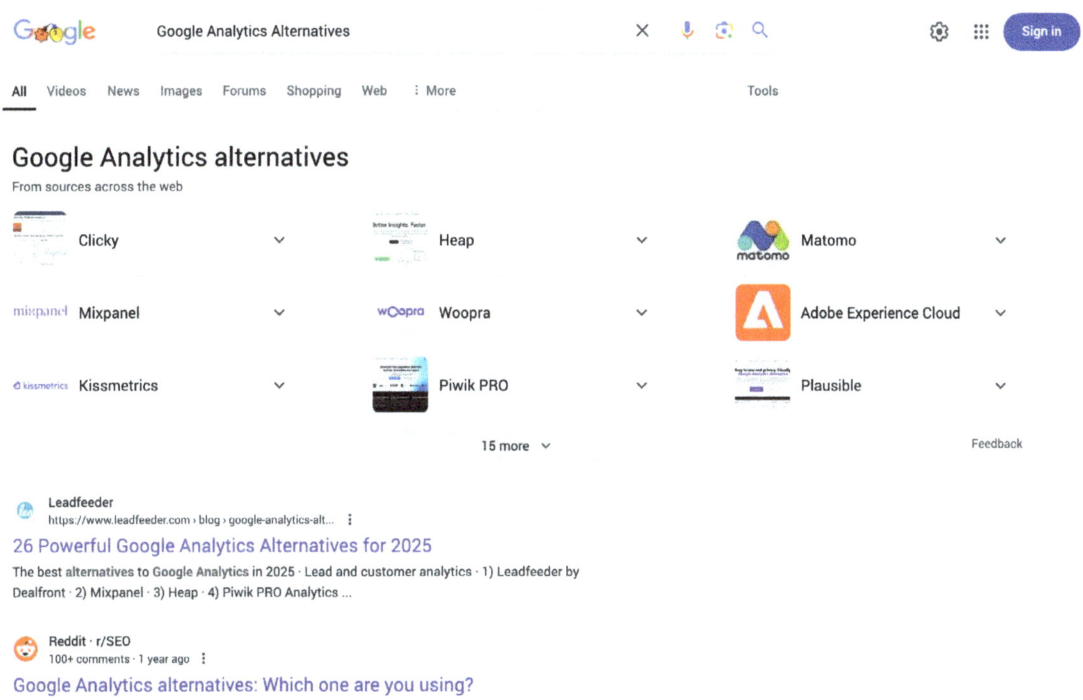

You'll see a number of vendors (e.g., Semrush, HubSpot, and Leadfeeder) with their own lists that just happen to feature their products at number one. Hat tip to their content teams, but those tools are clearly not GA alternatives. Some lists also include tools in the same overall space but not web analytics tools (e.g., session capturing and heatmaps, SEO tools, etc.).

This being 2026, maybe we should skip Google altogether and ask ChatGPT instead? Its listed alternatives are a bit better than the Google Search results, but still not great.

ChatGPT lists some tools that I do not consider direct GA replacements (Kissmetrics), as well as some that are very niche or that I would not recommend.

> Can you give me a list of good Google Analytics alternatives? Just a list of names please.

1. Matomo
2. Piwik PRO
3. Mixpanel
4. Plausible Analytics
5. Heap
6. Adobe Analytics
7. Fathom Analytics
8. Amplitude
9. Snowplow Analytics
10. Open Web Analytics (OWA)
11. Clicky
12. Simple Analytics
13. Kissmetrics
14. Countly
15. Woopra

The ChatGPT list has quite a bit of overlap (two-thirds) with the tools in this guide. That turns out to not be coincidental, as when doing more detailed research on GA alternatives, it cites this book as a source.

Before we identify possible alternatives to GA, we need to define what GA actually is and the space it occupies. GA has a ton of features that allow it to be compared to a number of different types of tools. However, just because UA could do rudimentary heatmapping doesn't mean we should consider heatmapping tools like Clarity or Hotjar as GA alternatives. Similarly, GA can monitor site speed via real user monitoring (RUM), but that doesn't make web performance tools like SpeedCurve or New Relic GA alternatives.

By our definition, an "alternative" is something that can replace a significant amount of the GA core functionality and could be used to fully replace GA for many different websites. That might trim a few from our Google and ChatGPT results, but that constraint alone doesn't cut nearly enough from our list of 120+. To narrow it down further, let's try to analyze what products compete with GA within the marketplace.

Who are these competitors? When measured in terms of overall installation base, nobody can rival GA. Nonetheless, looking at alternatives, sorted by popularity, is an effective way to filter down our options.

Technology research tool BuiltWith (https://builtwith.com) tracks the tech stacks on millions of websites via crawling and reports on how many of those sites use which tool. From this data, we can see that GA is indeed by far the most popular analytics tool. It's not even close.

We will reference these numbers from BuiltWith (with permission) throughout this guide, but readers should keep in mind that they're just a best guess from a third-party service.

I'm limiting my search to the top 1M sites to focus on sites that are more likely to actively manage their analytics and actually use the products in question.

Other services, such as Wappalyzer, W3Techs, and Datanyze, generally agree with BuiltWith, but there is quite a bit of variance—especially with the less common tools. All the major services agree that GA is far and away the most widely deployed, but the order of the rest of the field varies. You can see a couple of examples of their different rankings in the table below.

Tool Rank Per Service

	BuiltWith	Wappalzyer	W3Techs	Datanyze
Matomo	#4	#5	#3	#4
Adobe	#10	#7	#10	#6

Tool detection is tricky. As tools have become more adept at evading ad blockers and browser protections like Safari Intelligent Tracking Prevention (ITP), they have become harder to detect in general. If a tool allows customization that will evade detection by an ad blocker (such as changing the script names or running server-side), then it will also likely evade detection by these third-party monitoring tools. Tools that have changed names over time also cause issues for detection, such as AT Internet to Piano Analytics, or Omniture to Adobe Analytics.

I've put less focus on these installation numbers than I did in the first edition of this book. I feel the overall quality of these numbers has decreased to a point where they are useful only as a very broad snapshot of the marketplace. In particular, trying to use the numbers over time for trending has become very unreliable. They remain helpful to get us a list of what the top tools in general are, and that's what we're using them for here.

In evaluating alternatives, I drew a line in terms of popularity at 0.1% out of the top one million sites. This means we'll skip over alternatives with fewer than roughly 1,000 deployments in that dataset. This excludes some relatively well-known products, like Simple Analytics (https://www.simpleanalytics.com), Woopra (https://www.-woopra.com), Gauges (https://get.gaug.es), etc.

Our list of evaluated tools has also changed a bit from the first edition. TWIPLA (https://www.twipla.com; formerly known as Visitor Analytics) now fails to meet the installation-level requirements. I've also removed Snowplow and Chartbeat, the former since it is more of a general-purpose data collection platform than a web analytics tool, and the latter because it is targeted to the niche market of news sites.

Replacing those three, to keep our total number of tools at fifteen, are the following: Adobe Analytics, Piano, and Umami. Adobe and Piano were both tools I wanted to review in the first edition, but I was unable to. Both of those tools' install bases appear to be significantly under-represented in the BuiltWith numbers. Umami is an open source, simplified web analytics tool similar to Plausible and Fathom.

I'm also focused on tools in the Western market, and as such, I exclude the following popular tools: Yandex Metrica (Russian), Baidu Analytics (Chinese), and Naver Analytics (Korean).

websites. That might trim a few from our Google and ChatGPT results, but that constraint alone doesn't cut nearly enough from our list of 120+. To narrow it down further, let's try to analyze what products compete with GA within the marketplace.

Who are these competitors? When measured in terms of overall installation base, nobody can rival GA. Nonetheless, looking at alternatives, sorted by popularity, is an effective way to filter down our options.

Technology research tool BuiltWith (https://builtwith.com) tracks the tech stacks on millions of websites via crawling and reports on how many of those sites use which tool. From this data, we can see that GA is indeed by far the most popular analytics tool. It's not even close.

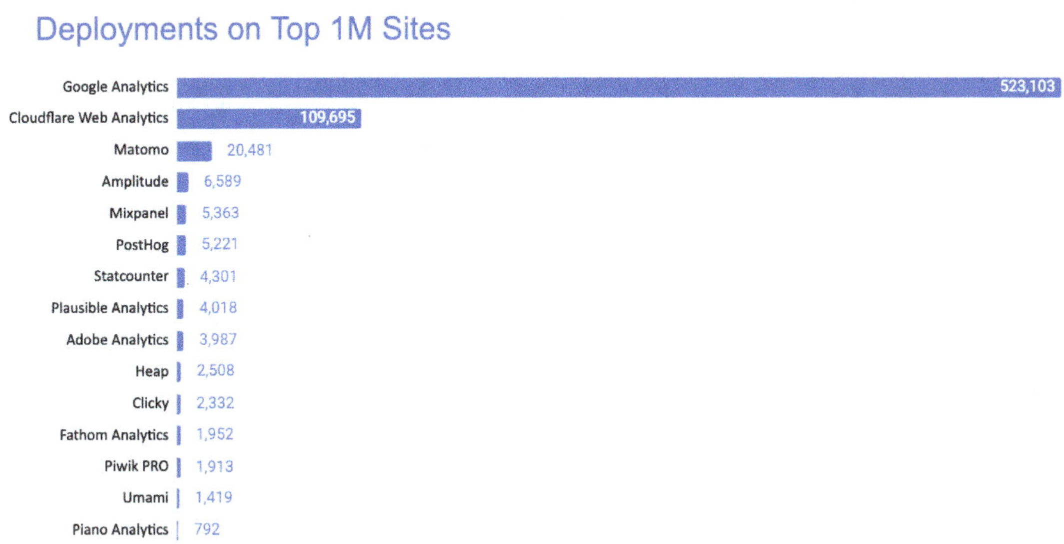

We will reference these numbers from BuiltWith (with permission) throughout this guide, but readers should keep in mind that they're just a best guess from a third-party service.

I'm limiting my search to the top 1M sites to focus on sites that are more likely to actively manage their analytics and actually use the products in question.

Other services, such as Wappalyzer, W3Techs, and Datanyze, generally agree with BuiltWith, but there is quite a bit of variance—especially with the less common tools. All the major services agree that GA is far and away the most widely deployed, but the order of the rest of the field varies. You can see a couple of examples of their different rankings in the table below.

Tool Rank Per Service

	BuiltWith	Wappalzyer	W3Techs	Datanyze
Matomo	#4	#5	#3	#4
Adobe	#10	#7	#10	#6

Tool detection is tricky. As tools have become more adept at evading ad blockers and browser protections like Safari Intelligent Tracking Prevention (ITP), they have become harder to detect in general. If a tool allows customization that will evade detection by an ad blocker (such as changing the script names or running server-side), then it will also likely evade detection by these third-party monitoring tools. Tools that have changed names over time also cause issues for detection, such as AT Internet to Piano Analytics, or Omniture to Adobe Analytics.

I've put less focus on these installation numbers than I did in the first edition of this book. I feel the overall quality of these numbers has decreased to a point where they are useful only as a very broad snapshot of the marketplace. In particular, trying to use the numbers over time for trending has become very unreliable. They remain helpful to get us a list of what the top tools in general are, and that's what we're using them for here.

In evaluating alternatives, I drew a line in terms of popularity at 0.1% out of the top one million sites. This means we'll skip over alternatives with fewer than roughly 1,000 deployments in that dataset. This excludes some relatively well-known products, like Simple Analytics (https://www.simpleanalytics.com), Woopra (https://www.-woopra.com), Gauges (https://get.gaug.es), etc.

Our list of evaluated tools has also changed a bit from the first edition. TWIPLA (https://www.twipla.com; formerly known as Visitor Analytics) now fails to meet the installation-level requirements. I've also removed Snowplow and Chartbeat, the former since it is more of a general-purpose data collection platform than a web analytics tool, and the latter because it is targeted to the niche market of news sites.

Replacing those three, to keep our total number of tools at fifteen, are the following: Adobe Analytics, Piano, and Umami. Adobe and Piano were both tools I wanted to review in the first edition, but I was unable to. Both of those tools' install bases appear to be significantly under-represented in the BuiltWith numbers. Umami is an open source, simplified web analytics tool similar to Plausible and Fathom.

I'm also focused on tools in the Western market, and as such, I exclude the following popular tools: Yandex Metrica (Russian), Baidu Analytics (Chinese), and Naver Analytics (Korean).

Is your perfect alternative out there but not yet popular enough to be on our list? It's possible, but we are likely covering a tool that is similar—and there are downsides to picking something without a significant user base, as we'll talk about later.

If you're looking at these installation numbers and still thinking they seem off, consider the following:

1) Our dataset is just the top one million sites. From GA's install numbers, that sample of the top 1M sites accounts for a small subset (~2%) of all GA installations.

2) Just because a crawl detects a tag on the page doesn't mean the site actively uses the tool. BuiltWith detects 2.9M sites that still run the long-defunct `ga.js` version of Google Analytics. That tag was replaced by `analytics.js` 12+ years ago and has zero compatibility with GA4. If a site hasn't updated its GA tag in 12 years and isn't collecting data in GA4, can it really be said to be a GA user? Unfortunately, in the BuiltWith numbers, it would still be counted in the GA column.

3) False negatives are more likely than false positives. When BuiltWith scans a site, it's unlikely to think a tool is there when it's not. However, the scan can easily miss cases of unusual implementations, sites that block their crawlers with anti-bot protections, server-side, etc. Meaning our alternatives likely have more installations than BuiltWith can detect. For example, Statcounter publicly claims that 1.5 million sites use its tool, but BuiltWith is only aware of around 270,000 sites actively using it.

I'm not exactly divulging industry secrets by saying GA is ubiquitous, but it may be surprising the extent to which GA is *so* far ahead of its competitors—and it remains so in nearly all market segments, even after the UA sunset. GA is installed on two times as many websites as all the other listed GA alternatives *combined*.

But the number of installations isn't everything. Far from it.

In the digital analytics community, tools like Adobe Analytics, Matomo, Amplitude, etc., are considered direct competitors of GA. For many years, GA vs. Adobe was thought of as the Coke vs. Pepsi of the analytics world (at least in the US), yet GA is installed on something like 70 times the total number of sites as Adobe Analytics. Or take Cloudflare Web Analytics, which is #2 in popularity on our list, yet is hardly ever mentioned, and is frequently mistaken for other analytics products within the Cloudflare suite. Matomo is installed on three times as many sites as Amplitude, yet Amplitude has far higher revenue. Matomo is estimated in the $1–10M yearly revenue range (per Crunchbase), whereas Amplitude is a public company that reported more than $340M annual recurring revenue in Q3 2025 (https://investors.amplitude.com/news-releases/news-release-details/amplitude-announces-third-quarter-2025-financial-results). Revenue isn't everything either, but it's safe to say that most businesses would choose revenue over install base if given the choice.

Free users are a major driver of these counts, and we're comparing paid and free versions together. Scanning a website externally can't reliably determine if it runs paid GA360 or free GA, so a true apples-to-apples comparison of paid installations only is impossible. Cloudflare Web Analytics is always free, and it's likely that many of the people who have it installed don't even realize they do.

Mindshare is even harder to measure, though I've made an attempt to do so by measuring online discussion volume. For this book, I built a dataset of about 450,000 analytics-related comments on Reddit and Y Combinator's Hacker News. I trimmed that down to a set of 2,300 that expressed opinions about GA alternatives. We'll talk about what those comments actually said in Chapter 33 - Crowd-Sourced Opinions, but just looking at comment volume may be helpful to measure what tools are being discussed in the tech community.

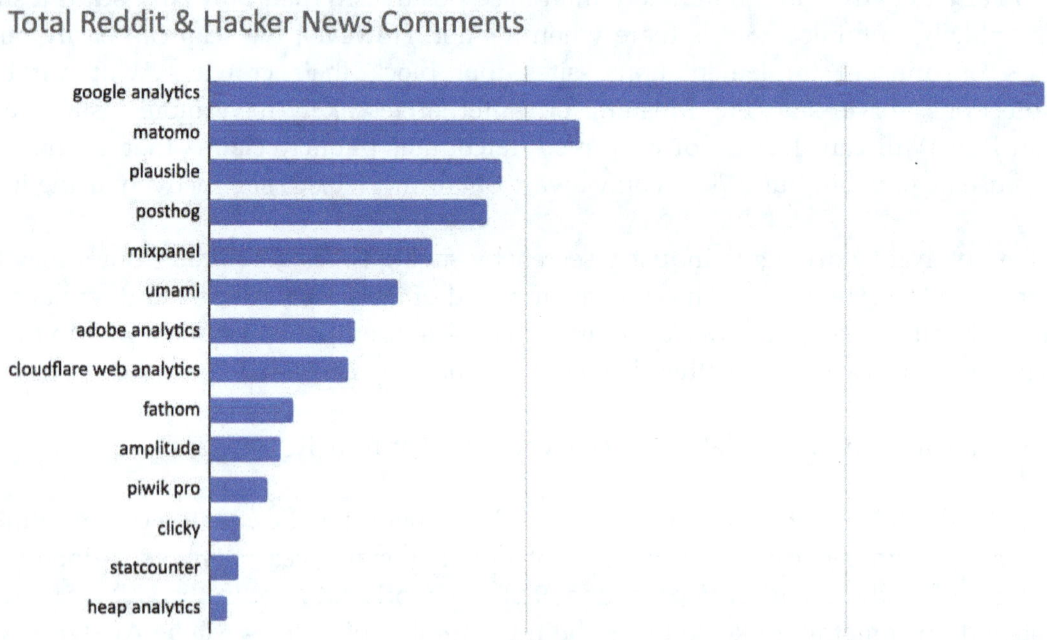

Again, GA is the most talked about by a lot, but many other tools are also being discussed. However, it's important to remember the source of this corpus. Reddit and Hacker News are both populated with tech types and developers, more than analysts. Hacker News, especially, is focused on startups and software engineering, so it's not surprising to see open source solutions near the top. This would be different if we looked at something like the wonderful Measure Slack (https://www.measure.chat), which is focused on digital marketing analytics. In that Slack, Umami has been mentioned in only four threads (twice by me)—whereas Adobe Analytics has its own channel with about 80k messages.

No matter how we measure it, GA will be at the top of any popularity list by a huge margin. It's used by sites from the biggest on the internet to your neighbor's dog's blog. The point of this book is to convince you that there's a rich variety of tools out there beyond just GA. Despite its status as the default analytics tool, it may very well not be the best fit for your use case.

We'll evaluate all of these tools individually in the second part of this guide, but first, we'll dig into the technical details of the questions we might consider as part of our evaluation process. Creating a framework that helps us understand the tools, technology, and market in general is going to help us make a much more informed decision.

Chapter 3 - The Google Ecosystem

Before we start talking about alternatives, let's define what we might be leaving behind. While we will evaluate GA4 itself as a product later in the book, we'll first take a look at how Google Analytics fits into the industry ecosystem as a whole.

Universal Analytics (UA)

The previous version of Google Analytics, known as Universal Analytics, helped define and then shape the field for almost 20 years before its sunset in 2023. In many scenarios, the term "analytics" by itself is used to mean Google Analytics. Peruse a digital marketing chat group or subreddit, and you will see users ask questions about "my analytics" without ever explaining that they are using GA. This is due to the long dominance and ubiquity of UA.

In addition to this dominance, UA also served as the entry point into analytics for many practitioners, creating a legacy that will be with the industry for a long time. UA's approach to analytics influenced how many people think of analytics in general. Universal Analytics was a multifaceted, extensible product that could be tweaked to perform a wide range of tracking and reporting functions. By no means was it a perfect product, but its industry impact was huge. Some of the alternatives we look at in this book follow UA's approach more closely than others, but all have been influenced by UA.

Between UA's legacy and the lack of enthusiasm for GA4, there can be a tendency to look back at UA with rose-colored glasses. At the time of UA's sunset in 2023, it was clear the field had moved on, and UA had not kept up. Even before UA became a moribund legacy product, it was a tool that went both wide and deep, and not always in a good way.

Google Analytics

When we think about our analytics tooling, we need to take into account all of its potential users and data, not just our personal use cases and preferences.

Let's consider a couple of different common use cases for GA:

Case one: You're a small business owner who just launched a WordPress site. Your developers set up GA4 and send you an invite with no further instructions. You log in and are greeted by a wide variety of standard reports, the blank slate that is the Explore section, and no idea where to start, what's useful, or how anything works. Simply finding the data you are looking for can be an insurmountable challenge.

Case two: You're a product manager for a large ecommerce site with millions of pageviews per month. You ask your analytics team to utilize GA to tell you about the performance of certain product bundles, segmented by campaign source and country. You're running into sampling issues and frustrations with GA data imports for calculating the marketing ROI. In this case, you're outgrowing the same product that was much too complex for the small business owner.

These two cases both use the same version of the same product (free GA), despite their different requirements and pain points. The large ecommerce site likely has the budget for an enterprise-level analytics tool, but isn't paying for one because they think they can mostly get what they need from free GA. This is how we ended up with a tool that isn't ideal for either use case. It's also market-distorting, causing users to think something as powerful as GA *should* be free.

Analytics tooling shouldn't be a one-size-fits-all scenario, nor should we pick and deploy a tool before we know what we want it to do. We also shouldn't expect it to be free at levels beyond the most basic installations.

Considering the Google Ecosystem

Looking beyond GA can feel risky because of how deeply embedded the Google ecosystem is within so many organizations. Not only are many people already familiar with GA itself, but it's integrated into many popular tools—those provided by both Google and others. This is the biggest competitive advantage of GA, and something alternatives can't fully replicate.

GA itself is part of the Google Marketing Platform (GMP). This means tight integration with Looker Studio, Google Tag Manager (GTM), and the Google Ads services (Campaign Manager, Search Ads, Display & Video).

Additionally, GA can link to Google tools outside the GMP: Google Ads, Google Ad Manager, Search Console, AdSense, Google Play, Merchant Center, and BigQuery. In particular, the BigQuery integration has become crucial to advanced GA4 usage. It's probable that more than one of these is critical to your business, which is a huge advantage for Google.

You're not required to use different parts of the platform together, but there are many synergistic benefits if you do.

Beyond the ease of integration, there are some data connections, like Google Ads to your GA4, that can't be fully replicated outside of the Google environment.

One point of integration that *doesn't* exist is between GA and Google Search results rankings. In other words, *there is no SEO benefit from running GA.* There's long been a rumor that Google uses things like the bounce rate from your GA to inform Google rankings, but Google has denied this many times. Here's a tweet from Google's Search Advocate John Mueller, making this very clear:

There's additional confirmation for this assertion, as when thousands of leaked Google Search API documents were leaked in 2024, and there was no reference to GA data being used for rankings (https://sparktoro.com/blog/an-anonymous-source-shared-thousands-of-leaked-google-search-api-documents-with-me-everyone-in-seo-should-see-them/).

Another less obvious integration is the data integration with Google Signals and DoubleClick, which enables demographic reporting features within GA. This type of demographic information is largely unavailable from alternatives because they lack an advertising network and the unifying login system necessary to generate demographic data. While integration could be done with analytics tools and other third-party demographic information providers, I'd advise against it. In addition to the expense of acquiring the data, it's a serious privacy liability. Ultimately, GA demographic data is interesting, but typically not actionable.

Adopting an alternative will make integration with the other parts of the Google ecosystem I mentioned earlier more difficult. Many options offer API integrations to some Google services, but before committing to another tool, you should enumerate those points of integration and how mission-critical they actually are.

For example, several of the alternatives we look at offer the ability to pull in data from Google Search Console (GSC). Since that information is also available from GSC or BigQuery, it may be unnecessary to do an integration with your analytics tool.

The most commonly used integration in GA is likely with Google Ads. When that connection is enabled, you can use granular details about your Google Ads campaigns that can't be replicated by other tools' connections to Google Ads. Many tools are capable of attributing a referring URL with a Google Click Identifier (GCLID) to Google Ads (no UTMs needed), but only Google can easily look up the details of that `gclid` and its associated campaign and cost data.

Despite the integration advantages that GA has with Google's extensive ecosystem, there is very little that doesn't have near equivalents in other tools.

There's no need to be trapped in an analytics tool that isn't a good fit just because you use the Google ecosystem for other things.

Chapter 4 - It's Time to Consider Alternatives

After listing out all that unique functionality, do we really want to try an alternative? Should we just stick with GA4 and be done with it? Considering the number of pages left in this book, you should be able to deduce that my answer to this question is a strong "no."

One of the primary points of this guide is that we should stop looking at GA as the default choice for all circumstances. GA should be viewed as one potential solution among many other valid selections. With a wider variety of high-quality analytics platforms than ever before, choosing GA without considering your options could mean missing out on something else that is a better fit.

GA4 is not well-liked, but does that mean the GMP is in trouble in general? Do we need to jump ship? Following the analytics news over the last few years might lead one to believe there's some kind of mass migration happening away from GA.

Google Analytics was declared to have violated the EU's General Data Protection Regulation (GDPR) in many EU countries, and major fines were levied.

https://noyb.eu/en/noyb-win-first-major-fine-eu-1-million-using-google-analytics

GA is in violation of US–EU data transfer rules (Schrems II)... Then it isn't (US–EU Data Privacy Framework, DPF)... Then maybe it might be again (US Privacy and Civil Liberties Oversight Board, PCLOB).

https://cdt.org/insights/what-the-pclob-firings-mean-for-the-eu-us-data-privacy-framework/

Between 2021 and 2024, there was a data leak of 4.7M users' personal info out of GA for advertising purposes.

https://www.bleepingcomputer.com/news/security/blue-shield-of-california-leaked-health-data-of-47-million-members-to-google/

There have been repeated complaints about data reliability and processing delays.

https://www.seroundtable.com/google-analytics-real-time-reporting-broken-again-39919.html

Despite this, GA and the broader GMP isn't going anywhere. GA's market share likely *has* shrunk after the release of GA4, but not massively. BuiltWith reports a loss of 7% of market share in the top 1M from fall 2023 (post UA sunset) to 2025. Other services (e.g., W3Techs) offer similar reports.

While the quality of the numbers from BuiltWith et al. leaves much to be desired, I am inclined to believe there has been a real drop in market share for GA. Due to its huge market footprint, even a 5% loss of sites for GA represents a slice of the market bigger than any of our alternatives (aside from Cloudflare).

While this drop might not be a huge blow to Google Analytics, it is a huge opportunity for the rest of the market. The challenge for other tools is capitalizing on that and capturing those sites as new customers!

It's worth noting that we are only measuring the presence of the GA tag, so sites that have migrated away from GA but continue to run it for backup or legacy reporting would still be counted as GA users. If you add another tool to run in conjunction with GA or even just never bother to turn off the old tag, you are still counted as having GA. We're not measuring *how* a site uses GA, just that the tag exists.

My experience with GA "alternatives" historically has meant another analytics platform run in parallel with GA, rather than as a replacement for GA. For example, you could run both GA and Amplitude, with the marketing team using GA and the product team using Amplitude. While this may be an unavoidable reality for many organizations, as anyone who has worked on sites with multiple "single sources of truth" can attest, it can also be a big pain point. If it's possible to replace GA completely, great, but running multiple platforms (especially during a transition) is a viable way to move forward as well.

To be a true alternative, a tool should be able to replace GA in a significant percentage of use cases. That doesn't mean everyone using an alternative is going to dump GA—in fact, the majority of sites likely won't—but they *could*. As mentioned, in some lists of alternatives you'll see things like session capture tools (e.g., Hotjar or Clarity), search engine marketing (SEM) tools (e.g., Ahrefs or Semrush), log analyzers (e.g., GoAccess or AWStats), or platform-specific analytics (e.g., WordPress stats or HubSpot Analytics). These are not alternatives to GA in any broad sense, and their inclusion in articles about GA alternatives further complicates an already complex situation. We're focusing on true alternatives, even though those other tools do cover functionality that exists within GA.

Let's discuss the three major issues driving users away from GA.

Reason One: Google Analytics 4 Is Disappointing

There's no sugar-coating it: users simply don't like GA4. In our crowd-sourced opinions chapter, Chapter 33, we look at thousands of user comments, and GA has by far the worst overall sentiment ratings. My own detailed review is in Chapter 19.

Google forced free users off of Universal Analytics onto GA4 starting July 1, 2023, and paid users a year later. Any forced upgrade will cause a user base to re-evaluate whether or not the product they have is right for them. If the new version is perceived as inferior to the old, then the impact of a forced migration is doubled. GA4 wasn't backwards compatible, and auto-migrations from UA to GA did not always go smoothly.

To understand the context a little better, let's do a quick recap of the history of GA (see the table below for a summary). In order to understand why the backlash to GA4 was so strong, we need to contextualize the legacy of UA. This history can be confusing, especially since versions before 4 weren't given version numbers at the time. GA4 is the first to use a new data model and the first with a number in its name (although Universal Analytics is sometimes now referred to as "GA3"). "Universal Analytics" is a broader term sometimes used to mean "any version of GA previous to 4," so I will use the term "UA" unless I am referring to a specific historical version. Technically, Google itself now refers to GA4 simply as "Google Analytics," but especially in this context of product history, that would be incredibly confusing, so I won't do that.

Version	Web Tracker	First Released
Original Measurement Framework		
"GA1" Urchin	urchin.js	2005
"GA2" Classic	ga.js	2007 (async in 2009)
"GA3" Universal	analytics.js gtag.js	2012 2017
Next Gen Measurement Framework		
GA4	gtag.js	2019 (as "App+Web")

Google encouraged users to update web tracking script tags with each new version, but upgrades previous to GA4 were always backwards compatible. This meant you could still run `urchin.js` on your website and collect data into the same property as your modern `gtag.js` implementation. If you ran `urchin.js` you would miss out on a huge number of features, but it would still work, and the data would be contiguous. You could have a GA property running from 2005 to 2023 with active data in the same single property, even if that data had been collected by four different web tracking scripts (`urchin.js, ga.js, analytics.js, gtag.js`).

GA4 broke this backwards compatibility and created a new data model different enough that they didn't even import the old data into the new properties. It's understandable why people who had GA on their site for many years were upset that they could no longer do things in the same way.

However, it's also understandable why Google would want a blank slate that allows it to get rid of all that legacy technology and data. The end of UA did *feel* abrupt, but `gtag.js`, which is compatible with both GA3 and GA4, was released all the way back in 2017. App+Web, which became GA4, was released in 2019. Google encouraged people to update their tagging and get ready for GA4 for quite some time, but it wasn't until the UA sunset was really underway that many people started to pay attention.

In March 2023, Google started automatically creating GA4 properties for UA users who had not yet done so (https://support.google.com/analytics/answer/12938611). Some sites that used `analytics.js` were required to update their tags, but you could do nothing and continue to collect GA data in most cases. Even more than two years after this automatic migration, I frequently run into sites that run `analytics.js` and never touch the auto-migrated setup at all, despite the issues that using the old `analytics.js` tracker with GA4 causes. In November 2025, BuiltWith still identified over 11M sites with `analytics.js`!

On July 1, 2024, Google started the process of removing old UA properties and data. Today, that data is totally gone. Considering that Google ran free data collection for upwards of 50% of all websites with unlimited historical reporting for almost 20 years, you can understand why it wanted to reset that. Beyond just the volume of data sitting in a legacy system, consider the liability and compliance issues involved with hosting that veritable mountain of historical data.

Google made an attempt to rein in that data volume with its change in data retention policies for UA in 2018, and it has curtailed it further with GA4. Full event data is now only retained for a max of 14 months in free GA4, although standard reports will still allow for unlimited look-back on processed and aggregated data.

Google Analytics' full history dates back even before the first public launch of Google Analytics in November 2005. This first version of GA was based upon Urchin, a web analytics tool dating back to the late '90s.

Anyone who has worked in software development knows how hard legacy and technical debt is to remove. The legacy of Urchin still continues long after its demise with terms like *UTM* parameters ("UTM" originally stood for "Urchin Traffic Monitor") and *UA-xxxx* property ids ("UA" originally stood for "Urchin Account"). The legacy doesn't only exist in the terminology; a user of Urchin from those early days would recognize a lot of the product's approach and design patterns in many of the tools inspired by Universal Analytics.

If you're interested in the history of Urchin and how it became Google Analytics, there's a great history of the company written by one of Urchin's founders, Scott Crosby, here: https://urchin.biz.

Not only does GA4 make users start over with a new property and different paradigm, but the rollout and timing of the forced migration left many GA users feeling stranded. GA4 is, in my opinion, an ok piece of analytics software. If it had been named something else (like Google Product Analytics) and not presented as an upgrade to UA with forced migration, it's likely people would think it was a decent tool, or at least one that had a lot of potential.

Reason Two: Privacy

Another reason GA users are looking elsewhere is that people don't trust Google when it comes to privacy. This is sensible. Google has an astonishing amount of data about users across its broad platform of offerings, and a mixed record of data stewardship.

That said, GA as a standalone product has surprisingly limited data:

- GA works largely with aggregated data rather than individual users.
- GA doesn't permit personally identifiable information (PII) to be stored and will actively remove it if it finds it (though it doesn't excel at this identification).
- GA doesn't provide access to user IPs and restricts storing IPs.
- GA doesn't capture data with high granularity. This means it doesn't support actions like screen capturing, mouse movement, dwell time, etc. It can do some of these if customized, but not by default.

This is less invasive than many other analytics products and far less so than most ad networks. The issue is that GA *is* part of Google, the largest ad network in the world.

It's easy to improve privacy on GA, though in my experience working with thousands of installations, most do not. Turning off Google Signals and the advertising features in GA is the best single thing that can be done to improve privacy and reduce the amount of data sharing, but as those features are also one of the biggest benefits of using GA, they are commonly enabled. Anonymizing IPs is also now always done in GA4, but anonymizing IPs doesn't hide a user's IP from being seen by Google.

It's possible to sanitize sensitive data sent via the GA JavaScript sensor before it's sent to Google, and in particular, when combined with a server-side proxy, that can be a very effective way to improve GA's privacy. However, these sorts of more involved methods have the downside of increasing the possibility of measurement errors, as well as adding the need for significant ongoing maintenance.

Any discussion of privacy in analytics tools should also talk about what funds the tool.

GA is free up to a very high level of usage. UA had a limit of 10 million hits per month, and GA4 has no hit limit at all. To compare, 10 million hits with Matomo Cloud would cost about $1,900 per month. Google has amazing infrastructure and economies of scale on its side, but GA still requires significant resources to support, and we should consider what Google might get out of that investment.

The reason for this effort on Google's part is the benefits GA brings to its advertising business. For all its other activities, Google (and its parent company Alphabet) is an advertising company first. Alphabet's most recent quarterly earnings report (Q3 2025, https://s206.q4cdn.com/479360582/files/doc_financials/2025/q3/2025q3-alphabet-earnings-release.pdf) showed it made 72% of its whopping $102B revenue from ads, meaning Alphabet is currently making around $815,000,000 **per day** on advertising.

GA and the greater Google Marketing Platform help support this ad ecosystem. In fact, Google seems to consider GMP part of the advertising product line. Alphabet's 99-page yearly investor report (10-K form: https://s206.q4cdn.com/479360582/files/doc_financials/2024/q4/goog-10-k-2024.pdf) doesn't even contain the word "Google Analytics," and the only reference to GMP is this: "Our customers generally purchase advertising inventory through Google Ads, Google Ad Manager, Google Display & Video 360, and Google Marketing Platform, among others."

I say this not to criticize Google, but to emphasize that Google is in the business of selling ads, not analytics software. You can, of course, pay for GA, but that's not a significant revenue stream for Google. GA exists as a free product to help the industry spend more money on advertising in general and to help those ads perform better. It can also be argued that features like GA4's free BigQuery export (up to 1M events/day) help bring customers into the Google Cloud Platform. GCP is Alphabet's second largest source of revenue after ads, representing 15% of that $102B top-line number.

Everyone loves getting something for free, but when I think about free GA, I think of my site visitors' data as subsidizing the cost of the tool. Google, meanwhile, would look at it more in the context of improving Google Ads sales and efficiency.

Ultimately, Google has stifled competition in the web analytics market by offering so much functionality for free. This has made it incredibly difficult for any alternative (outside of the large enterprise space) to compete with GA. With UA, Google got everyone used to an incredibly high level of functionality and performance at no cost.

If you want strong customer privacy to be part of your analytics platform, you have to give up that subsidy and pay for your analytics tool.

Reason Three: Legality and Compliance

Privacy isn't the same thing as compliance, though certainly they are connected. Google's difficulties in balancing its need to monetize GA data with users' privacy have led to years of discussion on how to legally use GA around the world. The main thrust of this discussion has been about GDPR compliance, culminating in multiple data protection authorities in the EU declaring that GA violates the GDPR because of its data transfers to the US. Austria, Denmark, France, Italy, and others have declared those data transfers to be problematic, and either implicitly or explicitly recommended moving away from GA. As these kinds of regulatory actions take a long time to work through the system, these decisions are largely based on UA, not GA4—though the core issue of US data transfers largely remains with GA4.

In 2023, the new EU–US Data Privacy Framework aimed to solve these transatlantic data transfer issues, which had been highlighted by the Schrems II decision from the EU. Yet many of the underlying incompatibilities between how the EU and US regulate data continue, meaning that the DPF doesn't provide the most solid of footing.

The IAPP (International Association of Privacy Professionals) is a quality, neutral resource for up-to-date and detailed information about this issue: https://iapp.org/resources/topics/international-data-transfers/.

If you're confused by all of that and thinking that avoiding GA in the EU altogether seems like the simplest solution, you're not alone.

In June 2022, the French data protection authority (CNIL, which translates to the National Commission on Informatics and Liberty) published a FAQ explicitly saying that GA's data transfers were against the GDPR. We can see that, measured shortly after that decision until now, GA's usage in France has gone down by 18%, whereas worldwide it is up 1%. Please note that that 1% increase worldwide shouldn't be taken as market share growth, as that is measured across *all* websites, not just the top 1M we are normally considering using the BuiltWith data (it doesn't allow segmentation by country and site popularity at the same time).

GA Usage Decline in France

Total GA Sites (BuiltWith)	August 2022	November 2025	Change
France 🇫🇷	824k	676k	-18%
Worldwide 🌐	30.0M	30.2M	+1%

The regulatory solution provided by the new EU–US Data Privacy Framework in 2023 did not bring French sites back to GA. Even though these GA transfers were only explicitly ruled unlawful in France for something like 16 months (February 2022–July 2023), the uncertainty continues.

Consider that 600k+ sites in France still use GA, only a small handful of sites were contacted by the CNIL, and, ultimately, no fines were ever issued (according to https://www.enforcementtracker.com). That same database of GDPR enforcement shows a total of only four fines total related to GA (Germany, Sweden x2, and Belgium). Using GA in the EU does not appear to be a big risk currently, but it is *some* kind of risk, and that alone is a good reason to look elsewhere.

The degree of risk can be hard to judge. These compliance issues are complex and operate in an intricate space that overlaps both technical analytics engineering and international law. I find it unreasonable to expect the analysts and engineers responsible for tool evaluation and implementation to also evaluate the legality of their toolkits, especially considering how quickly the landscape is changing. Analysts aren't lawyers, and organizations shouldn't depend on our interpretation of the legal landscape for compliance. An organization's legal decisions should be informed by its analysts' expert knowledge, but ultimately, the responsibility for decisions around compliance should remain with the legal team.

This complexity is a strong incentive to switch to something else. GA's competitors know this, and many have focused on privacy and compliance in their features and marketing.

So far, actions in the EU—many stemming from the initiative of the privacy advocacy organization NOYB ("none of your business")—have focused on GA and the Meta Pixel, and in particular its data transfers to the United States. This doesn't mean that switching to Adobe Analytics or something else US-based would make a site compliant, but staying away from the vendors with the worst privacy records (like Google and Meta) can decrease regulatory scrutiny, even if that does not directly mean compliance.

While the EU is the leader in this arena, much of the rest of the world is following after it in some fashion or another. With GA4, Google has taken some steps to try to improve compliance, but at a fundamental level, it will remain problematic, due to its inclusion in the Ads platform and the United States' weaker data protection laws.

Chapter 5 - Types of Tools

Before we start digging into individual product evaluations, let's spend some time considering the kind of questions we'll ask in the process. These questions and discussions will focus on the technical architecture and paradigm that a tool fits within rather than specific functionality details.

The first question to answer is what general category of analytics tool we think we need. This is only the first step in the requirements process, but each step along the way can help us narrow down the list and hone our thought processes.

Categorization can be challenging, as tools don't tend to fit cleanly in one predefined category. Many tools have features that span multiple product categories. A tool that focuses on product analytics might also have some great web analytics features. A different tool that focuses on application performance monitoring might also do app analytics. Additionally, the categories a tool focuses on change over time and may not even align with how the product is being marketed.

With GA4, Google moved its product away from traditional web analytics and more towards product analytics. GA4 is event-based, defaults to users rather than sessions, and can do both mobile and web—all features more generally associated with product analytics. Google doesn't actively use *either* of the terms "web" or "product" when it describes GA4.

Tools like Amplitude and PostHog that started in the product or app analytics realm have also added features that push them more towards web and marketing analytics. Even though all three of those tools (GA4, Amplitude, PostHog) have a lot of the same features, I've placed GA4 in the "comprehensive web analytics" category and the latter two in "product analytics." While it's not always clear what category a tool fits in, defining the categories themselves is helpful in the process of understanding requirements.

Web Analytics

We'll start with web analytics. By "web analytics" I mean the aggregate measurement of websites, focused on traffic acquisition and on-site behavior.

Comprehensive Web Analytics

The "comprehensive" modifier here is to differentiate these robust and configurable tools from the "simplified" category. Comprehensive web analytics tools are also much more likely to have additional tools as part of a suite, rather than *just* reporting on websites. Many tools in this category are parts of suites that contain things like tag management, audience management, compliance tools, etc.

These tools also likely have the ability to report on mobile apps, not just websites, although it's likely that websites remain the focus.

Detailed reporting and the ability to heavily customize that reporting is a core part of this category as well. These tools have lots of metrics and dimensions, and UIs that place those things directly in the hands of the analyst.

The first version of this book referred to this category as "traditional" web analytics, which is a helpful way to frame the differences between this category and the product analytics tools. However, it also had a connotation that this approach is outdated, which it's not.

Simplified Web Analytics

This sub-category of web analytics represents a different approach than comprehensive web analytics, not just a more basic and limited product. Good examples of tools in this category have made purposeful decisions on what to leave out, and how to measure and report on what is most commonly needed without a lot of overhead. Here, simplicity rules.

So what makes a tool fall under this as opposed to the "comprehensive" category? The simplified approach includes the following: fewer metrics tracked, fewer options for customization, a more basic data model and reporting interface, and less information stored about users.

Simplified tools are what the majority of sites overall should be using. These tools are easier to implement and better for privacy, and their output is easier to understand. While the *overall* predominance of sites should be using simplified tools, the readers of this book may well find that most of the sites they work with require more sophistication.

"Everything should be made as simple as possible, but not simpler." Whether Einstein actually said this famous maxim or not, the point is very clear. But when it comes to selecting software, people tend to put too much emphasis on the latter "not simpler" part. Many of us have experienced the pain of dealing with some tool that lacks a particular feature or option that we want, and this can lead to introducing more complexity than we actually need just to avoid that *potential* pain.

In other words, maybe you need 11 metrics. You find a good match, but that tool only has 10 metrics. Instead of figuring out how to work around that one "missing" metric, you upgrade to a tool with 100 metrics to make sure you are covered, and are soon drowning in its complexity.

Picking a more complicated tool to avoid having to work around a small number of missing features from a simpler tool is a common pitfall. A small amount of work to set expectations and some compromises on what stakeholders have asked for can really pay off in the long run by allowing a simpler and more efficient tool to be used.

We all know GA tracks a lot of stuff, but did you know that it currently has 460 metrics and dimensions—and this is actually *less* than UA had (https://developers.google.com/analytics/devguides/reporting/data/v1/api-schema)? Plausible has around 40 metrics and dimensions, an order of magnitude fewer.

That total count of 460 may well vary over time, and many of these dimensions in GA are specific to certain integrations, like those used in Google Ads, Campaign Manager 360, Display & Video 360, etc. Looking at the full list shows both how much GA is tracking that many sites don't need, as well as how much of GA's focus is around integration with other Google Ad platform tools.

We see the complexity this depth of tracking options creates every time we log in to GA. Compare the historical list of UA's 115 standard reports to a simplified tool like Statcounter's 8 standard reports. The simplicity of Statcounter and others in this category can be incredibly helpful for self-service users who aren't analytics experts.

Since tools in this category are generally much easier to create and manage, there are a plethora of options to choose from. We're analyzing six tools in this group—Clicky, Cloudflare Web Analytics, Fathom, Plausible Analytics, Statcounter, and Umami—and there are plenty more out there. Implementation in this category is relatively easy, and the costs are low, so you can test a couple of options and see what you like without a lot of effort.

Product Analytics

The other major analytics category is product analytics tools. The difference between web and product analytics can be hard to pinpoint, because there's significant overlap, and many tools don't fall clearly in one category or the other. It's a continuum, but I've done my best to fit each tool in the classification it aligns best with.

Here's a high-level comparison of what each type is most focused on.

Web Analytics	Product Analytics
Pageviews first	Events first
Sessions and unique visitors	Users, customer lifetime
Web-based	Cross-platform
Focused on inbound and marketing	Focused on product usage and retention

You can certainly measure events with a web analytics tool or track mobile app data with your web analytics tool; it's a question of focus and perspective. Tools that label themselves "product analytics," such as Heap or Amplitude, share functionality with "web analytics" tools and, with the decommissioning of UA, have been incentivized to close that gap even further.

Are web analytics and product analytics converging under one umbrella? I think it is likely for larger tool suites, especially since there is limited new development happening within the traditional web analytics category, and product analytics tools continue to add features.

Mobile App Analytics

While this category may seem self-explanatory, it can be a little confusing. Historically, mobile apps were measured with entirely separate tools from those for websites. You would run UA on your website, and then something app-specific, like Flurry, AppsFlyer, or Firebase, on your app, and the two datasets would be completely separate.

Newer tools like Amplitude, Heap, or GA4 combine web and mobile app reporting into the same measurement and reporting framework. You can utilize a JavaScript snippet tag on your website and an SDK (software development kit) within your mobile app to report to the same analytics property. GA4 was first named "App+Web" to explicitly highlight that kind of ability.

Since we're focusing on alternatives to GA, we won't look at mobile app analytics specifically. However, if you want to unify your mobile app and website analytics, you should consider a solution like many of the product analytics and comprehensive web analytics tools that are designed for both web and app.

A Note About Categories

Ok, so what about "marketing analytics," "digital analytics," or variations thereof? In my table above, I have "focused on inbound and marketing" as a feature of web analytics, rather than considering them as separate "digital" and "marketing" categories. Does that mean that those two categories are just part of good ol' web analytics? In this part of my taxonomy, those two categories are more like feature sets within other categories. Yes, they are more likely to be a part of "web," but they could be a part of any category.

At the risk of undermining my own argument, remember that categories are helpful as part of our decision framework, but they are just a conceptual tool. As analytical people, we can sometimes get hung up on the details of a taxonomy rather than looking at the actual items we are categorizing as a whole. Categories can be helpful to help frame your thinking, but that doesn't mean you have to limit yourself to investigating tools in just one product category.

Chapter 6 - Pricing

After functionality, the price of a product is typically at the top of my (and many others') list of concerns. Due to the complexity of pricing and a frequent lack of transparency, it can be difficult to determine how much a product costs until you get pretty far along into an evaluation.

I've wasted significant time looking into "enterprise" products that don't publicly show prices, only to discover an offering is totally out of my price range. Many vendors protect their rate cards like trade secrets, which frustrates and confuses potential buyers. Some vendors even take the approach of limiting price disclosure in an attempt to squeeze the maximum price they can out of each customer.

In this guide, I try to be as detailed about pricing as possible. I report any publicly available pricing and do my best to compare each tool's pricing model so you can understand how well each fits your budget and use case.

While it may seem like tools of a similar type should have comparable costs for the same use case, this is not always so—and a tool's pricing model can make or break affordability.

Most pricing models are based upon a combination of traffic volume and feature limitations. Still, the way that traffic is metered can make a big difference in how much the product costs, depending on your site's pattern of usage. The table below shows the main pricing models and examples of products that use them.

Pricing Meter	Example Products
Hits/events/actions	Matomo, Mixpanel, PostHog, Piwik PRO, Umami
Pageviews	Statcounter, Clicky, Plausible, Fathom
Sessions, monthly tracked users (MTUs)	Amplitude, Heap

While some tools may use the word "hits," some use "events," and some use "actions," they are generally all the same thing when it comes to metering. Even pageviews can mean nearly the same thing; for cases like Plausible and Fathom, events are charged as pageviews.

Hit levels per user will vary as a function of the complexity of your setup. In other words, the same traffic can become more costly if you decide to track more on each page. Similarly, session or user-based pricing can vary based on the usage patterns of your site. Thus, the best-matched pricing model for your use case depends upon how your users interact with your site, as well as how you instrument your tracking.

Here's a quick comparison based on current pricing to illustrate, using the "Plus" plan from Amplitude (user-based meter) and PostHog (hit-based meter).

Site A is a business-to-business software-as-a-service (B2B SaaS) website with highly engaged users active on the site almost every day. It has 25k monthly users, with an average of 400 events per user (10 million total events):

- Amplitude base cost: $311 / mo. (user-based pricing)
- PostHog base cost: $1,080 / mo. (hit-based pricing, product analytics tier)

Site B is a business-to-consumer (B2C) ecommerce site with significant traffic but lower user engagement. It has 100k monthly users, with an average of 20 events per user (two million total events):

- Amplitude base cost: $1,061 / mo. (user-based pricing)
- PostHog base cost: $248 / mo. (hit-based pricing, product analytics tier)

Both sites are in the same league in terms of overall traffic, but the best product choice from a budgetary perspective depends on the way that users interact with the site.

Four hundred events per user might sound like a lot, but if you track multiple events for users who return frequently over a month, it's not an unusual usage pattern. Think about how many events per month a single user might create in their Facebook account—it could be many thousands for an active individual.

If your traffic pattern is more middle-of-the-road, picking a tool based on the pricing model may matter less, but it's still important to understand how the pricing model works and not focus solely on functionality.

Whatever the usage meter, it is very frustrating to pay for bot traffic. Session and user-based meters can be particularly susceptible to bot inflation, since in many cases, bot traffic is a low-events-per-user scenario.

Like most buyers, I'm a fan of transparent pricing and consider it a positive selling point. I don't want to schedule a call with an outreach associate, who then needs to loop in their regional manager, who has to sync up with their subject matter expert sales engineer to start working on calculating a price. I don't want to get stuck with overages because there's no clear rate card or a way to self-upgrade. I just want to know the price to see if it will fit my budget! Yet that number can be difficult to obtain, especially when there are many features and sub-components that may need to be licensed and sized independently.

It's understandable that it may require time and effort to nail down a price for an enterprise installation quote. If you're implementing a tool across an organization with complex requirements and huge volume, then you may need help from the vendor in figuring out what components you should have to meet these needs. Still, many times, the pricing is kept private for reasons that primarily benefit the vendor: acquiring a lead, being able to offer a "deal" to close a sale, being able to change pricing models without disturbing existing customers, etc. That's the vendor's prerogative, but it doesn't help me as a buyer. I've rated all the different vendors we are looking at from most to least transparent here:

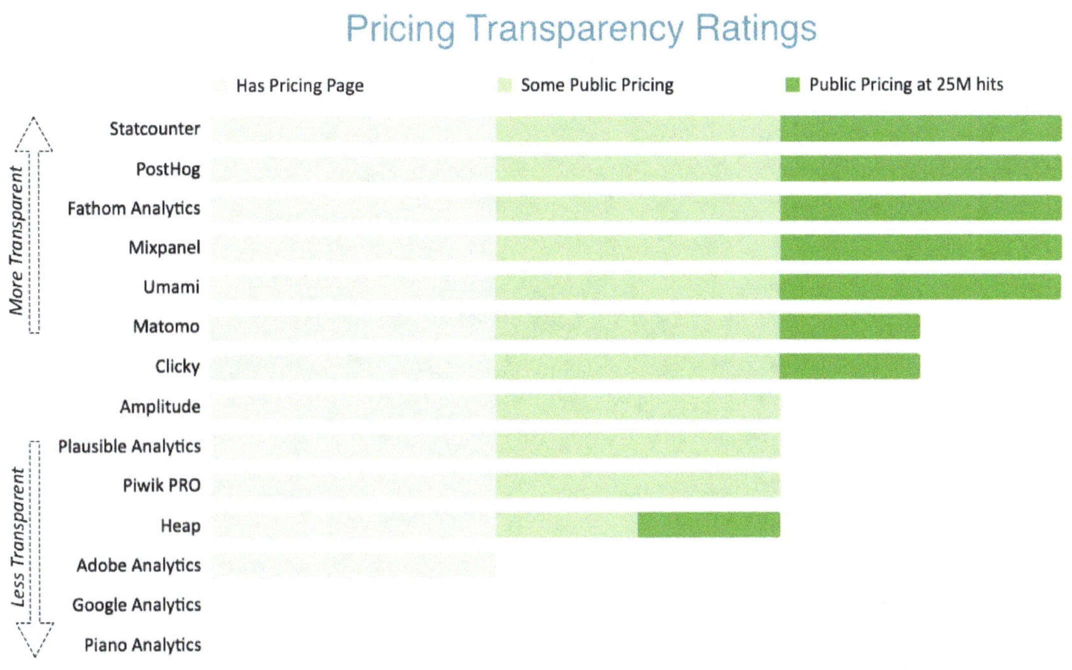

I've given out a few partial credits here, e.g., if a platform does have available pricing but requires you to log in to see it.

While there's a clear pattern here—more enterprise-oriented vendors like Adobe, Google, and Piano have less transparency—it's nice to see PostHog and Amplitude bucking that trend, even if in Amplitude's case, it's only the lowest-tier plan that has pricing available.

Despite my desire for pricing transparency, it's also clear how helpful sales engineers can be when onboarding to a complex product. If we look at more comprehensive digital platforms like Piano or Adobe Experience Cloud, it can be hard to wrap your head around which of the many individual tools and modules you need without engaging with the vendor. For example, PostHog has very high pricing transparency, but working with its pricing calculator can feel quite confusing. Within the PostHog calculator, there are eight products, with a total of 22 form fields to fill out to calculate a price—enough to feel overwhelming if you aren't familiar with the platform.

In this guide, I refer to cases where the vendor does not publish the price, but it is generally known, as "reportedly," and mark the price in italics. For example, "Google Universal Analytics 360 reportedly started at *$12,500* per month." As far as I know, Google didn't publicize that price, but it was widely circulated.

I report all prices in cost per month, regardless of whether or not a yearly contract is required. That means if something is only available yearly or discounts are offered for yearly agreements, that won't show in the prices I report. This may generate some inconsistencies between products that offer monthly discounts when purchased yearly, etc., so consider the prices listed in this guide as a starting point for informational purposes only.

Chapter 7 - Event Tracking Methodology

In terms of event tagging, there are two basic strategies: manual tagging and automatic event tracking. Sometimes this is called explicit vs. implicit, where explicit refers to manual tagging and implicit refers to automatic. Both options have their strengths and weaknesses.

Which option sounds better to you?

Option 1: Manual Event Tracking (Explicit)

Pro

You start with a blank slate: no events are tracked automatically, allowing you to construct the exact event structure you want and track only what you need. You avoid firing wasted events that nobody will use, which also improves reporting, since only the metrics purposely constructed are present.

Con

It takes significant instrumentation work to gather "basic" data, then still more work when something new needs to be tracked. Getting over this initial implementation hump can be difficult and sometimes cripples a tool's adoption if the implementor fails to grasp the necessary groundwork.

Option 2: Automatic Event Tracking (Implicit)

Pro

Every event is already captured and ready to go. Each click, form submission, and pageview is already a tracked event waiting for reporting. If the development team launches a new feature without letting you know, it's automatically reported with no new event coding needed. When a business stakeholder decides they want reporting on a certain element, you already have historical data and simply need to select which event to pull information from.

Con

It introduces a jumble of events you'll never need, making tracking more confusing. Sometimes capture doesn't work properly: maybe your auto-tracking is missing stuff it shouldn't, or even worse, maybe it is picking up things like personal private information that it shouldn't. Since everything is supposedly automatic, you may come in without a plan and end up with something that doesn't address the questions you need answers to. If you are paying by event volume, you're paying for a bunch of events you don't use.

How to Decide

Many tools are somewhere in the middle, and nearly all support manual event tracking on top of whatever the built-in options are. Still, thinking about how you want to handle this kind of instrumentation is important when selecting a tool. If you are in an organization with a mature and well-staffed analytics practice, then manual can be more appealing, since there may already be schemas to comply with, and doing some manual tagging instrumentation isn't going to be difficult for you. If you are at a small organization without an analytics team and nobody even knows what you should be tracking until after your new site has launched, then automatic tracking can be better, as it requires less work to get going and less planning.

Within the Google Analytics world, GA4 has moved towards the automated/implicit realm with its enhanced measurement feature. Enhanced measurement is an option that can automatically track things like page scroll, outbound clicks, form interactions, etc. In UA, this existed as an external library called auto-track, which has been improved and extended for inclusion in GA4. Sometimes enhanced measurement doesn't work properly (especially with regard to form interactions), but it can be an easy first step to capture much of what you may want to.

In general, each category has different levels of automated event tracking. In many cases, automatic event tracking is a configurable option, but limited in what it can capture. GA4 is a good example of this: it can automatically track the things we just mentioned above, but there is no option to auto-track every single interaction. In the table below, I lay out three of the tool categories from Chapter 5, and the tracking approaches they tend to take.

Approach per Product Category

Category	Approach
Comprehensive web analytics	Captures pageviews, limited auto-tracking, extensive manual event tracking.
Simplified web analytics	Captures pageviews, minimal (if any) auto-tracking, limited manual event tracking.
Product analytics	Highly variable. Some tools don't even capture pageviews by default, some capture every click.

While seemingly a small difference, this tracking approach can become an important deciding factor. Especially when looking at product analytics tools, make sure to investigate what is captured automatically vs. manually so you aren't surprised by what needs to be done to launch the tool successfully.

CHAPTER 8 - SUPPORT & INTEROPERABILITY

As its users can attest, Google's customer support is nearly non-existent. GA does, however, have a tremendous community with knowledgeable users willing to offer solutions. Additionally, if you pay for GA360, you'll likely receive excellent support from your GA reseller (since you can't buy GA directly from Google), but you still won't get much help directly from Google.

If you want to do something uncommon in GA, odds are you can find a post or snippet from someone else who has already done that precise thing and provided their solution back to the community.

When we move to a GA alternative, we lose that rich community. This is a major downside to consider when thinking about how you'll implement, troubleshoot, and support an alternative. Some alternatives have larger communities than others, but you shouldn't expect things like a vast library of how-to articles from third parties or lots of free tag manager templates and recipes.

On the other hand, many of the vendors of these alternatives do provide excellent support. When evaluating products like Amplitude or PostHog that have generous free tiers, you should consider what kind of support you'll need; you may want to pay for a support plan instead of counting on blogs or ChatGPT. It can also be true that the quality of content in the new community can be excellent, even if it doesn't rival the sheer size of Google's community. Many of the tools we discuss have a lot of quality content being created about them. In particular, Adobe, Piwik PRO, Amplitude, and PostHog stand out in this regard (though it should be noted that PostHog's community is focused around developers, not analysts).

In addition to less community support, integrations with outside software platforms are scarcer outside of GA. Whether you are looking for integration for a chat widget on your site or pulling data via an API into a third-party dashboard software, these connections are harder to do with a GA alternative and require more research.

Let's go through some examples of typical integrations.

Back-End Examples

When referring to "back-end" analytics integrations, I mean data pipelines to or from our analytics platform. Here are some example scenarios:

- Analytics tool -> Funnel.io -> Google BigQuery -> Power BI
- Analytics tool -> Looker Studio
- Analytics tool -> Supermetrics -> Google Sheets

With GA, we take it for granted that nearly any third-party software or tool will have an integration. We can't make that assumption with an alternative.

When evaluating a GA alternative as part of a data flow pipeline, consider that we only need a connector from that alternative to the next step in the pipeline—although the alternative's data schema will affect the whole data flow. In our first data flow example above, we don't need our new tool to have a connector for BigQuery and Power BI, just Funnel. Though if we are replacing GA in an existing data pipeline, we need to remember that the schema we get from the alternative won't match what we got from GA.

Let's look at how many of our 15 alternatives can connect directly to these common third-party tools with an existing available connector.

- **Funnel.io**: 5 out of 15 (Adobe, GA4, Matomo, Piwik PRO, Mixpanel)
- **Looker Studio**: 8 out of 15 (Adobe*, GA4, Matomo, Piano, Piwik PRO, Plausible, Amplitude*, Mixpanel*) **through a third-party paid marketplace connector*
- **Supermetrics**: 7 out of 15 (Adobe, GA4, Matomo, Piano, Piwik PRO, Amplitude, Mixpanel)

While the number of connectors has shown a lot of improvement since the first edition of this book, it still shows fewer than half of our alternatives having connectors to these three very commonly used platforms. The comprehensive web analytics category shows extensive coverage, simplified web analytics shows minimal coverage, and product analytics shows moderate coverage.

A couple of tools (Heap and Cloudflare Web Analytics) currently have no data-reporting API at all, which is needed for many pipelines, and I consider to be a baseline expectation of a reporting platform.

Beyond just data-reporting connectors, many of these tools also support exporting event data to external datastores. Sometimes that is more valuable than a reporting connector, which may explain why some of the product analytics tools, like PostHog, have limited data-reporting connectors but extensive ability to route data to other locations. PostHog can connect for free to BigQuery, Postgres, Snowflake, Redshift, S3, and others. This can obviate the need for a connector tool, like Funnel or Supermetrics, but if your existing flow is dependent upon those tools, then an export may not help.

Front-End Examples

From WordPress plugins, to live chat integrations, to ticket-buying platforms—if it has an "enable third-party stats" option, odds are it'll be Google Analytics. As an example, let's look at Gumroad, the platform on which I sell this very book. Gumroad allows me to add a GA property id and/or Facebook (Meta) Pixel. On the happy occasion when someone adds the book to their cart and checks out, it sends events for each step to GA, allowing me to report on the whole checkout funnel. You can see a screenshot from Gumroad below.

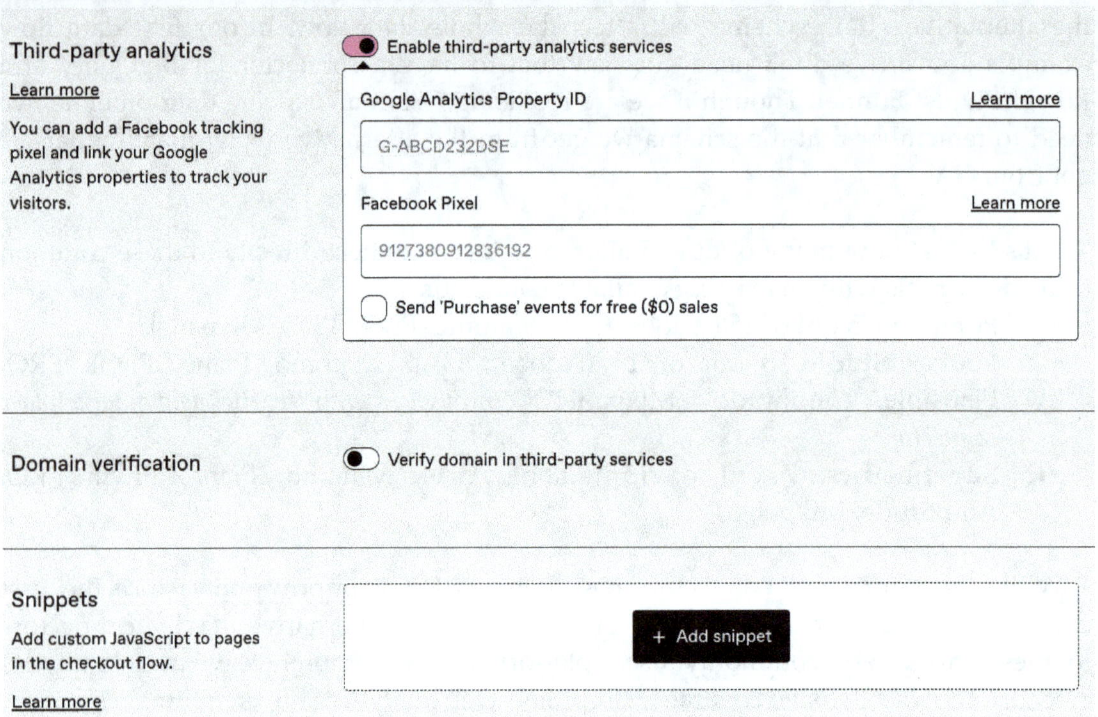

There is also the option to add "snippets," but unfortunately, those tags only show during checkout, so I would not be able to get pageviews recorded from tools other than GA4 or Facebook. The snippets option is designed for ad conversion tracking, for example, if I had purchased ads for my book on LinkedIn and wanted to show their conversion pixel on checkout. Meaning if I wanted to integrate Piwik PRO, Mixpanel, or another tool on the Gumroad landing page, I couldn't do that.

I simply can't imagine Gumroad settings ever having a "select your analytics platform" dropdown with a bunch of tools listed, though maybe it will expand snippets to work on any page rather than just checkout. Considering how many integrations like this still show the option to add a Universal Analytics property id years after the sunset, we can see how hard it is for third parties to keep up, even with the ubiquitous market leader.

In a world where there's not a single dominant platform like GA, we will need to rely on open standards more. Easier said than done, but there's already the start of one in the form of the data layer. The data layer is a JavaScript object that is part of a webpage and acts as glue between that page and a tag manager. There was a start towards developing a standard in a W3C community group report from 2013 (https://www.w3.org/community/custexpdata/2013/12/16/final-report-customer-experience-digital-data-layer-v1-0-ready/), but it was never turned into an official standard, and what's used today in GTM and elsewhere is a bit different from that original proposed standard.

Somewhat confusingly, Google has called its version of the data layer just "the data layer or "dataLayer", and even though this is a very widely used version of a data layer and seems like a universal standard, it is not. Adobe has its own (Adobe Client Data Layer), Tealium has its own (Universal Data Object), etc.

If Gumroad had generic data layer event pushes built into its platform, then we could easily implement any analytics platform we wanted via a tag management system (TMS) of our choosing. Certainly, using an open standards version of a data layer would be ideal, but anything that a TMS could consume would be enough.

This would mean that your TMS could handle all of the tool-specific instrumentation work. You want to upgrade from GA3 to GA4? Redo the tags inside your TMS. You want to run both GA4 and Amplitude? Create new Amplitude tags in the TMS tied to the same preexisting events and triggers.

Data layers have great *potential* to allow interoperability, but with all the different competing standards and lack of implementation in web apps, we still have a long way to go to take advantage of that potential. Even beyond just the JavaScript object structure, there are also different sub-standards within the different types of data layers, defining a wide range of different events and attributes that could be used. In other words, even when two different sites are both using Google's dataLayer, they might be naming the events themselves something quite different on each site.

This lack of interoperability highlights the overall importance of support and community. Whatever ecosystem we've been using (but especially Google's) we may start to take for granted that everyone is doing things following a particular playbook. When we switch to a different vendor, we've got to learn a new playbook—and for that, we will rely on that new vendor's support and community. Even for vendors that have replicated much of the Google playbook (e.g. Matomo, Piwik PRO), we will find that some things are different, and we need to be prepared to find resources to solve these inevitable issues.

Chapter 9 - Reporting Interfaces

One of the biggest complaints about GA4 is the reporting interface. People find it confusing and difficult to work with. Conversely, one of the things people love most about GA4 is the free data export to BigQuery and working with the event-level data there.

This highlights a growing divergence in the ways different people work with analytics data: reporting inside the tool, or pulling the data into another platform and transforming it or combining it with other data. Before we pick a tool, we need to understand how we're going to use it.

Let's split this up into four different usage patterns: built-in default reporting, custom reporting, reporting outside the platform, and exporting the data for use elsewhere.

Built-In Default Reporting

Historically, this was the only way to do things. You log into the tool, find which built-in report has the numbers you're looking for, and that's it. There may be the ability to customize reports and menus, but mostly this pattern is about using the defaults.

This remains a totally valid way to do things, and the best way to keep things simple. Accordingly, this is the primary mode in which all the simplified web analytics tools are designed to be used. In addition to the ease of setup here, there's another advantage in relying on universal defaults. If you move from one organization to another and they both use the same tool's built-in reports, you already know how to work with the data. It's also easier to find help if you need it.

Sometimes customization just adds work and confusion. For example, creating a bunch of different report collections in GA for different data consumers can flummox those different teams when they communicate with each other about reports and confuse people who have experience with the defaults from other installations. Customization can also add maintenance work.

Custom Reporting and Metrics Definition Within the Platform

An example of this usage pattern is the Explore reports in GA4, or really any platform where you build up custom reporting within that platform. You could be starting with a template or a blank screen and a list of metrics, but customization is the expected way to use the tool.

This approach entails more than just extending a template; it goes along with defining things like custom metrics and dimensions within reporting. This goes hand-in-hand with custom reporting, since built-in reports will not contain these sorts of additional fields. The more we customize our data schema overall, the more we have to customize the reporting on that data.

Many of the more enterprise-oriented tools we will evaluate take this approach, such as tools like Adobe or Piano that have excellent report-building tools within the platform and are intended for use by professional analysts. Similarly, in the product analytics category, this is the typical mode of operation, since flexibility is such an integral part of those tools.

Reporting Outside the Platform via Data Reporting APIs

Using a dashboarding/business intelligence (BI) tool *outside* of the analytics platform would fall under this category. This would fit examples like Looker Studio, Power BI, Tableau, etc. This category also includes patterns like using connectors like Supermetrics to pull data into Google Sheets or Excel, or even using a WordPress plugin to view your analytics data within the WordPress admin dashboard.

The key feature of this usage pattern is that you're still using the reporting abilities of your analytics platform, but you're consuming the data somewhere else. With this approach, we're still reliant upon the platforms' own definitions and reporting algorithms.

This can be a very appealing method, although there is also a common trap here of building yet another dashboard that may never be consumed and has to be maintained.

Exporting the Data for Use Elsewhere

Now we're entering the realm of data engineering. In some ways, this can be a subtle difference compared to the previous item, but the big differences are that we're a) dealing with something closer to raw data rather than aggregated reporting, and b) we're intending to ingest or transform the data somewhere else, not just report on it.

Beyond my obvious love for categorizing things and making lists, the point of this exercise is to spur thinking about how you and your organization plan to use and maintain this analytics data.

Before committing to a platform, you should figure out who owns what part of this process. Your organization can have great plans for a data pipeline merging raw analytics data with internal customer relationship management (CRM) data. But is your organization staffed to actually implement that? After implementation, who is going to maintain it? What good is a sophisticated new data schema if nobody has allocated any resources to make changes to that schema down the road? Just buying a tool that supports these plans doesn't always solve problems; sometimes, it creates them.

Similarly, who will be the consumers of this reporting? Going back to our GA4 example, some of the frustration has to do with putting data consumers into the wrong part of the reporting platform. Expecting non-analysts to work with Explore reports when they would be better off with a simple Looker Studio report, for example.

The tool selection process isn't something that should happen in a vacuum; it requires input from multiple stakeholders.

Chapter 10 - Self-Hosting

The level of control and potential cost savings of hosting your own analytics can be very appealing. Fans of self-hosting can make this approach sound like "full data ownership at discount prices!"

That actually does sound great—should we all be self-hosting our analytics tools?

Like most things in this book, the answer is that it depends on your use case. My general advice is that self-hosting is not worth it, but consider the following questions:

- Do you want to access the live data store?
- Do you want to customize your installation beyond what's normally possible?
- Do you think running on your own servers is the only way to ensure full compliance?
- Does your organization already run its own servers and have strong proficiency in DevOps?
- Are you running at mega-scale with a tight budget?

If your answer to some or all of those is yes, then maybe self-hosting could be a good option for you.

Knowing the precise method and location of the data you store isn't always possible with cloud-hosted analytics, and hosting it yourself can help provide that control. If we self-host, we know where the data is—it's on our servers. We aren't subject to the whims and vagaries of the vendor; we have control. The data may still be on a public cloud like Amazon or Google, but we know a lot more about where and how it's hosted. Self-hosting can get us closer to what most people mean when they say "full data ownership."

In the broadest sense:

- Data *ownership* = control & rights
- Data *sovereignty* = controlling legal jurisdiction
- Data *security* = how safe the data is

What does "data ownership" truly mean, though, in different scenarios? My broad-strokes definition aside, there's no universal legal definition. I'm not a lawyer or a privacy expert (as is probably very clear throughout this book!). To me, data ownership refers to the following categories:

- Who *collects* the data.
- Who has *access* to the data, both read and write.
- Who can *use* the data for their own purposes, including deriving economic value from the data.
- Who *controls* the legal rights to grant the preceding: including access, use, etc.

Despite what some may think, Google *does not* claim ownership of the data in your GA account. In the Google Analytics Terms of Service (https://marketingplatform.google.com/about/analytics/terms/us/), it defines "Customer Data" as the data collected by GA, and proceeds to say "Google will not share **Your** Customer Data" (bold is my emphasis, capitalization is Google's... for some reason).

Yet Google does have access to this data, and it does utilize this data for its own economic purposes. Most notably in the form of the GA advertising features, the data that is used for its advertising network.

That doesn't feel like full ownership, and it certainly doesn't give you full control.

What about other cloud-hosted commercial tools, like Amplitude, Piwik PRO, etc.? These tools tend to give more control and better privacy for your data in comparison with Google. With these platforms, you know that your customer's data isn't going to be used to build an ad audience for someone else.

Still, do you really "own" the data? Your data is on the vendor's server, and you won't typically have access to those servers or databases directly. You may be able to export the data out of those servers, but you don't have access to the raw data live. Your raw data is also deleted based upon the vendor's rules, not yours. For example, if you are on the Piwik PRO core plan, your raw data will be deleted after 14 months. How can it delete it if you "own" it?

Some vendors, like Piwik PRO, also offer private cloud hosting. This means that you're hosted in the cloud, but on dedicated resources. While this can offer some additional data security and performance advantages, from an ownership perspective, the difference is limited.

If you still want more ownership, what about a scenario like running Matomo on your own Amazon Web Services (AWS) Linux servers? Matomo is an open source product, meaning we can see the code, data structures, and ultimately all the data collected. Does that give us full ownership? My answer now is "mostly yes." Your data is still on a physical server that may also host data from other organizations, and AWS still has some (highly limited) ability to access your data.

If we moved that same Matomo installation to hardware we owned ourselves, then that would provide the highest level of "ownership" as we've defined it.

We've got a pretty good hierarchy of data ownership now, from least ownership to most:

1. Cloud-hosted, where your data is also used by the vendor (e.g., Google Analytics)
2. Cloud-hosted, where your data is not shared (e.g., Amplitude, Piano, cloud-hosted Matomo, etc.)
3. Private cloud-hosted, where your data is on dedicated hardware (e.g., some Piwik PRO plans)
4. Self-hosted on a public cloud provider (e.g., Matomo on AWS)
5. Self-hosted on private cloud, or your own hardware (e.g., Matomo on your hardware hosted at a colocation facility)

Whatever level we're at for ownership, this may not give us the data *sovereignty* situation we want. Defining "sovereignty" can also be quite complex, but a simplified explanation would be "what country's laws apply to your data." Wherever you host your data, it's subject to someone's rules—you just get to choose whose. Far and away, the most common use of the term "data sovereignty" is in the context of European organizations being concerned about their data hosted on services run by US-based companies.

This boils down to concerns that US law does not provide the same level of data protection that EU laws do. For example, a US-based provider like Amazon could be forced by the US government to hand over data on its servers.

Take Matomo Cloud, for example. Matomo is a New Zealand-based company that hosts its cloud service in the EU. But Matomo utilizes Amazon Web Services to do its cloud hosting, and Amazon is a US-based company. Could the US government use US law (like the Clarifying Lawful Overseas Use of Data Act, or the CLOUD Act) to legally request this data that exists on an AWS server in Germany and compel Amazon to hand it over?

It's possible it could, at least by the government's own definition of what is legal. The "by its own definition of what is legal" bit is a very important part of what data sovereignty means. Who gets to decide what the rules are? As the US has become an increasingly unreliable partner in international agreements, it's a legitimate concern to worry about data under what the US thinks is its jurisdiction.

In response, many of the so-called "hyperscalers" like AWS, Azure, and GCP are attempting to create segments or spin-offs of their services with different data sovereignties. For example, Amazon launched what it calls the "AWS European Sovereign Cloud" in the fall of 2025 (https://aws.eu). This is an attempt to create a completely separate EU-based AWS hosting service that is free from non-European influences (a.k.a. the US). This seems like a logical response to years of wrangling over data transfers and EU judgments about the adequacy of other countries' data protection regulations.

Do these efforts by AWS et al. provide the sovereignty that EU organizations are looking for? I couldn't say, but it's no surprise that companies like Piwik PRO have chosen an easier route to sidestep this complex question and are in the process of switching from Microsoft Azure to Sweden-based Elastx.

When it comes to web analytics, I find the concerns about data sovereignty and the US to be a bit overblown. Could the FBI come for my AWS-hosted-in-Germany Matomo data? I suppose, but I'm not storing any PII in there to start with, and the CLOUD Act would require the FBI to submit to a warrant, so it'd need a good reason. Additionally, hosts like AWS do have safeguards in place, as the perception that data on their servers isn't safe from prying eyes in the US government is bad for business.

On AWS' CLOUD Act page (https://aws.amazon.com/compliance/cloud-act), it claims that "AWS has not disclosed any enterprise or government content data stored outside the U.S. to the U.S. government since we started reporting the statistic in 2020." There are a few concerning caveats in that: it's not clear what it means by "enterprise" data, it only started keeping track in 2020, and the explicit naming of "content data" makes it seem likely that it *has* handed over metadata.

As I said, AWS has at least some access to what you host with it. If nothing else, it is physically in the possession of the hardware. AWS doesn't provide any ability for itself to log in to your systems unless you grant it to it (if you've ever locked yourself out of an ec2 instance, you may have learned this the hard way). AWS also cannot decrypt anything where the customers own and control the encryption keys (though this would require you to make sure you aren't using AWS-managed keys, which most do).

AWS can and does hand over data to governments that provide search warrants, but there aren't all that many of these requests. AWS disclosures (https://d1.awsstatic.com/Security/pdfs/Amazon_AWS_Information_Request_Report_H1_2025.pdf) show that in the first half of 2025, it received 1,619 legal orders to disclose data. India (31%), the US (31%), and Germany (13%) were the top countries of origin. Across all countries, almost all of the requests (99.3%) were for meta (aka "non-content") data. Meaning almost all of what Amazon is disclosing to governments is metadata about accounts, like who owns the account, rather than the contents of the account.

Having a lack of back doors is very important to data security. Government-mandated encryption back doors that allow snooping at scale are especially problematic, in my view. End-to-end encryption, like what can be achieved on AWS if you manage your own keys, means that AWS has no ability to hand over your content data, because it can't decrypt it. Hosting data in countries that have such laws in effect, like China and Russia, should be avoided, but at the time of writing, none of the tools we are talking about are based in countries with such laws.

While the US certainly has a spotty history with data privacy and data regulations (Snowden, NSA, Facebook, etc.). I don't personally find US sovereignty alone to be reason to switch to an EU-based provider.

There's a well-known saying that the cloud is "just someone else's computer." I have mixed feelings about this aphorism. On the one hand, I like it because it's a reminder that there's nothing magical involved in cloud hosting; it's all just a computer in a rack in a data center somewhere. However, I also dislike the saying because it neglects the differences in architecture and the massive benefits of cloud hosting.

Cloud hosting at its best implies your data will be hosted in a redundant way across multiple servers with transparent scalability and edge optimization (that is, doing as much as we can closest to the end user). So, if the end user is in Germany, we'd want them to connect to a computer in Germany and have the data processed as close to that point of collection as possible.

That's part of the cloud promise. For our purposes of comparison, the difference is who runs and pays for the servers: if you run the servers, it's "self-hosted"; if your vendor runs the servers, it's "cloud-based." An oversimplification, but accurate enough for our purposes.

Sometimes the tool vendor will use the term "on-premises" (or just "on-prem") rather than "self-hosted." When "on-premises" is used, there's an implication to me that the servers are *not* on a public cloud like AWS or GCP—though, unfortunately, that is not always the case. I find this to be unnecessarily confusing terminology since, from the vendor's perspective, there's little difference.

In general, my recommendation is to let someone else manage the server unless there's a good reason not to. Having full control over the tool is enticing, but typically more trouble than it's worth. My perspective on self-managing may be colored by spending many years as the person who received the 3:00 a.m. text when a server went down. My feelings about being woken up at 3 a.m. aside, consider what your organization's core competencies are.

To summarize, what are the reasons someone *would* choose to be self-hosted?

Compliance

Sometimes you need complete control over the data to ensure you're following the rules, and self-hosting is the only way to guarantee this.

Privacy and Security

Self-hosting doesn't necessarily mean better privacy, but it can. This is a double-edged sword, because when you self-host, you're also responsible for the security of these services (patching the servers, maintaining security groups, firewalls, etc.). There are certainly risks involved in trusting a vendor with your data, but unless your organization has a strong security team, the vendor will likely be more capable of handling security issues related to the hosting of its software.

Price

If you run a high-volume site, it *can* be significantly cheaper to self-host. However, do remember to consider the total cost of ownership (TCO), not just that of the servers alone (https://en.wikipedia.org/wiki/Total_cost_of_ownership).

Let's look at a Matomo Cloud example for a site with 10 million hits per month.

	Matomo **Cloud**	Matomo **Self-Hosted**
Base monthly cost	$1,900	$0
Premium plugins (estimate)	$0	$100
Server cost	$0	$715
Total cost	**$1,900**	**$815**

In this case, for a reasonably high-volume site, it seems we'd save more than 50% through self-hosting. Base Matomo costs us nothing, though there are paid plugins which add expenses (which ones you need will vary, so $100 a month is just an estimate), as well as the cost of the servers. The $715 monthly charge is based on a simple AWS estimate I made here:
https://calculator.aws/#/estimate?id=b8568e9b2b755ea8d-d831030e3bc2b6cb8607785 (where the majority of the cost is in the MySQL RDS database, and I exclude smaller costs like bandwidth).

Now, considering the TCO, we can start with the fact that the $815 monthly estimate doesn't include the cost of people. Who sets up the hosting? Who manages the backups? Who patches the servers and opens tickets with AWS when something goes wrong? Even if you have someone on staff now with the requisite expertise, what happens when that person leaves? With self-hosting, you take on plenty of additional responsibility. What *looks* like 50% cheaper may end up being much more expensive than cloud-hosted when all costs are accounted for.

Control and Customization

Self-hosted means you can tweak elements of your installation in a way that most managed cloud hosting would not allow. Just like with privacy, this can have serious blowback if done incorrectly.

Additionally, the level of customization will depend on whether the product is open source or not, which we'll talk about in the next chapter.

Integration With Existing Infrastructure

This is a similar point to our last one about control and customization, but focuses more on communication and data transfer.

Do you need to tie something in your analytics stack to a core element of your infrastructure? With self-hosting, your analytics data can sit in the same network as your other data. This allows for faster (and cheaper) data transfers, safer and more secure data access, plus other benefits. This kind of integration is not necessary for most installations; however, when it is, self-hosting may be the best way to bring datasets close to each other.

Databases

I'll close out this chapter with a short appendix about databases. The majority of these tools have ended up at a limited number of hosts (AWS, Azure, Hetzner, etc.). There's also a limited number of database platforms that our data actually ends up on. While the difference between a Linux host running on AWS vs. Hetzner is pretty transparent when it comes to the functioning of an analytics server, the database itself can have more impact.

We're looking at 15 different tools in this book, yet they only end up in nine different databases. If we increased the number of tools, the number of databases would go up more and more slowly. If we looked at 50 different tools, we might only be talking about a few additional databases.

Database Use by Platform

Storage Database	Populari-ty	Type	Licensing	Used by Analytics Platform(s)
ClickHouse	#30	Column-oriented	Open source	Piwik PRO, Plausible, PostHog, Cloudflare
MySQL	#2	General-purpose relational	Open source	Matomo, Statcounter, Clicky
SingleStore	#98	Hybrid row & col-umn	Propri-etary	Heap, Fathom
Snowflake	#6	Column-oriented	Propri-etary	Piano
Apache HBase	#32	Wide column key-value	Open source	Adobe Analytics
Postgres	#4	General-purpose relational	Open source	Umami
Google Bigtable	#100	Wide column key-value	n/a	Google Analytics
ARB	n/a	Proprietary internal	n/a	Mixpanel
Nova	n/a	Proprietary internal	n/a	Amplitude

The popularity rankings are from the DB-Engines database information site (https://db-engines.com/en/ranking), where more info about all of these different database systems can be found. Certainly, databases are an important topic, and I think the list here is interesting, but a deeper discussion is far beyond the scope of this book.

The tools that support self-hosting all use either ClickHouse, MySQL, or Postgres. This is logical as those are popular open source products. In particular, MySQL is highly available on shared hosting plans and easy to set up and maintain.

Somewhat incongruously, Adobe Analytics uses Apache HBase, which is also an open source product. The newer Adobe Customer Journey Analytics product no longer uses HBase, but rather a proprietary internal database. GA4 uses its own product, Bigtable (which HBase was modeled after), though to be clear, this is a totally different database system than BigQuery, where GA4 exports end up living.

As we will see when we review individual tools, the functionality of the database has a big downstream impact on the functionality of the analytics tool. That doesn't mean that any of these databases is inherently superior to any other, and just like the analytics tools themselves, the best fit is based upon the particular use case.

Chapter 11 - Open Source

I've long been a proponent of open source tools. I've volunteered for open source projects and contributed code. However, open source isn't always the best option for your analytics tool. All things being equal, I recommend the open source option—but in many cases, there are other more important considerations. Moreover, many open source tools in this space are not *fully* open; and lack the kind of community you may associate with famous open source projects like Linux, Apache, etc.

I encourage you to think of a tool being open source as an additional feature that may or may not be helpful to you. Supporting open source is a good thing, but tool selection is about more than picking the one that ticks the most boxes. How does a tool being open source help to meet your particular needs?

Let's dig into some of the common benefits associated with open source tools.

Price

Open source = no cost, right? Turns out this one is not as simple as it seems. We talked about server costs in the previous chapter, but servers are not the only additional expense. Many GA alternatives are "open core" software (https://en.wikipedia.org/wiki/Open-core_model), a sub-type of open source where the core of the product is open, but some features and add-ons are closed source and commercial. For example, Matomo currently has 19 different paid premium add-on features that are not open source, e.g., funnel reporting starting at $229/year.

On the business side, this has been a great way for open source vendors to make money and continue to improve their products. From the consumer's point of view, it means you need to be careful about what part of the product is free, both in terms of cost and access to the code.

Avoiding Vendor Lock-In

Some make the argument that "even if the vendor goes away, you won't lose access to the product" or "if the vendor drastically changes pricing model, we'll have options."

If we're talking about the major open source projects like Linux, they absolutely can outlast any vendor or contributor. However, the open source alternatives we look at in this guide—Matomo, PostHog, Plausible, and Umami—are all closely tied to their vendors, meaning vendor-sponsored developers perform the vast majority of work on the product. So, if the vendor goes away, the funding for that developer time disappears as well.

Customizability

Customization is much harder than it sounds. Contributing meaningful code to an open source project is no simple task. If you don't want to contribute back, forking your own version is a very bumpy road to go down. So, unless you have excess developer time and highly specific needs, customization alone is not a compelling reason to opt for open source.

Security, Privacy, and Verifiability

Open source doesn't inherently make a project more (or less) secure; it makes it more transparent. This transparency has the potential to be both good and bad for cybersecurity; the overall outcome depends on how the project is managed. The same can be said for privacy, though the ability to self-host can be very good for privacy and compliance. Data governance is clearest when you have total control. Open source is always more verifiable—you don't have to blindly trust what a vendor says about the technical details of the product when you can just check the code yourself.

These are all potential benefits that may or may not manifest in any particular tool. A vibrant community of contributors *can* be an outgrowth of an open source project, but that doesn't guarantee it'll happen (in fact, it usually doesn't).

Within open source, there's a lot of attention and interest paid to the particular license that a project uses. With the four open source tools we are evaluating, they all use variations of the GNU GPL (more restrictive) or the MIT License (less restrictive). The table below describes the open source tools in this book and their license details.

Open Source License Type per Tool

Tool	License	License Notes	Functionality Excluded
Matomo	GNU GPL v3	Modifications have to also be GPL, can't derive a closed source product.	19 premium features including A/B testing, activity log, cohorts, funnels, etc.
Plausible Community Edition	GNU AGPL v3	Same as regular GPL but includes network use as distribution.	Newly added features, 4 premium features, advanced bot filtering, etc.
PostHog	MIT	Do what you want as long as you include the original copyright and license notices.	A significant number of advanced features bundled into the "Enterprise Edition."
Umami	MIT	Do what you want as long as you include the original copyright and license notices.	None.

See https://choosealicense.com/licenses/ for more details.

An Open Source Test Case: Fathom Versus Plausible

Let's analyze a case that is as near to "all other things being equal" as you're likely to see. Fathom and Plausible are very similar products, as we'll talk about more in the individual project evaluation chapters. While of course not identical, they're probably the closest of any two products we evaluate, open source or not. One of the more significant differences is that Plausible is open source while Fathom is not.

You can download the Plausible source code from GitHub (https://github.com/plausible/analytics) and run it yourself, totally separately from Plausible. You could fork it and do whatever you want, short of using the code as a basis for your own commercial product, which is restricted by the GNU AGPL open source license.

How does this affect you as a user? Let's evaluate against some of our previously stated potential benefits:

Price—Minimal Difference

As both products have a low price point, you wouldn't save much money and would take on some work if you decided to self-host your version. If you then modified your own version, it would be *significantly* more work. In most cases, it would cost you more to maintain a modified version, considering the developer time required.

Vendor Lock-In—Plausible Offers a Slight Advantage

Plausible employees are the main contributors to the tool's source code. Other individuals have committed code, but the tool lacks a large community that could maintain the product in the absence of the vendor. If Plausible went out of business tomorrow, you'd be better off shifting to another product, as the Plausible code would likely no longer be actively developed. However, having access to the code would give you the option to continue to run the product as is, though that's not without its own risks.

Customization—No Difference for Most Use Cases

Want to customize the product? Do you or your development team know Elixir? That's what the core of Plausible is written in, and it's an uncommon language. Elixir runs on the Erlang virtual machine, which is also not very widely used. These are, in my opinion, strong technologies to run an analytics platform on, but they can make it difficult (and expensive) to find a developer. The project's language is not the only problem, but it's representative of the kind of issues you'll have when you customize the tool. AI development tools may make it easier to generate code and features, but that code still needs to be reviewed and understood to be trusted and reliable.

You'd also need to learn the structure and standards of the project, especially if you want to contribute your modifications back to the main project. It's highly preferable to contribute patches back. Not only because it's good for the project, but it also helps keep your version from diverging from the main version. If you have diverged, it makes updates the main version gets harder to apply to your customized version.

Whether or not this is an advantage depends on your use case. Let's say you run a large content-hosting platform and site builder, which we'll call "Trianglespace," and it has thousands of hosted sites. If you wanted to offer easy-to-use web analytics to all your customers on Trianglespace, you'd probably choose Plausible over Fathom so you could self-host at scale and customize it to your needs. The individual sites on Trianglespace might be small, but the operation overall would be large, with a lot of technical capacity.

While there are certainly benefits in some use cases, most potential users will experience no direct benefit from Plausible's open source status.

The Popularity of Open Source Tools

Since we've discussed install base as a measurement of market share, we should also talk about popularity within the open source community. This is a good way to determine if a project has stability and will continue to be maintained and updated.

The typical way to gauge popularity is through stars on GitHub, which shows how many users on that site have a project's repository saved to their favorites. Stars don't mean someone has contributed code or installed the project; it's more like saving a bookmark.

As of October 2025, Umami is the most popular open source GA alternative, measured by GitHub stars. This is an interesting change from the first edition of this book, when Matomo was at the top of the list. Matomo is now the *least* starred out of our four open source options, being slightly edged out by Plausible.

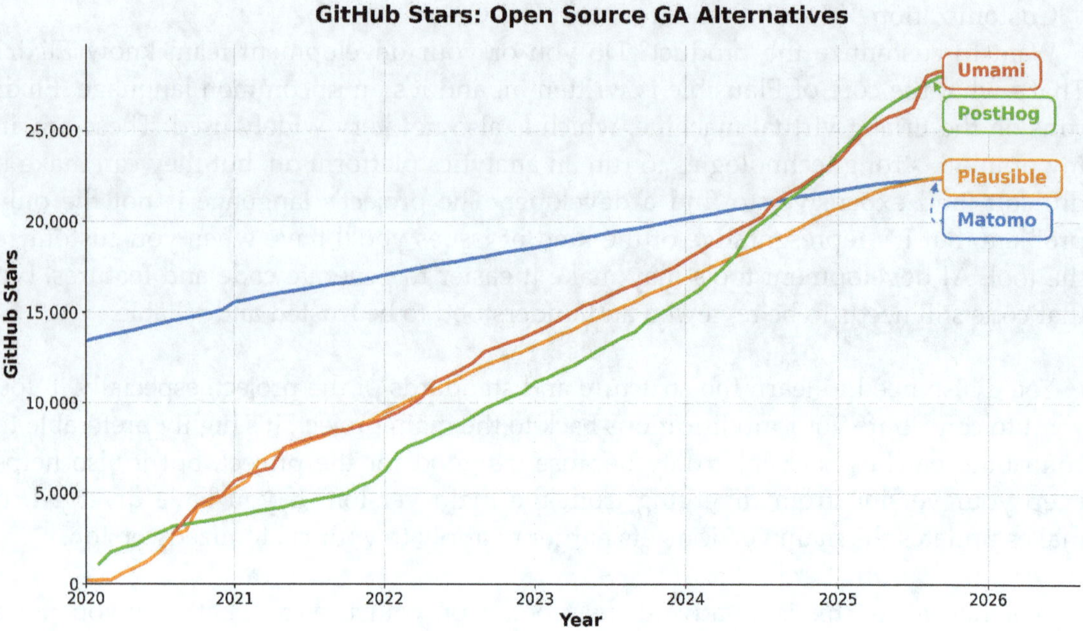

Data from ossinsight.io

If we compare the number of stars to our number of deployments detected by BuiltWith, we see that, in fact, the popularity is flipped. Matomo has by far the most detected installations, and Umami the least. So while Umami and PostHog are both very popular and growing in the open source developer community, that popularity has not fully translated to as much popularity among analysts and decision-makers.

Another chart I'd like to show is the number of pull request creators over time, which illustrates the vitality of the developer community around an open source project. For those who are not familiar, a pull request is what happens when a developer submits a patch for the project maintainers to accept. This could be a significant code change, with hundreds of lines of code needed to fix a core issue with the project, or it could be a one-line fix of a typo in documentation. The numbers of pull request creators show the total of how many different users have submitted changes to a project.

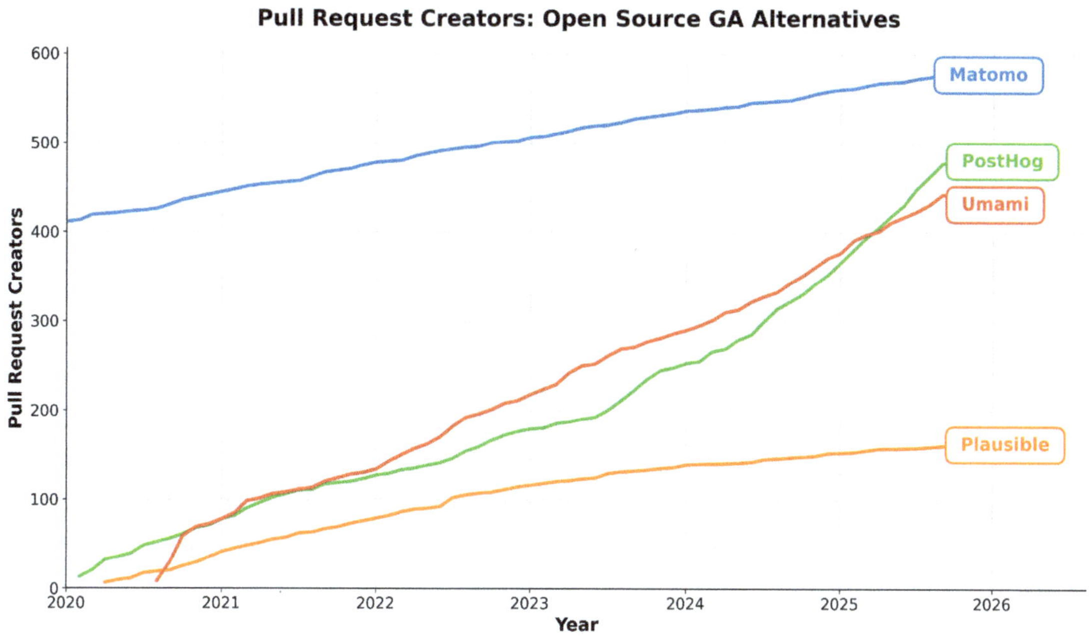

Data from ossinsight.io

This second graph highlights the robust and growing open source community around both PostHog and Umami. In particular, the velocity of PostHog in the last year is very impressive. Matomo is still at the top, with the most total individual contributors, but as a much older project with a GitHub history going back to 2013, it had a huge head start.

Plausible's much smaller number of contributors, despite its popularity, aligns with Plausible's overall approach to open source, which is not quite all-in in the same way. It focuses more on its hosted cloud offering than on the self-installation of the open source "community edition" of the product.

While the number of stars and the number of pull request creators are indicative of a project's open source community vitality, they can also be a bit misleading in terms of who is doing the bulk of the work. While Umami has over 400 different contributors who committed *something*, 80% of commits were made by the three brothers who founded the company. This is a very typical pattern.

As with the install base stats, popularity is just one metric, but it's something to consider when evaluating a product to predict how it may endure and improve over time. Whatever tool we pick, the amount of data we may amass in that tool and the work put into instrumenting and customizing it strongly incentivizes us to pick something that will stick around and continue to improve for a long time!

Chapter 12 - Tracker Speed

Every analyst will tell you that the speed of reporting within a tool makes a big difference in how pleasant a tool is to work with. If your tool is slow to return numbers, you can be sure it will be doubly slow, exactly when you need to finish your reporting on the first day of the month. But what about the speed client-side, the tracking code itself running on the end user's browser? Does that matter?

Fair warning, this chapter gets pretty deep into the weeds on things like network speed and browser internals, and the upshot is that it doesn't typically matter all that much.

It's a commonly made argument (in particular by the simplified tools) that GA's JavaScript is bloated, and removing it can speed up your site. Some will even make the claim that removing GA can help improve your SEO, since site speed can indeed affect SEO.

So is it true that GA can slow down your site? It's undeniable that GA4 (especially when you count GTM as well) contains a lot of JavaScript. GA4 is about 142kB compressed (415kB uncompressed). A GTM container, which only includes the Google tag for GA4, is 106kB compressed (301kB uncompressed), for a combined total of 700k+ of JavaScript. The compressed version is what's typically transferred over a network connection, and the uncompressed version represents the full size of the script's contents.

Compare that to a tool like Fathom, which, at a tiny 2.5kB compressed (6kB uncompressed), is something like 50x smaller than the GA4 script. This isn't the 1990s, though, and downloading a few hundred kilobytes isn't a big deal. So unless you're still using the 56kbps modem you bought back then (mine is in a closet somewhere, still working on a Wolfenstein 3D download), that's not a lot of data. Combined, those two Google scripts are 248kB (compressed `gtag.js + gtm.js`), which would take about 50ms over a 100Mbps connection for just the data (excluding all the other parts of the transfer, like DNS, latency, server response time, etc.). Speedtest.net reports the current world median broadband connection is 115Mbps, and mobile is 103Mbps.

In a simple real-word test with my exceedingly average ISP connection speed, the GA4 `gtag.js` script actually downloaded consistently *faster* on average (70ms) than the Fathom `script.js` (81ms).

This is because I'm in Columbus, Ohio, and there is a nearby Google data center, whereas to get the Fathom script, I'm connecting to a bunny.net content delivery network (CDN) node in Charlotte, NC. Bunny.net is a well-regarded CDN; it just happens that in this case, Google is closer and being routed better. This distance has caused network latency to become a bigger factor than the size of the scripts. As network speeds get faster and faster, the latency introduced by physical distance can become a higher overall percentage of the time spent.

There is little effective difference between 70ms and 81ms, and your network connection will be different. When it comes to effective JavaScript performance, it has more to do with what's *in* the JavaScript and what the browser has to execute than the size of the script alone. Obviously, there is a strong correlation, though, where larger scripts do more and require more from the browser.

This is where we need to look at what the user actually experiences in the browser.

From a web performance perspective, the metric Google Search uses for rankings is Core Web Vitals (CWV), intended to represent the user's speed experience. I imagine many of us are familiar with this term (if not the specifics of its definition), as it officially became part of the Google Search algorithm in 2021 (https://developers.google.com/search/blog/2021/04/more-details-page-experience).

By itself, Google Analytics has a near-zero impact on Core Web Vitals. To be clear, that doesn't mean it has a zero impact of performance, just how Google measures performance.

Below is an overview of the components that make up Core Web Vitals, as provided by Google:

From https://web.dev/vitals, content unchanged under CC license: https://creativecommons.org/licenses/by/3.0/

Here's a breakdown of the terms in the image:

- Largest Contentful Paint (LCP) measures *loading* performance. To provide a good user experience, LCP should occur within 2.5 seconds of when the page first starts loading.
- Interaction to Next Paint (INP) measures *interactivity*. To provide a good user experience, pages should have an INP of 200 milliseconds or less. This replaced First Input Delay (FID) in March 2024.
- Cumulative Layout Shift (CLS) measures *visual stability*. To provide a good user experience, pages should maintain a CLS of 0.1 or less.

The metrics that combine to form Core Web Vitals are intended to cover the three basic parts of web performance: loading, interactivity, and visual stability. If you look closely at the performance metrics Google chose, you may notice that it doesn't include anything about the final completion time of a page. Google is focused on how long it takes users to see the biggest part of the page and then interact with the page, not the total time for every element to finish loading.

As long as a page renders its largest section and becomes interactive quickly, Google has no problem with additional late-loading content, provided this late-loading content doesn't shift the page around or eat up enough processing power to slow browser interactions. This is a reasonable way to measure things. However, it's also friendly to ads, which effectively leaves a hole in Google's rules, allowing ads to slow the user experience without hurting Core Web Vitals scores.

In terms of the component metrics of Core Web Vitals:

- GA doesn't affect LCP because it's not a render-blocking script.
- GA doesn't affect CLS because it doesn't insert any content into the page.
- GA *can* sometimes affect INP, but is typically limited to very slow mobile devices or cases where there are either excessive amounts of JavaScript on the page or very inefficient JS.

Still worried that GA might be affecting CWV? It's easy to test. Create an HTML page with no components on it other than a stock GA tag. Then, run it through a performance testing tool such as webpagetest.org. I did just that, and here are the results:

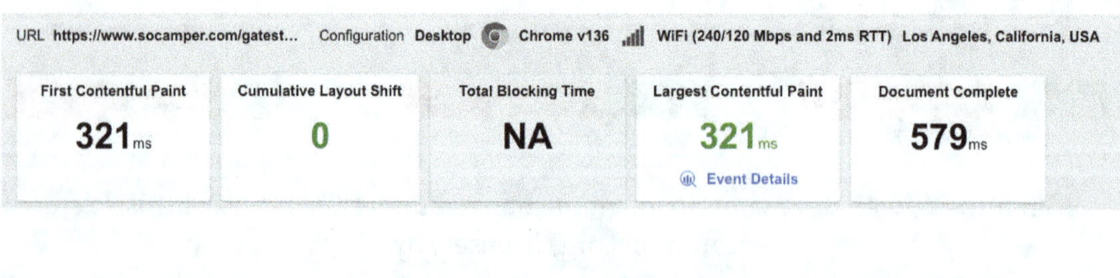

This test shows nothing that would negatively impact Core Web Vitals:

- LCP—321 ms (happens before the contents of the GA tag were seen by the browser, because it knew the GA tag was a non-render-blocking tag)
- CLS—0 (meaning no content shifting)
- Total Blocking Time (TBT)—0 (meaning no potential interactivity pauses, and thus 0 INP)

Total Blocking Time is a new metric to this discussion. How come our testing results show the metric TBT instead of the official CWV metric Interaction to Next Paint? The two metrics measure very similar things, but in different ways. INP is a real-world field measurement of how long a user actually waited for the browser to realize they've done something. For example, if you're loading the amazon.com home page and start typing into the search box, but have to wait to be able to type because the browser is still churning on page processing, that time would be counted as INP. TBT is how much time the automated headless test counted there being enough browser resources used, such that any additional code execution would have to wait. In an automated test like that, there's no opportunity to measure INP, because there are no user interactions (https://www.semrush.com/blog/google-inp/). TBT shows us where there could potentially be interactivity pauses that would affect INP.

Because Google bases Core Web Vitals on actual user measurements, your users' actual experiences are more important than a lab test like the one I did. Assuming most of your users don't use very underpowered devices, the JavaScript from GA alone shouldn't impact INP. GA *can* exacerbate an existing JavaScript problem, though, so if you have a ton of JS already, running GA adds that much more processing. It's a marginal effect, however.

We may have just busted another SEO myth, but we can't let analytics tools completely off the hook for performance. The more trackers we put on the page and the more things we try to intercept and track, the more we risk analytics actually causing a noticeable slowdown.

Say, for example, you run 15 analytics tools all on the same page—not something I'd recommend, but exactly what I did with our test sites for this guide. How will that affect web performance?

Here's a test simulating an iPhone 13 at 4G speeds with all 15 tools on a blank page:

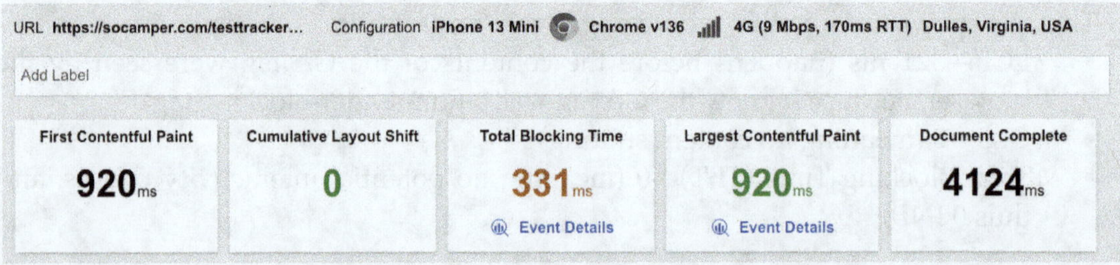

Loaded down with all 15 tools (including some that run session capture as well as web analytics, which contain particularly heavy JavaScript), we see some effect on performance. All the metrics other than layout shift were degraded. We'd likely still be in the green for Core Web Vitals, but it's now taking over four seconds to complete a page with literally nothing on it.

We've *potentially* altered INP, but it's not too bad. Even with 15 trackers, we have only mildly affected one of the three core CWV metrics.

Looking at the waterfall performance chart for that webpage with 15 trackers shows the impact more clearly:

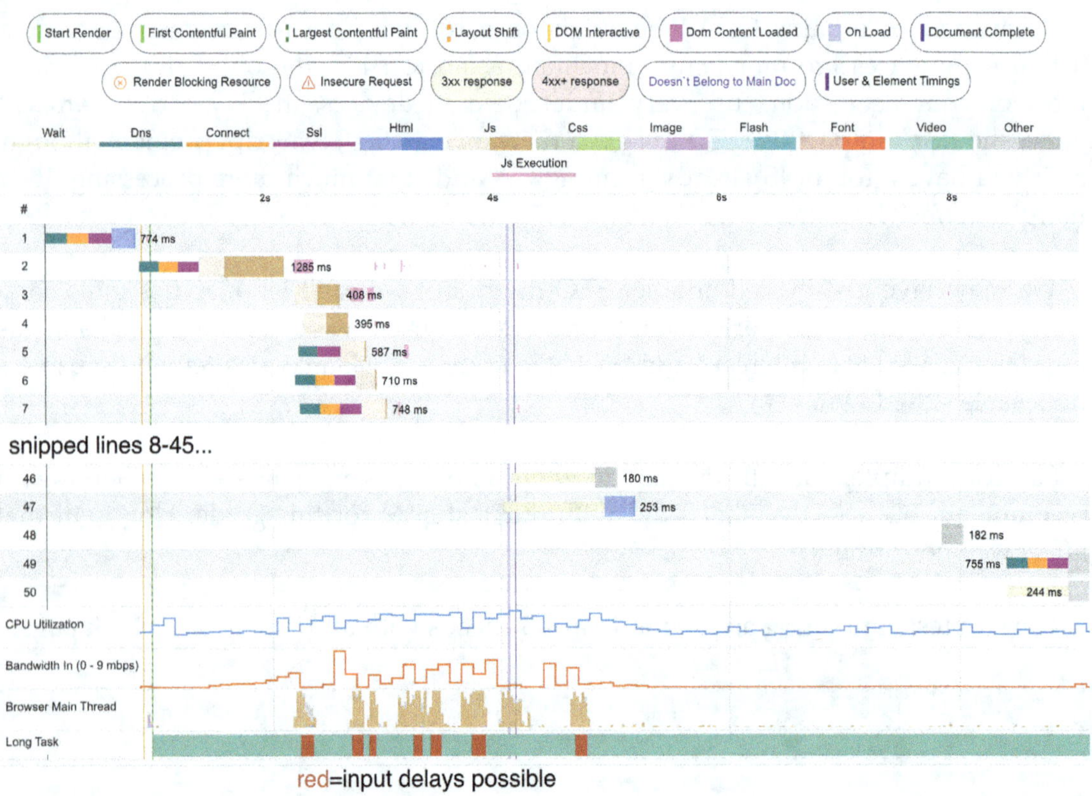

Ok, so maybe "more clearly" is an exaggeration, as performance waterfall charts are notoriously hard to read. Still, we see that the total time the page takes to load has shot up from 600ms to over 4 seconds to get to document complete. More critically, there are a bunch of periods where long tasks are hogging the browser's processing (shown as the red/dark bands under Long Task in the graph above). This means in this example, these tools could be degrading the user experience if a user were trying to do something during those times. Note that I've purposefully simulated a less powerful device and connection (iPhone 13 over 4G) to show how these slowdowns can happen.

So, don't run 15 analytics tools, duh. That might seem like a ridiculous number of analytics tools, but plenty of sites run at least that many trackers when you include *all* the tags on a site, especially ad tags with chaining. The average number of trackers per site is seven (according to Ghostery: https://whotracks.me/websites.html), but it's a wide distribution, with many sites running far more. It's not unusual to see hundreds of additional requests on sites with significant ad chaining.

Since there may be many more tags on the site other than the analytics tag that we are responsible for, we want to avoid *our* tag being the problem. In addition to limiting the total number of trackers, we need to make sure the ones we recommend perform well.

How do we evaluate tracker performance? Reiterating what we've already covered, the main aspects we should look at are the following:

- Tracker size
- Tracker complexity and chaining
- Physical location of the servers

Tracker Size

UA was 50k (uncompressed), which is a reasonable starting benchmark. JavaScript tracker size can vary significantly based on what the tracker does and what features and plugins you enable. For example, when enabling session capture, PostHog loads an additional 247k in JavaScript, but that's not included in the base tracker code, and I don't count it in the chart below, which describes the tracker code size (not including additional features or tag management).

Base Tracker Code	Uncompressed JS size (K)
GA4 (gtag.js)	415
Heap	334
Matomo	208
PostHog	170
Mixpanel	98
Amplitude Analytics	97
Piano Analytics	89
Piwik PRO	67
Google UA (analytics.js)	52
Adobe Analytics (AppMeasurement.js)	41
Statcounter	36
Cloudflare Web Analytics	20
Clicky	13
Fathom	6
Umami	3
Plausible Analytics	3

The GA4 code is indeed quite large—you can see where the claims of bloat come from. The huge increase in size in comparison to UA is in part because the `gtag.js` also includes Google Ads functionality.

Tracker Complexity and Chaining

Once it's downloaded the JavaScript, the browser has to execute that code. Sometimes that code will also chain in additional JavaScript. For example, when `gtag.js` was used to run your UA, it loaded `gtag.js` and then also chained in `analytics.js`, making using `gtag.js` slower, with more overhead than calling `analytics.js` directly.

Server Location

The physical location of the servers involved in site analytics is of increasing importance, though much more for legal compliance than site speed. We'll talk about site speed impact here and the compliance issues in Chapter 14 - Consent.

From a site speed standpoint, we want the server recording the analytics measurement data to be as close to the end user as possible. If our end user is in Australia, we'd like the server that collects the measurement calls to be in or near Australia. This is what I referenced earlier when talking about edge delivery, and it's the same concept as content delivery networks for things like images and Cascading Style Sheets (CSS) delivery.

Let's say the end user is in Perth, Australia and our analytics measurement server is in Ashburn, Virginia, US (AWS' largest data center). That means every tracked event click sends data across a vast distance of 18,500km (11,500 miles). That would take 123ms to do a round trip as the crow flies at the speed of light.

Our data packets bounce around much more than these imaginary crows capable of relativistic speeds, so in reality, we're looking at more like 300ms of latency added to every request. If instead we had our data collection happening at the AWS zone in Perth, we'd save our data packages quite a trip. The data processing and ultimate home for the data could still be in Virginia, but our end user in Perth doesn't have to wait for that data transfer to happen.

Extreme distance causes slowness and increases the chance that the measurement requests might not even arrive. Three hundred milliseconds may not sound like a lot, but that's just the overhead, adding a hefty tax onto server and browser processing time of every request.

We want our analytics reporting system to have endpoints distributed around the world, transparently routing measurement requests to whatever endpoint can most quickly serve the user. Many analytics tools have taken into account this kind of edge routing, but some are better at it than others. Google is, unsurprisingly, extremely good at this kind of thing, setting a pretty high bar for our alternatives. If we're self-hosting, we need to consider this as well, especially as it can substantially increase prices. This can also be a great time for server-side tagging to come in, as we can offload slow, high-latency network calls to be done in a server-to-server fashion. We'll cover server-side more deeply in Chapter 15 - Server-side.

Of the 15 tools, only Piwik PRO and Matomo were sending my measurement data somewhere outside the US while I was in the US (the former to Stockholm, SE, and the latter to Frankfurt, DE). Piwik PRO Enterprise supports US hosting, and when it was self-hosted, you could host Matomo anywhere you want to, but both companies have chosen to host their basic cloud plans in Europe. They've chosen to do this because they've decided that the compliance concerns are more significant than the site speed concerns. Because much of the JavaScript tracker download process and measurement data sending happens with minimal impact to the user experience, this is not an unreasonable decision. Especially from the East Coast of the United States, the network performance to either of those locations is pretty good. If you were in Japan or New Zealand, you might feel differently.

Chapter 13 - Tracking Methods

Underpinning any discussion about tracking, consent, and compliance are the technical details of tracking methods. While technology itself shouldn't drive our decisions, it is helpful to understand the fundamentals of how these different methods work. Some tools even support multiple methods, though we will focus on their default tracking methods.

The three primary visitor tracking methods used by the tools in this book are the following:

- Cookies
- IP + User-Agent
- Referrer

Cookies are the most used by a significant margin, as you can see illustrated in the bar chart below.

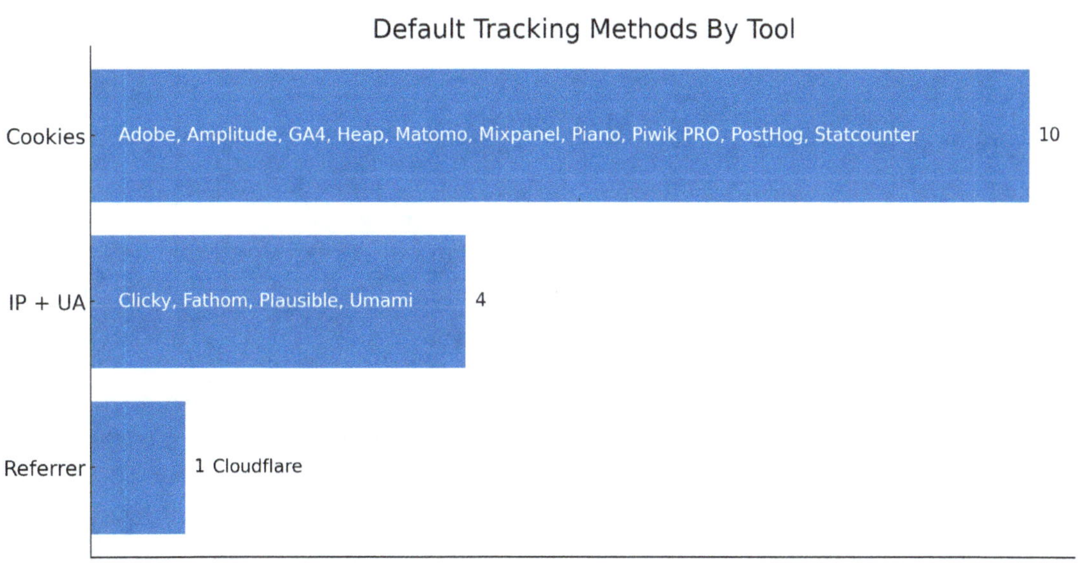

We will also discuss browser fingerprinting, as it is still used by some tools (none in this book) and is relevant to the discussion about IP + User-Agent tracking. The discussion is also focused on identifying anonymous users, since once a user logs into your site or has otherwise self-identified, tracking works differently.

Method One: Cookies

Cookies are the most common method for user tracking, used by the majority of the tools evaluated in this book. You're likely very familiar with them already, so I won't spend too much time on explanation.

Ok, that was a lie. I'm going to get into some nitty-gritty details here, if only because I've read too many site privacy policies that refer to cookies as "small text files." Cookies aren't small text files, and as analysts and tracking experts, we should understand the fundamentals of this particular method.

Cookies are name-value pairs and associated metadata stored in users' browsers, allowing for state to be maintained between individual requests.

While that description doesn't roll off the tongue like "small text files," it's a lot more accurate. Cookies haven't been stored in a text file for at least 10 years, and it was only old versions of Internet Explorer that did so, as individual small text files.

Modern browsers typically store cookies in a local SQLite database, which is a serverless database system that stores data in a single file. This is a regular file that the browser can then do SQL queries against. In fact, you could run queries on the file yourself from command-line or any SQL tool that supports SQLite.

Here's a command to see how many sites I have a GA cookie for:

```
$ sqlite3 "./Google/Chrome/Default/Cookies" \
"SELECT COUNT(*) FROM cookies WHERE name = '_ga';"
73
```

That means I've got GA cookies from 73 different sites. I can't pull the actual values quite so easily, because they are saved by the browser in an encrypted format. Still, it is just a regular SQL database.

Cookies were designed specifically to bring state to HTTP, so using cookies to identify users between individual web requests is exactly what they were made for.

I'd argue that using anything *other* than cookies requires some justification. The typical reasoning given is that the laws and regulations are about cookies, so if we use something else, we don't need to follow the same rules. This is a flawed interpretation. As we discussed in the last chapter, the rules are mostly designed to be technologically agnostic.

Insofar as cookies have a bad reputation, it's because of how they have been misused, rather than any inherent issues with the technology. Or at least this is true when we are talking about first-party cookies. Third-party cookies used for cross-site tracking *are* a misuse of the original design and purpose of cookies, and browsers shouldn't support them. You don't have to take my word for that statement; the inventor of cookies, Lou Montulli, said the following in an interview a few years ago (https://hiddenheroes.netguru.com/lou-montulli):

> Montulli recalls being shocked when he first encountered the DoubleClick implementation in the late 90s. "My first thought was: 'Holy shit, that shouldn't be possible—**we tried to design cookies so that would not be possible**,'" he says. "After I dove in and figured out how DoubleClick was doing it, we started talking about the ways in which we could respond. We ended up taking the path of creating a set of tools to allow users to see and control the ways in which cookies can be used."

After about five years of work towards abandoning third-party cookies, in 2024, Google about-faced and announced that Chrome will continue to support them. Edge also still supports third-party cookies, though its built-in tracking protection will block many attempts to set third-party tracking cookies (including Google's). Safari and Firefox do not allow third-party cookies. A good resource to track how different browsers treat cookies is https://www.cookiestatus.com.

Fortunately, web analytics does not require third-party cookies, and doesn't generally use them. Let's look at how GA uses cookies as an example. In GA, the basic building block of the device reporting identity is a cookie, specifically a cookie set on the domain of your website that looks like this:

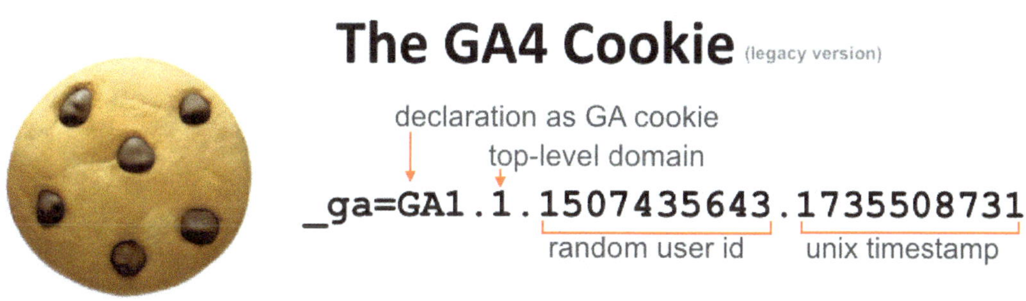

As with any cookie, this is simply a name–value pair (name=value). The name of the cookie is _ga, and the value is `GA1.1.1507435643.1735508731`.

- The initial "`GA1`" is a prefix to identify that this is a GA cookie, version one.
- The next "`1`" indicates the scope of the cookie. "`1`" means our cookie was likely set with the default "auto" setting for the cookie domain in GA4 and works on the top-level domain. If the tag used a manually set domain, e.g., "example.com," then this would be set to "`2`," and when manually set to

www.example.com, with three levels in the domain it would show that with "3."

- "1507435643" is a randomly generated user id from GA4.
- "1735508731" is a Unix timestamp, showing that this user id was generated on Dec 29, 2024.

In May 2025, Google changed its cookie format to something more complex that looks like this:

```
_ga_CFNYPCL3Q0=GS2.1.s1751547179$o1$g1$t1751547871$j58$l0$h0
```

It's still just a name–value pair; the complexity has just been increased in the format. The original format is more instructive of how cookies are used generally, which is why I'm still using it as an example. Please see David Vallejo's explainer if you would like to see a breakdown of the new format (https://www.thyngster.com/google-analytics-4-cookie-format-change-from-gs1-to-gs2-explained).

As David explains in his article, the new GA4 format follows better practices when it comes to serializing the data. This means that the data stored as the cookie value is packed up in a way that allows more flexibility and robustness.

However the cookie is formatted, how it is used for tracking users is straightforward: it's an identifier that is sent along with every request.

Method Two: IP + User-Agent

The very first visitor counting metrics were introduced by log analysis tools in the 1990s. Tools like Webtrends (released in 1995) and Webalizer (released in 1997) started counting total visitors in addition to just hits and pageviews. At first these tools counted the unique IP addresses in the web server log file. For example, take a look at this log file snippet:

```
128.135.189.8 [21/Feb/1997:15:16:27] "GET / HTTP/1.1" 200 5397 "Mozilla/4.02 (Win95; U)"
128.135.189.9 [21/Feb/1997:15:18:41] "GET / HTTP/1.1" 200 5397 "Mozilla/3.01 (X11; I; Linux)"
128.135.189.9 [21/Feb/1997:16:23:33] "GET / HTTP/1.1" 200 5397 "Mozilla/3.01 (X11; I; Linux)"
65.60.216.104 [21/Feb/1997:18:16:01] "GET / HTTP/1.1" 200 5397 "Mozilla/4.02 (Win95; U)"
```

IP-based log analyzers like Webalyzer would count three visitors, since there were three unique IPs. In 1995, this was a reasonably accurate way to count individual visitors—or at least individual computers—since at the time, IP addresses weren't widely shared between multiple computers. Network address translation (NAT), the technology that allows for the use of non-routable IPs (such as 192.168.1.100) on devices behind a router, was proposed in 1994 but took years to become commonplace. Proxies and IP sharing certainly existed, but were much less common than they are today.

Today, with NAT, many users all share the same externally facing IP. A company might have hundreds or thousands of users that all show up with the same external IP address, which would all show as the same IP to the remote web server and its logs. Internet service providers (ISPs) and especially mobile providers also use "carrier-grade" NAT (CGNAT), which allows for a similar kind of external-facing IP address sharing, but at a larger scale.

While Webalizer still exists and still counts IPs (it actually comes pre-installed on my current shared hosting account in 2025!), more advanced tools like Webtrends quickly realized that IP alone was not the most accurate method, and began using IP + User-Agent (as well as cookies). When adding User-Agent, cases where different devices are used on the same IP address are now seen as separate visitors.

After adding User-Agent to the identifier, all of a sudden, my iPhone is a different user than my desktop, and my office-mate running Windows shows up as a different user than me running MacOS—even though we all have the same external IP address.

When tracking migrated to client-side cookies in the early 2000s, this IP + User-Agent method was mostly left by the wayside. It was still used by logfile analyzers, but wasn't popularly used on the client side until its revival with tools like Fathom, Plausible, Umami, et al. in the post-GDPR era (2016–).

This revised version of IP + User-Agent has some changes from the original version. Firstly, it's done client-side via JavaScript tag, rather than via log processing. It also typically contains some additional privacy safeguards. A typical use of this method would create an identifier like this:

"Salt" means additional random text added to alter the output of the hash and increase cryptographic safety. Changing the salt means the identifier only lasts until the salt is rotated. So a daily salt rotation would mean identifiers only last for a maximum of one day. The inclusion of the site's domain means that the identifier can't be used for cross-site tracking. While this seems to be the predominant approach, not every tool that uses this method implements it the same way or even discloses its precise methodology. For example, Umami uses IP + User-Agent, but it has *monthly* salt rotation, so it can track the same returning user over multiple days.

Matomo and Piwik PRO use cookies by default, but offer IP + User-Agent as an additional method that can be used for users that decline consent. Clicky and PostHog support both cookies and IP+UA, but as alternatives to cookies, not working in conjunction with them.

There are a number of variations on this method. Some tools add additional factors to the identifier to improve the identifier's resolution. For example, Matomo uses `hash(salt + domain + IP + User-Agent + browser plugins + language)` as an identifier. Piwik PRO calls its version of this a "session hash" because it is designed to work for just one session and is never stored in its databases at all.

This addition of additional identification power ("entropy" in information-theoretic terms) can help distinguish users on the same network. For example, if you and your office-mate both run Chrome 131 on MacOS, but you also have Spanish set up as a language in your browser, then you would now be seen as separate users.

Language is just the user's language setting, but "browser plugins" is a somewhat misleading label. What actually happens is that the client-side JavaScript is checking for functionality that was historically supported by plugins: PDF support, QuickTime, Flash, etc.

"Plugins" like this don't really exist anymore, and to be clear, it's not checking for browser *extensions* (e.g., Ghostery or uBlock Origin), since it is not possible to directly do that with external JavaScript. It's also not using the Navigator.plugins browser API, which has been deactivated in most browsers for quite some time now and only returns a hard-coded list.

Matomo's method is still fairly restrained.

Is it browser fingerprinting? Matomo's FAQ very clearly says "Matomo does not use a fingerprint to track visitors," yet in the code, it refers to this identifier as a fingerprint, for example with a function called `getFingerprint()`. If Matomo is doing browser fingerprinting, then why wouldn't Plausible's method also be fingerprinting? After all, it's nearly the same thing, just with two fewer factors of identification.

As I've labelled this method "IP + User-Agent," it's evident I don't believe either of these methods should be labelled as "browser fingerprinting." This method lacks the invasiveness, identification power, and durability of true browser fingerprinting. We could accurately call this method "fingerprinting lite," or be even more pedantic and call it "transient low-entropy fingerprints," but I think it's confusing to associate it with the more invasive fingerprinting method.

While every tracking method has its drawbacks, I have a couple of specific concerns about IP + User-Agent.

IP+UA Issue 1: User-Agent Detail Reduction

Browsers are reducing the amount of information in the User-Agent string specifically because they want to avoid providing the kind of browser details that can be used for fingerprinting. Whether you consider IP+UA fingerprinting or not, efforts to restrict fingerprinting will also affect IP+UA. The table below lays out some clues as to whether the browser is using fingerprinting or not.

Is IP + UA Browser Fingerprinting?

Might Be Fingerprinting...	Might Not Be...
Can't be deleted or cleared by the user. Works in & out of incognito mode.	Not durable Can't be used for cross-site tracking Doesn't exploit wide variety of browser factors Focuses on "passive" factors

When I talk about passive factors, I mean things like IP and HTTP User-Agent that are sent with every single request and do not require actively inspecting the browser details with JavaScript like most fingerprinting methods do. Note that in some cases, tools are using the User-Agent as provided by JavaScript, not HTTP headers.

User-Agent detail reduction means that the idiosyncratic details that are self-reported by the browser get even weirder. Here are a couple of example

Safari 26 on macOS 15.6.1 reports as:

`Mozilla/5.0` **`(Macintosh;`** `Intel` **`Mac OS X`** `10_15_7`**`) AppleWebKit/605.1.15`** **`(`**`KHTML, like Gecko`**`) Version/26.`**`0` **`Safari/605.1.15`**

Chrome 138 on Windows 11 reports as:

`Mozilla/5.0` **`(Windows`** `NT 10.0; Win64; x64`**`)`** `AppleWebKit/537.36 (KHTML, like Gecko)` **`Chrome/138.`**`0.0.0` `Safari/537.36`

Bold means the information is correct and accurate.

`Red` means that the information in the User-Agent is purposefully incorrect for a legacy compatibility reason. For example, all major browsers start with "Mozilla/5.0" because during the early days of the web, sites used User-Agent strings for feature detection. "Mozilla/5.0" became a kind of shorthand in the 1990s, meaning that you were a "modern" browser, even though there was actually never a version 5.0 of Mozilla.

Grey means the information has been "reduced" to combat fingerprinting. For example, you could be on a Mac M4 with MacOS 16.1, but your HTTP User-Agent would still say Intel and MacOS 10.15.7. Chrome and Safari both have frozen parts of string, hard-coding it at a fixed, older version.

Working at odds against those privacy improvements, Chromium (Chrome, Edge, etc.) offers a workaround with the `getHighEntropyValues()` function in the User-Agent Client Hints API that can still give you the full data:

```
> navigator.userAgentData.getHighEntropyValues(["uaFullVersion"])
      .then(highEntropyData => {
          const userAgent = navigator.userAgent;
          const headerVersion = userAgent.match(/Chrome\/([\d.]+)/)[1];
          const apiVersion = highEntropyData.uaFullVersion;

          console.log("User-Agent HTTP Header Version:", headerVersion);
          console.log("High Entropy API Version:", apiVersion);
      });
<· ▶ Promise {<pending>}
  User-Agent HTTP Header Version: 131.0.0.0
  High Entropy API Version: 131.0.6778.205
```

The JavaScript above was run in the Chrome debugger, and you can see how Chrome still reveals the detailed info, though it is no longer passively sent as a part of each request, but has to be requested with JavaScript.

Safari and Firefox don't support this API. Brave (which is Chromium-based but with many privacy fixes) partially supports it.

IP+UA Issue 2: IP Addresses Don't Correspond Well to Individuals

In the IP + User-Agent method, the IP is providing most of the user identification power (entropy). Yet, IP addresses may change frequently, and can be shared by many people.

This has long been true, but as IP tracking and ad targeting have increased in recent years, there has been more use of virtual private networks (VPNs) to hide user IPs. This includes VPNs built-into browsers like Apple's iCloud Private Relay or Microsoft Edge Secure Network.

Method Three: Referrer

This is a method that doesn't create a visitor identifier at all, but creates an overall visitor count by looking at the HTTP referrer on pageviews. It's a very simple and limited method, but generally effective in terms of basic counts. As it has no identifier, it is by far the safest in terms of privacy and compliance.

This works because navigation from page to page inside your site should always pass a referrer of the previous page, so when there is no referrer or an external referrer like google.com, it's a good bet that this is a new visit. Cloudflare is the only tool we evaluate that uses this method, but there are other well-known tools like Simple Analytics that use it. This is a more recently developed method, as far as I could discover. Adriaan van Rossum, who founded Simple Analytics in 2018, told me that as far as he knew he was the inventor of this method, though he acknowledged that others may have developed it themselves independently as well.

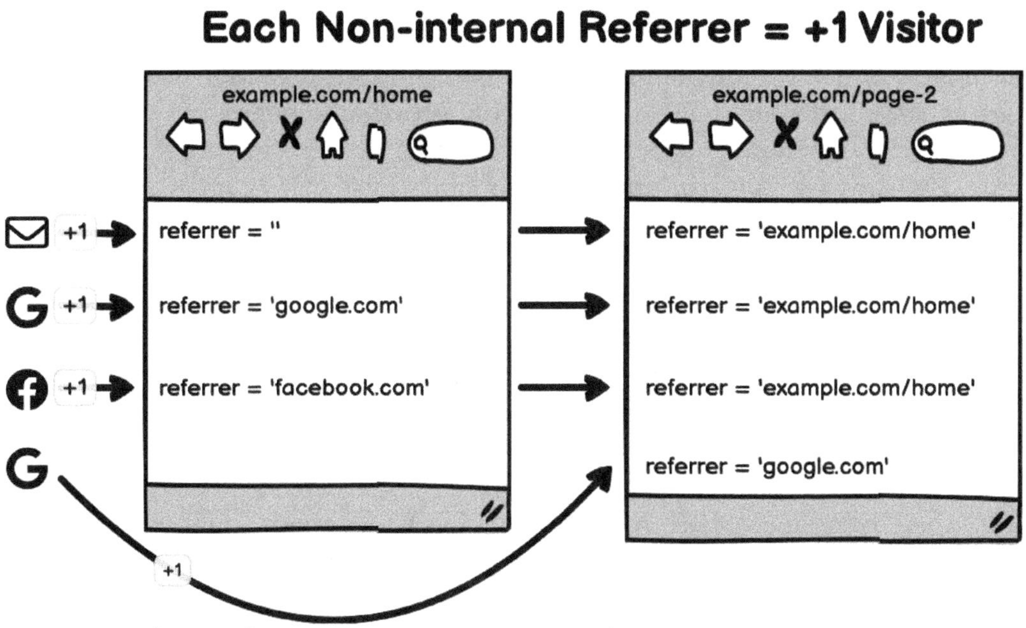

Because this method doesn't create an identifier at all, it is very safe to use without consent. If you think this sounds too simplistic to be accurate, I had the same reaction. However, I tested it against GA4, and found that the number of visits reported by Cloudflare was within 5% of GA4's session numbers, measured on a site with over a million sessions.

In exchange for improved privacy, there is no ability to track an individual user across their session (since there is no concept of a session). This means there's no ability to track a return visit vs a new visit, and no ability to do any kind of attribution. The latter is the reason why I don't generally recommend this method. In Cloudflare Web Analytics you could

- Track how many visits you received from Google.com
- Track how many pageviews you had to your conversion page/thank-you

but you *couldn't* track how many of those conversions came from Google. This is a deal-breaker for many use cases.

Method Four: Browser Fingerprinting

By our stricter definition, *none of the tools we evaluate use browser fingerprinting* to create a visitor id. The User-Agent method and its extensions simply don't collect enough information to create ids that are unique just based on information from the browser. True browser fingerprinting doesn't need to use IP addresses because the created fingerprint is unique enough without that IP, and it can even track users when IP addresses change. I consider IP + User-Agent to be a variation of tracking by IP address with some additional entropy, rather than tracking by inspecting the users' browsers in detail.

While fingerprinting is not popular in web analytics, it is widely used for other purposes. In 2024, I identified 38% of the top 100 sites' home pages that used fingerprinting methods. This number is in line with academic studies showing that over 25% of the top 10k sites use fingerprinting (https://umariqbal.com/papers/fpinspector-sp2021.pdf).

Most fingerprinting is used for advertising tracking, anti-bot, and anti-fraud uses—not web analytics. In the first edition of this book, I reviewed Visitor Analytics (now known as TWIPLA), which did use fingerprinting as its default method in 2022. TWIPLA has since changed its policies. It still supports browser fingerprinting, but no longer uses it by default.

In 2010, the Electronic Frontier Foundation (EFF) first brought public attention to browser fingerprinting with its "Panopticlick" project. Its follow-up, the "Cover Your Tracks" project, defines browser fingerprinting as follows (emphasis mine; from https://coveryourtracks.eff.org/about#browser-fingerprinting):

> "Browser fingerprinting" is a method of **tracking web browsers by the configuration and settings** information they make visible to websites, rather than traditional tracking methods such as IP addresses and unique cookies.
>
> Browser fingerprinting is both difficult to detect and and extremely difficult to thwart.
>
> When you load a webpage, you will automatically broadcast certain information about your browser to the website you are visiting—as well as to any trackers embedded within the site (such as those that serve advertisements). The site you are visiting may choose to analyze your browser using JavaScript, Flash and other methods (just like Cover Your Tracks does). It may look for what types of fonts you have installed, the language you've set, the add-ons you've installed, and other factors. The site may then create a type of profile of you, tied to this pattern of characteristics associated with your browser, rather than tied to a specific tracking cookie.

If your browser is unique, then it's possible that an online tracker can identify you even without setting tracking cookies. While the tracker won't know your name, they could collect a deeply personal dossier of websites you visit.

According to the EFF's definition, fingerprinting is about more than just IP tracking and involves using a variety of factors unrelated to what is sent in the normal process of browsing. We can see the difference simply in the number of factors used by fingerprinting services in the bar chart below.

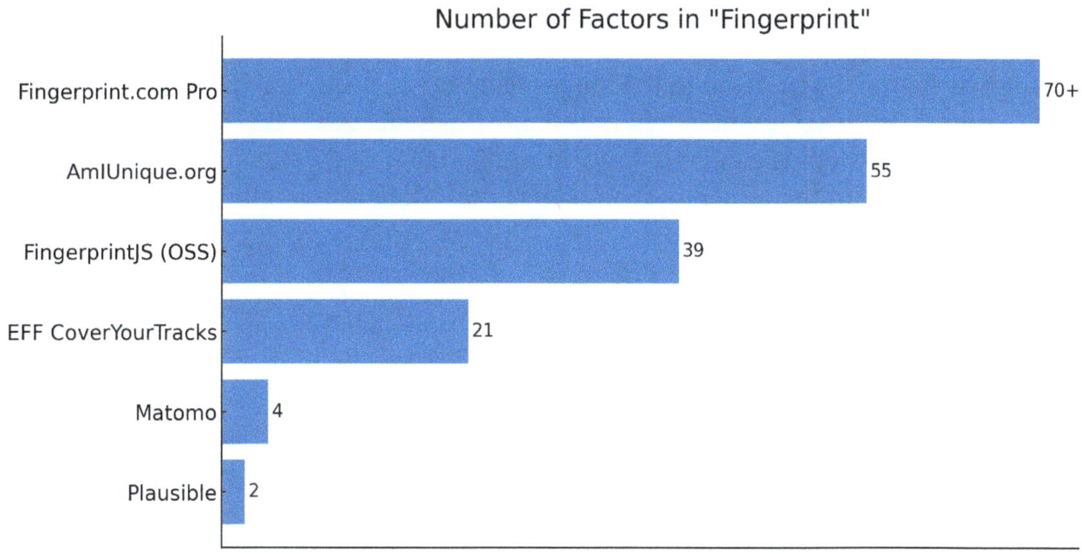

Services like FingerprintJS use not just the basic info like User-Agent, which is sent with every request already, but also much more invasive checks like checking what kind of fonts you have installed, your graphics card, or how many CPU cores your device reports having.

Fingerprinting is much more invasive and less favorable to privacy than standard first-party analytics cookies, and I don't recommend its use in analytics for the following reasons:

- Cookies can be deleted, but fingerprints remain constant until the browser itself is changed.
- Fingerprints are the same across different sites, opening a greater possibility for cross-site tracking than first-party cookies.
- Fingerprinting can detect the use of incognito mode and maintain the same fingerprint between regular and incognito mode.

- Fingerprinting looks at your browser in detail and creates a much more unique and durable identifier than any cookie. Fingerprinting relies on the use of JavaScript functions, sometimes in clever but borderline malicious ways.
- Browsers are actively working to stop fingerprinting. One could correctly point out that they're also trying to restrict cookie-based tracking, but the browser and web standards community recognizes the utility of first-party cookies—meaning they're looking to *limit* cookies but *eliminate* fingerprinting.

Fingerprinting, however, *does* have legitimate uses for anti-bot and anti-fraud purposes, which we'll talk about in Chapter 16 - Bot Filtering.

Congrats on making it through the longest chapter in the book! There's a lot of detail here to digest, but if you remember anything from the last chapter or two, it should be this: the technical details can be helpful to understand, but, ultimately, *how the data is used* is more relevant than the fine-grained technical details on methods.

Chapter 14 - Consent

Throughout this guide, we talk about consent, compliance, and privacy in a broad sense. We'll go a bit deeper in this chapter, especially with regard to consent.

Whether or not you need to ask a user for consent before recording their data remains one of the most polarizing and difficult questions to get a clear answer to when implementing an analytics tool.

While I'd love to be able to give you a simple yes or no answer here, this topic can get pretty complicated, and I'm not a lawyer. I'm especially not *your* lawyer. This subject can also change very quickly. At the time of writing, in late 2025, there are discussions happening in the EU about how to simplify regulations and streamline consent. I'm hopeful that the idea of setting preferences more globally in the browser could eliminate the need for per-site prompting, but that's not where we are right now.

Consentless Tracking

If you do any tracking that can persistently identify users, you are required to get user consent in many places, most notably the EU. The EU's ePrivacy Directive (formally the Privacy and Electronic Communications Directive) coupled with the GDPR are the most relevant regulations here, and require the following (cribbed from https://gdpr.eu/cookies):

> Receive users' consent before you use any cookies except strictly necessary cookies.
>
> Provide accurate and specific information about the data each cookie tracks and its purpose in plain language before consent is received.
>
> Document and store consent received from users.
>
> Allow users to access your service even if they refuse to allow the use of certain cookies.
>
> Make it as easy for users to withdraw their consent as it was for them to give their consent in the first place.

The United States is a much different story, as there is no federal data protection law but instead an incomplete patchwork of state laws. Currently, no individual state laws require the same kind of "accept/reject" consent prompt that the EU requires, though many organizations have decided to implement that sort of prompt globally for simplicity and safety purposes.

As of October 2025, 16 US states (CA, CO, CT, DE, IA, MD, MN, MT, NE, NH, NJ, OR, TN, TX, UT, VA) have active data privacy and protection laws (https://iapp.org/resources/article/us-state-privacy-legislation-tracker/). The California laws (the California Consumer Privacy Act, CCPA, and the California Privacy Rights Act, CPRA) are the most notable, being the first passed and the template that many other states have followed. Each set of state laws is different, however, and treating the California law as if it were the missing federal law isn't always going to be correct.

Most of us are not data privacy experts. We don't have deep knowledge of the GDPR or the enforcement date of Nebraska's data privacy law on our calendar (it was January 1, 2025, in case you missed it). When it comes to implementation, we have become reliant upon tool vendors as well as consent management platforms (CMPs) and their interpretations of these laws.

Let's take a quick look at two of the most popular CMPs (CookieYes and OneTrust) and their own sites' cookie banners as shown in California vs. the EU.

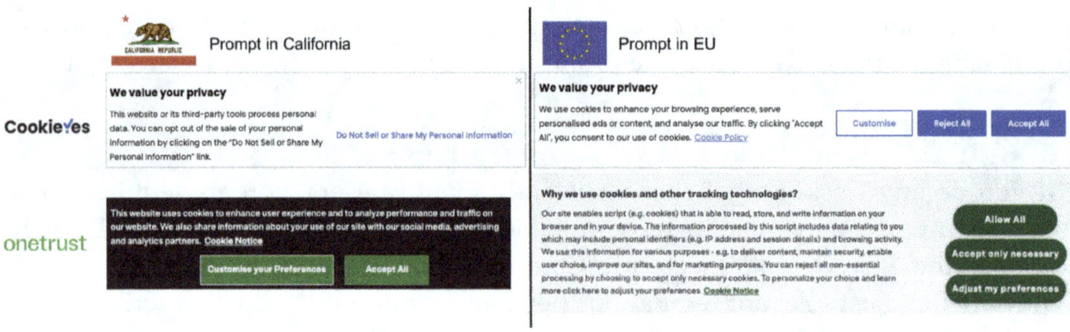

Both CMP vendors take a similar approach: a relatively clear "accept/reject" in the EU and a default accept in California. The way the vendors have set up their EU banners is clear: no analytics cookies before consent, and analytics cookies are not to be classified as "necessary." In the example of CookieYes and GA4, they still allow GA's so-called "cookieless pings" if analytics cookies are rejected. OneTrust does not run GA.

If implemented properly and without dark patterns, a GDPR-style banner can definitely have a positive effect on user privacy. It's bad UI, annoying, and I fundamentally question its concept of "informed consent"... However, it's miles (kilometers?) better than the California version of the prompts, which isn't actually consent at all.

The California banner is not a consent prompt but a privacy notice, with a link to opt out of personal information selling. For CookieYes in California, it allows GA4 cookies no matter what you select, even if you select the "Do Not Sell or Share My Personal Information" option.

One thing I really like about the California approach is the mandate that sites need to be listening for the Global Privacy Control (GPC) header. This is a simple signal from the browser in the form of an HTTP header (`Sec-GPC`) or JavaScript flag (`navigator.globalPrivacySignal`) that indicates whether the user consents or not, universally across all sites. If you're not familiar with the GPC header, it's more or less the same as the defunct Do Not Track (DNT) header: a browser preference that sends an HTTP header with every request indicating your tracking preferences. One of the main reasons for DNT's failure was that it had no enforcement, so having GPC already established in law is a good first step.

California's privacy laws (as well as those of Colorado and Connecticut) require GPC support, and, indeed, both of the CMPs above do listen for it and treat it as an opt-out signal if you're in the United States. Among many issues with GPC, however, is that it's currently only supported in Firefox and Brave (https://caniuse.com/?search=sec-gpc), so ~95% of users don't even have the option to send that header without using a browser extension. There's also the same issues that existed with DNT: it's not controllable by site (at least with how Firefox and Brave have implemented it) and when a browser chooses to turn it on by default (as Brave has done with GPC and Internet Explorer did long ago with DNT in 2012), it throws a wrench into a system that is largely built upon the idea of opting out.

Obviously, the world is much bigger than the EU and the US. The IAPP currently tracks data protection and privacy laws for 144 different countries (https://iapp.org/news/a/data-protection-and-privacy-laws-now-in-effect-in-144-countries/), so you'll understand why we can't cover more than the two that are the most widely relevant for the likely readers of this book.

So, where does that leave us on the question of so-called consentless analytics? In this book, we've got multiple tools that claim not to need a consent banner, including Plausible, Fathom, and Umami. We've also got tools that normally use cookies but have cookieless modes that claim not to require consent, including GA4, Piwik PRO, and Matomo.

The statement "I don't use cookies, therefore I don't need consent" is an incorrect reading of EU rules. The rules are designed to be technology-agnostic, meaning it doesn't matter if you use cookies, localStorage, browser fingerprinting, or some yet-to-be-developed technology—it's about how the technology functions and if it can be used to identify someone and their personal data. The European Data Protection Board (EDPB) has issued guidelines (https://www.edpb.europa.eu/our-work-tools/our-documents/guidelines/guidelines-22023-technical-scope-art-53-eprivacy-directive_en) that clarify that the ePrivacy Directive, despite being known as "the cookie law," is applicable beyond cookies.

If your tracking method replicates similar tracking capacity to that of a cookie, then there's no question that you need consent for it in the same places you need consent for cookies. It also doesn't matter if your tracking tech is delivered client-side or server-side (which we'll go into more deeply in the next chapter); the rules remain the same.

Is there some point at which the tracking capacity of a tool has been reduced to a point such that you don't need consent? This uncertainty is the space in which the cookieless tools operate. Different tools make different claims, or avoid making explicit claims at all. For example, Umami makes this very unhelpful claim (https://umami.is/docs):

> Do I need to display a cookie notice to users?
>
> No, Umami does not use any cookies in the tracking code.

This doesn't discuss consent at all and is woefully inadequate guidance for users of the tool.

Plausible makes the case that its tool doesn't require consent, based on legitimate interest and the lack of resolution and durability of its identifier (https://plausible.io/blog/legal-assessment-gdpr-eprivacy). Fathom makes some of the same points (https://usefathom.com/legal/compliance/eprivacy-compliant-website-analytics), though it highlights the passive nature of its tracking data factors.

In particular, I find the "legitimate interest" argument to be pretty weak. You hear that vague phrase thrown around a lot as a justification for collecting data, as if invoking the word "legitimate" over and over makes it so. What that phrase is actually saying is that you have to *make an argument* that your use of the data is justifiable and reasonable. The phrase "legitimate interest" is not an argument in and of itself.

Here's the full section from the relevant part of the GDPR:

> Art. 6 (f): processing is necessary for the purposes of the legitimate interests pursued by the controller or by a third party, except where such interests are overridden by the interests or fundamental rights and freedoms of the data subject which require protection of personal data, in particular where the data subject is a child.

"Legitimate interest" has to be balanced against the user's privacy rights, and in addition, this GDPR section is explicitly about *processing*, not consent.

My issues with that phrase aside, Plausible and Fathom do both make good points. Also, I just checked, and I'm still not a lawyer. If you are in the EU or somewhere with similar regulations, you will want to discuss this with your own legal counsel.

These same arguments apply at least in part to all the other tools marked "IP + User-Agent" as the default visitor id in this guide. As of 2025, there have been no court cases I'm aware of that test these vendor claims.

Simple Analytics, a competitor with a different method, offers a counter-argument (https://www.simpleanalytics.com/blog/why-simple-analytics-is-a-great-alternative-to-plausible#are-ip-hashes-considered-personal-data), asserting that using a hash that includes an IP address means Plausible should be required to ask for consent.

I run Plausible on my company's own website without asking for consent, based upon the following rationale:

1. My company is based in the US and has no business interests in the EU.
2. A user id in Plausible is defined as `hash(daily_salt + website_domain + ip_address + user_agent)`, which, as we covered in the last chapter, means:
3. Raw IP addresses aren't stored.
4. Visitors can't be tracked over time; if the same person comes back the next day, their id would change.
5. Users can't be tracked cross-site, since the website domain is included in the hash.
6. In particular, those are passively collectable data points that are part of a default HTTP request and not the result of active JavaScript inspection of the browser.
7. Plausible is designed to collect a minimal amount of data, and is not connected to any advertising-related platform.
8. Introducing a third-party CMP would *increase* my users' data exposure. I trust Plausible with my users' data more than I would OneTrust, so adding a CMP like OneTrust would only add data exposure.
9. I maintain that running Plausible *without consent* is superior for users' privacy vs GA4 *with consent* when using advanced consent mode cookieless pings and a CMP.

That's my rationale, but you'll have to make your own choices. From my comments earlier in this chapter about the lack of US laws requiring consent, I probably could have just stopped at #1.

Even if you can find a solution you feel comfortable running consentless, consider that you may need consent for other things on your site. Do you use cookies or track personal information in any other way that would require consent management?

This is a deep topic where different experts have a variety of well-considered and strongly held opinions!

Analytics Tools, CMPs, and Tag Managers

Other than Piwik PRO, which offers its own CMP (https://piwik.pro/gdpr-consent-manager/), consent will likely be managed via a third-party CMP. Similarly, some suites include tag managers (Piwik PRO, Adobe, Matomo, and, of course, GA itself), but it's overall more common to use a TMS from a different vendor than your analytics tool.

For implementation, we need to consider our CMP and tag manager tools and how they work with our new solution.

Limiting Data Collection

So far, we've mostly been talking about consent in the context of regulatory compliance. That's, of course, critically necessary, but it's not the same thing as user privacy. Good regulation should improve user privacy, but we need data practitioners to get ahead and lead with good privacy practices rather than just being reactive to regulations.

Information security has a rule called the "principle of least privilege" (https://en.wikipedia.org/wiki/Principle_of_least_privilege) or the "principal of minimal privilege" (my preferred nomenclature). This rule states that each person or process should have access to the minimal amount of information and resources needed to do their function. Typically, this is used in the context of permissions in computer security to limit access.

For example, you may give an outside consultant read-only access at the GA view level to the only view they need to perform their analysis, instead of allowing edit access at the property or account level.

This same principle can and should apply to the data itself. What's the minimal amount of data I need to collect and store to accomplish the job at hand?

Introducing this limitation can easily become annoying, but we need to do our best to avoid taking the easy way out. In our GA access example above, if you're the analytics consultant receiving access and you discover you need to see a different view as well, or need to edit a filter or something, you'd have to go back and ask for more permissions, which is frustrating and time-consuming. Considering that user permissions are infrequently cleaned up, it's obvious what issues could arise from giving everyone admin access. A common problem is "privilege creep," where access levels *increase* over time rather than decrease.

Now think about how this rule would apply to data. If you don't need user IPs, don't store them. If you don't need historical access to raw data for more than 30 days, don't keep it. This approach aligns well with the "explicit" style of tracking we discussed previously. It's more work, but it's a substantial improvement for both compliance and user privacy. Minimal privilege is something that most projects intend to do, but few actually succeed in doing.

Beyond the rules, I'd encourage analysts to simply consider how they'd like their own data to be handled. We can get caught up in the details about what article of the GDPR says what and which browser cuts off cookies when, but starting from an empathetic approach, where we remember this data comes from real people, is the best first step we can take.

CHAPTER 15 - SERVER-SIDE

As an analyst, ad blockers are a huge pain and an ongoing source of data issues. As a user, I love my ad blocker and recoil at the idea of using the internet without it.

This is the cognitive dissonance underlying much of the discussion about content blocking, cookie restrictions, and their workarounds—most notably, server-side analytics.

So what is server-side analytics? Confusingly, when people talk about "server-side," what they are typically referring to is a scenario where client-side JavaScript is still used, but its tracking payloads are sent via a proxy server that sits between the browser and the measurement server. This tracking is still initiated by the client (i.e., the browser), but it's relayed through an additional server before it reaches its destination server. This can have the effect of making the analytics scripts and measurement appear to be first-party, from your own site, rather than via a third party like Google.

I would describe "true" server-side tracking as server-to-server communication that is initiated by a server, not the browser. For example, let's say you run a subscription service that costs $10/mo. and you have a billing program running on your server to automatically charge your renewing customers. As part of that script, you want to track renewal transactions in GA, so you have the script also send a server-to-server measurement protocol request with the transaction and the user id it belongs to. That's true server-side. That's also not very relevant to most user activities we're talking about, not generally what people mean when they say "server-side," and not what we're discussing in this chapter.

This chapter is about client-initiated, server-proxied analytics. The terminology is confusing, and the process itself can also be complex, leading many an analyst's eyes to glaze over when the topic is discussed.

While this additional server-proxy layer adds complexity, it also adds a lot of opportunities for innovation and streamlining measurement. Server-side benefits can include the following:

- Site performance increases by reducing the number of front-end requests. Instead of having 20 different client-side tags on your site that are each reading the same information and slowing the browser experience down, we could send that information just once to a server-side container and then have that server handle relaying that information to 20 different servers.
- Privacy improvements. If we are concerned about something like personal data reaching a measurement server or an overly aggressive vendor tag pulling data from sensitive page contents, we can have fine-grained control over what data the measurement vendors have access to, since we can place the vendor tag in the server-side container and control what is sent to that container.
- Other data cleaning and normalization functionality. There are a lot of interesting and innovative ideas that could make use of this newer paradigm, and analysts are still trying to learn about it and explore the possibilities. We could hide API keys that might otherwise be client-side, track offline conversions, enrich measurement hits with external data, etc., etc.

There are a lot of potential benefits, but the one benefit that is driving adoption of this technology is avoiding having tags blocked and cookie durations reduced. Much of the talk about server-side is to "recover lost data." This is a euphemistic way to talk about dodging ad blockers, avoiding consent management, and defeating browser cookie restrictions like Safari ITP.

For example, let's say that instead of directly calling the Google domains, we load our GA tracking tag from our own domain:
`example.com/server-side/my-tracker.js`
and send the measurement requests to
`example.com/server-side/send-data`
then, we have a much better chance of avoiding detection by the ad blockers.

Additionally, we could also call
`example.com/server-side/set-cookie`
And this would enable us to utilize HTTP headers to set (or extend) the cookies we need, rather than relying upon the standard JavaScript `document.cookie` calls, which may have their cookies shortened.

Done and dusted, we've solved ad blockers and ITP, right? Not even close! Not only have we not yet discussed additional protections like Canonical Name (CNAME) decloaking or algorithmic tracker blockers, but we haven't discussed the more important topic of users' privacy choices and compliance. *In no way does server-side tagging abrogate a site's responsibilities to respect user privacy!* In fact, it can make compliance harder, since it brings in more technical complexity. The signals that represent users' consent choices now have to be passed around to more places, and likewise, there are more places where you need to make sure user data compliance is validated. Consider that part of the reason that analytics measurement is now so complicated is, in fact, a response to a long record of not considering user privacy!

Ad blocking has been interfering with analytics data for a long time, and over that time, it has gotten much more widespread and complex. Site operators still want to know "how much data they are losing," a fundamentally flawed perspective that assumes they are somehow entitled to 100% of user tracking data, whether the user is ok with that or not. Measuring users who are explicitly trying to avoid tracking is both technically difficult and ethically questionable.

Let's dig into some actual request flows and see what happens to our measurement requests with an ad blocker. Our examples focus on GA, but are broadly applicable to any platform.

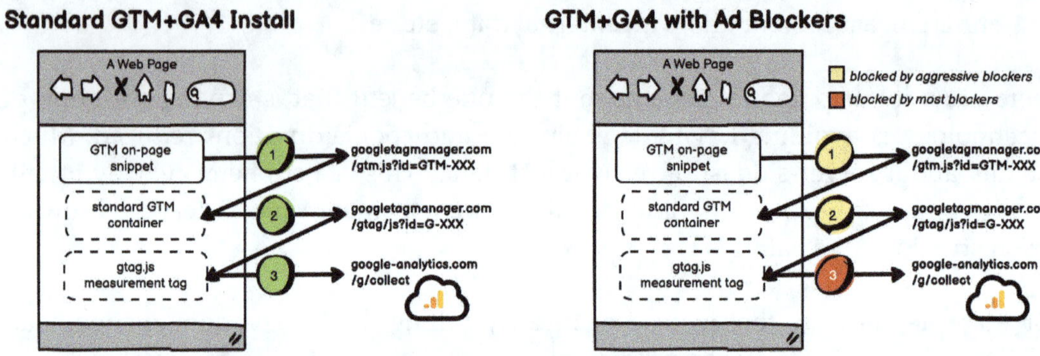

Note that the more aggressive blockers may also block GTM itself or the `gtag.js` file before it even starts sending measurement requests to Google! In the first example on the left, everything flows as expected. The browser loads the GTM container, retrieves the GA tracking code measurement tag, then executes that and sends off a measurement request to the GA back-end.

In the second case, with an ad blocker, there are three different opportunities for measurement to be interrupted. The browser might totally block GTM (#1), in which case none of your tags including GA would load. The browser might allow GTM but disallow the loading of the `gtag.js` tracking code (#2), or it might only block the measurement endpoint at google-analytics.com itself (#3).

How many users run ad blockers? Blockthrough reports 27% of desktop and 22% of mobile users in the US use an ad blocker, based on tracking actual usage (https://blockthrough.com/blog/2023-pagefair-adblock-report/). Asking users via survey tends to result in even higher numbers being reported, as users may want to appear more technologically savvy to surveyors, or may not have their blocker enabled all the time.

Several of the most popular ad blockers in the market don't actually block analytics trackers by default, so the effect on analytics will on average be lower than that 22–27% number. In an article on GA blocking I published in 2024 (https://www.quantable.com/analytics/whats-blocking-google-analytics-now/), I calculated that about half of ad block users were blocking GA by default. That would give us a *very* rough estimate of *about 12% of users in the US blocking GA* overall.

Your particular site's number will be highly dependent on your users' demographics. The more tech-savvy and privacy-conscious your users are, the more likely they are to block analytics trackers. For example, Plausible reported in 2021 that 58% of tech-savvy users from sites like Hacker News and Reddit blocked Google Analytics (https://plausible.io/blog/google-analytics-adblockers-missing-data).

How did we get to a point where so many users, especially technically sophisticated ones, are pushing back so strongly against analytics? While "web analytics" started as an IT function in the early years, it quickly grew to be more associated with marketing. As GA became the predominant tool, its association with advertising and Google's aggressive approach to user data became more clear—and users started to want to block analytics too, not just ads.

Ad blockers have existed for just about as long as there have been ads on the web. The first banner ad was in 1994, and the first ad blocker was in 1996, yet it wasn't until many years later that GA blocking became widespread, in the early 2010s.

The first well-known blocker that included Google Analytics was the Adblock EasyList (by Rick Petnel), available for AdblockPlus in 2006 (https://web.archive.org/web/20060831043622/http://easylist.adblockplus.org/easylist-modified.htm). Since Google Analytics itself launched in 2005, it wasn't long after GA started that some users were looking to block it. This early blocklist not only blocked GA, but it also included domains for Webtrends and Omniture. Nearly 20 years later, "EasyList" lives on and is one of the most widely used blocklists around, and it's grown massively in both size and popularity.

In 2006, EasyList was 281 lines long. As of 2025, the core EasyList is 63,931 lines long—excluding the auxiliary EasyPrivacy list, where analytics tools now live. The popular uBlock Origin ad block extension uses those lists and several others by default, summing up to a whopping *142k* rules active in a default installation of uBlock Origin.

EasyList is used in AdBlock Plus, uBlock Origin, Brave, and numerous other places. As mentioned, one important distinction is that EasyList splits out tracking tools into a separate list called "EasyPrivacy," which is *not* used by default by all blockers. The two most popular blockers, AdBlock and AdBlockPlus (historically separate products now owned by eyeo GmbH and effectively the same), don't have EasyPrivacy turned on by default—meaning many of those users do not block GA.

The default setup in Adblock and AdblockPlus requires you to click "Block additional tracking" to enable the blocklist that would include GA and other analytics trackers.

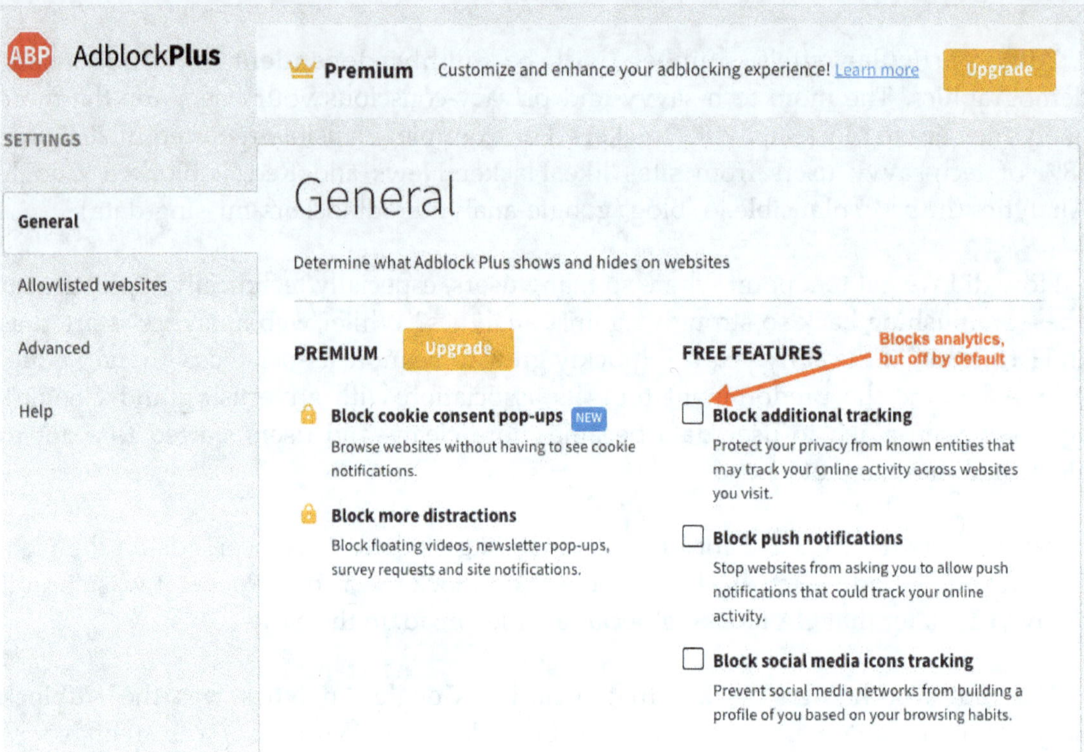

In other words, not all ad blocker tools block GA, and it can be hard to keep track of when they do.

Sometimes, tools point out when they are *not* on the ad blockers' lists. I would argue this is more of a measurement of that tool's popularity and age rather than a comment on its user privacy standards.

Aggressive blocking lists like EasyPrivacy aren't interested in investigating a particular tool's claims on its privacy-friendly data practices. If they can be considered a tracker, they go on the list. In the last chapter, we talked about how the design of Cloudflare Web Analytics is the most privacy-friendly we evaluate, since it doesn't have any concept of a user identifier. Despite this, all the major block lists include Cloudflare Web Analytics, as you can see in the chart below.

	EasyPrivacy	AdGuard Tracking	Ghostery TrackerDB	EFF Privacy Badger	DDG Tracker Radar	Disconnect	*blocked by*
Google Analytics	✗	✗	✗	✗	✗	✗	100%
Statcounter	✗	✗	✗	✗	✗	✗	100%
Clicky	✗	✗	✗	✗	✗	✗	100%
Amplitude	✗	✗	✗	✗	✗	✗	100%
Adobe Analytics	✗	✗	✗	✗	✗	✗	100%
Cloudflare	✗	✗	✗	✗	✗	✗	100%
Mixpanel	✗	✗	✗	⚠	✗	✗	83%
Matomo	✗	✗	✗	✗	✗	✓	83%
Piwik PRO	✗	✗	✗	✗	✗	✓	83%
Piano Analytics	✗	✗	✗	✗	✓	✗	83%
Heap	✗	✗	✗	✗	✗	✓	83%
Fathom Analytics	✗	✗	✗	✗	✓	✓	67%
PostHog	✗	✗	⚠	✗	✗	✓	67%
Google Tag Manager	✗	✗	✗	✓	✓	✓	50%
Plausible Analytics	✗	✗	✗	✓	✓	✓	50%
Umami	✗	✗	⚠	✓	✓	✓	33%
	16	16	14	12	11	8	80% <= overall rate

That's not to say there isn't some correlation between being more privacy-friendly and exclusion from blocklists, just that you should expect most trackers to appear on most lists eventually.

It's also worth nothing that half of these lists block Google Tag Manager. You could use a totally adblock-proof tag, but if you deliver it via GTM (or some other tag manager) it may still be blocked.

Even if you follow GA4's basic instructions on how to setup GA4 via GTM server-side tracking (https://developers.google.com/tag-platform/learn/sst-fundamentals/5-sst-setup-analytics), you're still going to have a lot of your measurement data blocked and degraded.

Let's re-create the diagram from earlier in the chapter for what happens with a default ssGTM setup.

Standard SS GTM+GA4 Install

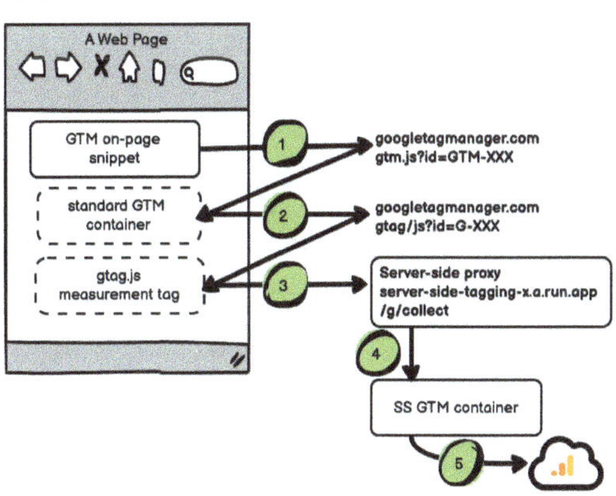

SS GTM+GA4 Install with Ad Blockers

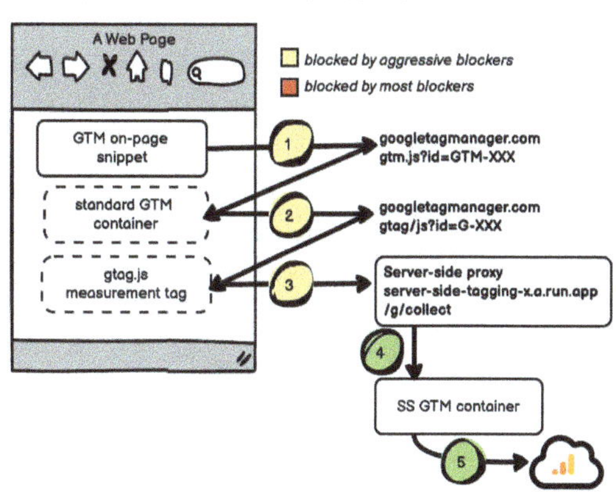

This basic server-side setup gives aggressive lists like EasyPrivacy several obvious chances to block the tag. This is a "worst of both worlds" scenario: many blockers will still be blocking the data, you've made your installation significantly more complicated, and you've added something that will require maintenance. More recent options like the Cloudflare Google Tag gateway (https://developers.cloudflare.com/google-tag-gateway/) are intended to both simplify this setup and avoid implementing a solution that doesn't solve your issues.

While many of our alternatives are technically capable of being deployed via a server-side proxy, some make this much easier than others. Plausible's WordPress plugin allows for the deployment of a server-side proxy with one click. Google Analytics is on the other end of the spectrum, with a very complex setup.

Note that using a simple proxy solution like Plausible's WordPress plugin doesn't allow you to take advantage of some of the additional benefits of server-side we talked about at the top. In that scenario, there's no server-side tag container and no ability to transform the data server-side; it just gets around the blockers. When it comes to full server-side *tagging*, you need a tag manager (or some other tag and data manipulation layer) deployed on the intermediary server as well.

This is a deep and technical topic that goes well beyond the depth we can get into with one chapter of this book. If you're looking to learn more, the "Server-side Tagging in Google Tag Manager" class from Team Simmer (https://www.teamsimmer.com/all-courses/server-side-tagging-in-google-tag-manager/) is a great resource.

Chapter 16 - Bot Filtering

The internet is full of bots, and we don't typically want them in our reports. They pollute our data, and can even raise the bill from your analytics tool. Yet most tools have limited capacity to stop or filter out the bot data.

Much of the issue is simply the huge volume of bot traffic. Imperva's 2025 Bad Bot Report (https://www.imperva.com/resources/resource-library/reports/2025-bad-bot-report/) says bots are responsible for 51% of web traffic, and Cloudflare Radar says bots are responsible for 31% (https://radar.cloudflare.com/bots). Both numbers are from very credible sources, but there's also no way to truly validate these claims, and it's likely that neither represents the "actual" number. If these companies really could identify bots with high accuracy, then they would be able to offer much more effective bot-blocking tools than they do. Both of those companies do, in fact, offer enterprise-level bot blocking services, and having used both of them in high-volume situations against real bot attacks, I can tell you that they are far from 100% accurate.

Does this mean that 30–50% (or more) of the traffic in our analytics reports is bot traffic? Thankfully, that answer is typically no. The full answer is complex, as there are a lot of different points in the analytics measurement process where website traffic can be filtered or excluded before it makes it into your final reports.

The grey "dead ends" in the following diagram show at what point traffic may end up missing from your reports. Whether it's a bot without JavaScript capabilities, or a human coming from a filtered internal IP, there are a number of different ways traffic can end up absent from your reports.

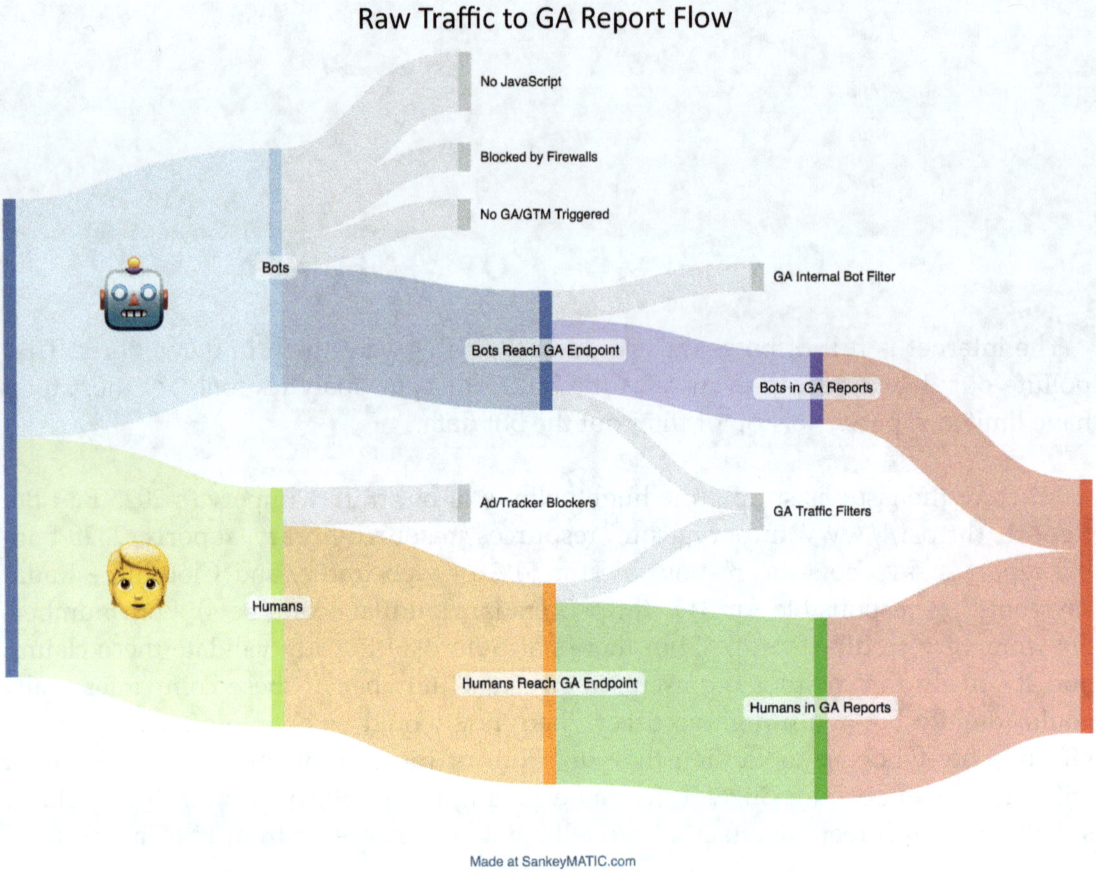

While this diagram is not comprehensive, I have listed many of the common cases of exclusion. It is also not intended to show accurate proportions, which vary greatly per site. One site might have 5% ad block users, and the next might have 40%. One site might be subject to constant bot attacks, and the next might be spared.

Once data shows up in a GA report, it can be very hard to differentiate human from bot, and it's not feasible to remove the data even if you could accurately identify it. In GA, one of the best ways to know if you have a bot issue is if you see lots of traffic from cities with big data centers (e.g., Ashburn, VA, or Boardman, OR), but that is a very limited data point: a warning signal, that's all. This method only works because those are locales with big data centers, but modest populations. According to datacentermap.com, Dallas, TX, has 193 data centers compared to Ashburn's 150, but seeing Dallas near the top of your most popular cities wouldn't be as notable (and nobody would suggest filtering out all traffic from Dallas). So, before you just exclude Ashburn from your reports and call it a day, dig a little deeper to see if you can really solve the problem rather than just hiding it.

For privacy reasons, GA doesn't track many of the data points that are required for effective bot filtering. GA doesn't store ISP data or individual IPs, and doesn't provide users with raw User-Agent strings, among other limitations. Privacy is, in fact, a big reason why analytics tools struggle with bot detection, as much of what is necessary for effective bot detection is not allowable in analytics under privacy regulations. The more intrusive data collection we need to stop bots is much beyond what we should be using for analytics, and the data needs to be treated differently.

As an example, we might need to do consentless browser fingerprinting to do effective bot detection. Fingerprinting before asking the user *would* be allowable under "legitimate interest" according to GDPR, but unacceptable for use in user analytics.

Some examples of bots that could show up in your reports:

- SEO monitoring tools
- Developer testing tools
- Ad validation or targeting
- Ad fraud
- AI bots
- General content scrapers

No tool is going to be 100% accurate in identifying bots, and part of the challenge is that the more aggressive the detector, the more likely it is to also include false positives of human traffic. The difficulty is that there are a large number of possible signals of bot behavior, but many are not definitive proof, but are rather simply indicative of a higher likelihood. Some of these factors include network data, browser-based data, data integrity, and behavioral data.

Network Data (IP Address, Network Connection-Level Information)

Is the user coming from a data center IP address? If they are coming from an IP that is registered to Amazon AWS, Google Cloud Platform, etc., then it's likely (though far from certain) they are a bot. Filtering out all data center traffic as "bots" means you will miss some amount of human traffic, as a data center IP could be a human using a VPN that routes its traffic via a data center exit point. With the increased popularity of VPNs and services like Safari's iCloud Private Relay, blanket filtering based on data center IPs can be problematic. Conversely, plenty of bots use IP addresses that appear to be residential IPs, so an IP belonging to a known consumer ISP also doesn't mean they are human. This is the probabilistic nature of bot filtering.

Beyond just the IP address itself, bot detection may also look at other aspects of the network connection. Let's take JA4 Transport Layer Security (TLS) handshake fingerprinting as one example. This method creates a hash using the TLS secure handshake during the HTTPS connection to attempt to differentiate end-user browsers like Chrome from programmatic clients like Python or curl. So if the passed User-Agent is

Chrome but the TLS handshake works like curl, then that connection could be a bot spoofing their user agent. This particular method requires direct access to that TLS handshake process, meaning that it needs to be run close to the web server, and this is much harder to achieve via a JavaScript tag.

Browser-Based Data

There are a vast number of possible signals here. An HTTP User-Agent is the most basic data point, but it's very trivial to spoof one. User-Agent is the first line of defense that most tools, including GA, use to keep out bots that are honest about being bots.

There are also other ways that browsers report their user agents: via Client Hints JavaScript API/headers, or `userAgent` in the JavaScript Navigator API. Simplistic checks look at just the HTTP User-Agent header, whereas more sophisticated checking may check multiple methods and make sure those methods return consistent data.

Data Integrity

In order to evade detection, bots frequently spoof (i.e., lie about) parts of the data they send. A significant part of bot detection is checking that the information the client is sending is actually valid and makes sense. Some examples:

The HTTP User-Agent declares the client is an iPhone, but JavaScript inspection shows an Intel graphics card, an impossible pairing.

- The IP address shows the client is coming from New York, but the browser time zone is set to China.
- JavaScript shows a large number of processors (indicative of a server), but the user agent indicates a small mobile device.

Behavioral Data

Humans and bots have very different browsing patterns.

Did the client hit 1,000 different unconnected pages in two minutes? Have they been hitting pages for 20 hours straight with exactly 10 seconds between each request? Did they hit every page on the site and never convert? Or maybe they converted 100 times in a row? These are some of the bot-like behaviors you might see. Part of what makes using behavioral data more difficult is that it's part of a series of events, and it's sometimes not available until later. For example, it may not become clear that a session is bot-driven until there have been 1,000 consecutive requests made and a rate limiter is triggered. We can't look at just one request and get that information, and we can't know from the first request that there will be 999 more coming.

If your head is spinning a bit right now, that's a natural reaction and consistent with being a human, not a robot.

Many of the analytics platforms we test only filter bots out that declare themselves as bots via their user agents. The table below shows some examples (focused on the open source options, which by their nature reveal more details about their anti-bot methods).

Tool	Method	Filter List
GA	Predominantly HTTP user agent, via Individual Address Block (IAB) list	https://www.iab.com/guidelines/iab-abc-international-spiders-bots-list/
PostHog	JavaScript user agent via its own list, some IPs	https://github.com/PostHog/posthog-js/blob/main/packages/browser/src/utils/blocked-uas.ts
Mato-mo	HTTP user agent, additional options like blocking by IP or Geo	https://github.com/matomo-org/plugin-TrackingSpamPrevention
Umami	HTTP user agent via third-party li-brary	https://www.npmjs.com/package/isbot

How effective is the kind of user agent-based blocking that most platforms rely on? As you might expect, it depends on the kind of bot traffic your site is receiving. The upside of user agent blocking is that it doesn't produce much in the way of false positives. Humans don't normally set their user agents to "Googlebot" or "Perplexity-Bot," etc.

So if GA uses mostly HTTP User-Agent, are there other alternatives we are evaluating that are significantly better than GA in terms of bot filtering? To evaluate this, I ran a test against all our platforms with four different types of sample bot traffic to see what got filtered out.

Level 1: Obvious Bot User Agents

This level contained simulated traffic with very obvious bot strings like "`Googlebot`," "`Screaming Frog SEO Spider`," or "`python-requests`." The requests were made consecutively from the same real residential IP.

Level 2: Human-Like, but Bot User Agents

Many automation and testing tools don't explicitly use words like "bot" or "spider" in their user agents, and otherwise have a human-looking user agent, but do still indicate they are bots, e.g.,

`Mozilla/5.0 (Macintosh; Intel Mac OS X 10_15_7), AppleWebKit/537.36 (KHTML, like Gecko)`**`HeadlessChrome`**`/136.0.7103.25 Safari/537.36.`

The "**`HeadlessChrome`**" indicates it's running in headless mode and should be considered a bot. In addition to the user agent above, I also used strings like `Perpexi-ty-User` and `PhantomJS`. As with level 1, the requests were all made consecutively from my own residential IP.

Level 3: Human User Agent, but Data Center IP

This level used currently popular real user agent strings, except all requests came in from an AWS data center IP. This is consistent with how many basic scrapers and attackers operate: they spoof the user agent coming from servers to look like real users.

Level 4: Human User Agent, Simulated User Behavior

This level used residential IPs via scraping proxy services, including simulated scrolls, clicks, and random pauses.

This traffic is intended to be hard to detect. It's still scripted, of course, but includes things like mouse movements and comes from a residential IP via a paid proxy service rather than a data center. I purposely did not try to close *all* detectability, but instead attempted to simulate typical advanced bot traffic attempting to circumvent detection. The chart below summarizes my findings.

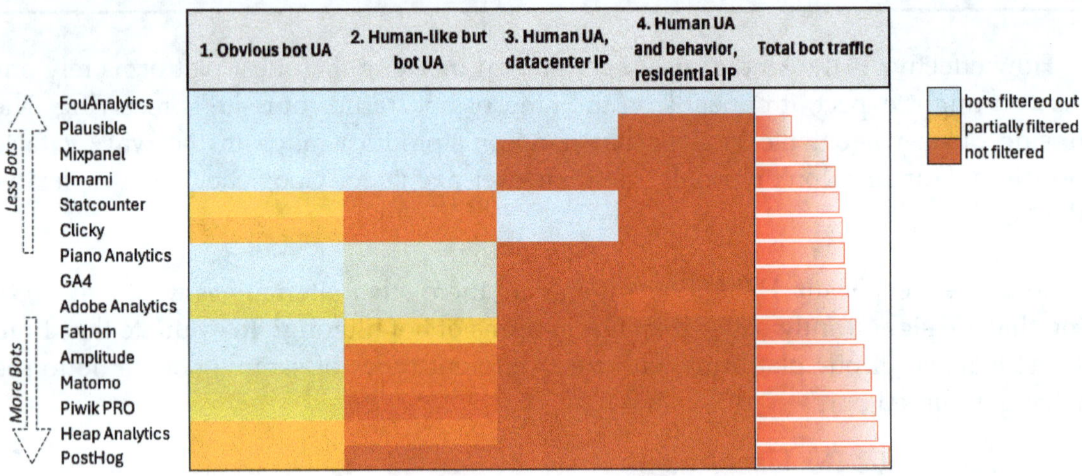

To benchmark the results against an actual anti-bot tool, I used the FouAnalytics bot detection service (https://fouanalytics.com). None of my simulated traffic fooled this purpose-built tool, indicating that our test traffic is all traffic that is *possible* to detect.

The results show GA4 as middle-of-the-pack. GA's user agent blocklist is ok, but it is unable to stop bot traffic with faked human-like user agents. Many of the more enterprise-y tools we evaluate (Piano, GA4, Adobe, Amplitude) in fact use the same blocklist subscription service from the IAB, which is why they all scored about the same.

While no platform was able to detect level 4 traffic, a few (Plausible, Statcounter, Clicky) were able to exclude the level 3 traffic. This is likely because they have chosen to exclude all traffic from known data centers like AWS, which, as we discussed earlier, may cause some real users to be excluded. It makes sense that it is tools in the simplified category that have chosen to filter that traffic, since enterprise tools like Adobe or

Piano are more likely to be used in business environments where real users are on corporate VPNs that could come from data centers. In other words, if Adobe or Piano implemented blocking based on data centers the same way Plausible has done, it might cause an unacceptable level of false positives.

I also want to note that while PostHog scored the lowest in our test, it was in some ways one of the most difficult tools to fool. PostHog uses JavaScript to discover the browser user agent, and does so in a way that trivial user agent spoofing does not fool. In other words, while PostHog's list of bot user agents wasn't very comprehensive, the tech it used to reveal the user agent was more sophisticated.

Overall, this means if you are suffering from bot traffic in GA4, don't expect an alternative to be necessarily much better—but it depends on the type of bot traffic. My testing, while structured, was synthetic and far from comprehensive.

To validate this test, I also ran a more "real-world" scenario. I purchased hundreds of dollars' worth of cheap, low-quality, and un-targeted display advertising. This drove thousands of visitors to my test site, but it was mostly ad fraud bots. FouAnalytics bot detection identified 65% of the traffic as bots, meaning the traffic was about two-thirds bots. As with our level 4 test, none of the analytics tools filtered significant amounts of this traffic out.

Yet there is a catch-22 here. Sometimes our web analytics tool is how we discover that there is a bot attack happening at all! Take my test example, where I paid for ads that ended up being low-quality bot traffic. If that traffic never appeared in GA, perhaps nobody would have realized they were paying for worthless bot traffic?

A customized setup, like server-side, can cause more bot traffic to show up. Bots that are specifically designed to ignore the GA/GTM tags could still end up showing up in your analytics if you have customized your setup.

For example, the SEO spider Screaming Frog is programmed by its developers to *not* fire GA, even when it is rendering other JavaScript tags on the page. Yet with a customized server-side GA setup, Screaming Frog might fire GA because it would no longer recognize the setup as GA. If the customized setup is intended to fool an ad blocker by no longer being identifiable as GA, it will fool Screaming Frog as well.

In that example of a customized server-side setup, consider the following: Screaming Frog would fire GA, but it still would *not* show up in GA because its default user agent "`Screaming Frog Spider/[version]`" would be excluded by GA (likely due to the word "spider"). Except many users *do* in fact change that default user agent, because otherwise it gets blocked by anti-bot firewalls, meaning then it would appear! Oh what a tangled web we weave, when we set the spiders to deceive...

If you have a bot problem, try to deal with it *ahead of* and *partitioned from* your analytics tool.

Ahead of, meaning identifying bots and stopping bad bots before they get to your site. For example, you could run a web application firewall (WAF) that has bot protection abilities, which can stop the bad traffic before it uses your site resources and muddies your analytics reports.

Partitioned from, meaning using something other than your user analytics tool to do the bot analysis. Most advanced bot protection tools have their own reporting tools that do their own bot reporting. Some tools also have the ability to score potential bot traffic in a way that can then be passed along to your analytics tool, which is ideal.

Chapter 17 - AI & The Future

The biggest change in tech since the first edition of this book in 2022 is certainly AI. But how does AI fit into analytics? The last couple of years have seen tech vendors add AI—in particular, large language models (LLMs)—to just about everything, and analytics tools have been no exception. Some of these additions have been very useful, but just as often, AI is being slotted in everywhere, whether anyone asked for it or not.

Everyone has a lot of opinions about AI, myself included. In short, my current opinion about AI in analytics is this: it's a very valuable tool, but not very good at analysis, and dangerous to outsource your thinking to. Here's a quick run-down of my view of where we're at now:

AI's Role in Analytics (2026)

Highly Useful	**Sometimes Useful**	**Danger Zone**
Creating code and SQL Help and research summarization	Chat-driven user interfaces Model Context Protocol (MCP) Anomaly detection	Doing analysis Finding insights No humans in the loop

What will this table look like next year? It's hard to say. Just a couple years ago, I didn't expect that AI would so quickly become as good as it is now at code and SQL.

But how good is it, really? How do we determine how "smart" these tools really are? The top models score very highly on things like math benchmarks, yet still struggle with seemingly trivial things like counting the number of "r"s in a word. While continuing to improve at things like knowledge retrieval and synthesis, models remain weak at the kind of analytical reasoning our jobs require.

Being an analyst involves many things that LLMs have shown themselves to be poor at. Here are a few examples:

- Working with unclear or incomplete questions
- Answering questions that are new and novel
- Thinking outside the box for simple answers, rather than doubling down on complexity

- Knowing when a question *shouldn't* be answered

To get an idea of how well these models work with the tools of our trade, I've done some basic benchmarking myself against how good the major models are at GA4. All of the top models are very good at basic GA4 knowledge, such as what's in the official GA4 certification exam.

I tested nine of the top models in April 2025, and every one would have hit the 80% correct mark required to pass GA certification (https://www.quantable.com/analytics/how-good-is-ai-at-ga4/). You might be thinking that's not a fair test, since the answers to the exam are out there on the internet and might be part of the LLMs' training set. A reasonable point, though humans taking the exam can also look stuff up on the internet. Either way, a quiz such as this is testing the use of the AI for knowledge retrieval far more than true problem-solving. If you want to accurately test "reasoning," you can't just ask questions the model has seen before or that are simple factual look-ups.

To test problem-solving in a scenario where the answers weren't already on the internet, as part of that same blog post, I created a much harder GA4 quiz. Only some so-called reasoning models, newer than OpenAI's o1 (released in Dec 2024), were able to get an 80% or better on this test. Currently, Gemini 3 Pro has the highest score on this test, with 93% correct. Gemini 3 Pro is also at the top of the LMArena.ai chat leaderboard and Artificial Analysis' (https://artificialanalysis.ai) aggregate intelligence ratings, two solid sources for model benchmarking.

Gemini 3 Pro is very good. In fact, all of the current top models (sometimes called "frontier" models to indicate that they're at the forefront of capabilities at the moment) are very good. The rate of change being what it has been, does that mean a year from now, when Gemini 4.5 is out, we'll look back and wonder how we thought Gemini 3 could have ever been considered good? Perhaps.

Looking at those same aggregate intelligence ratings in the chart below, we can see that 2025 was definitely the year that the other major players caught up with OpenAI.

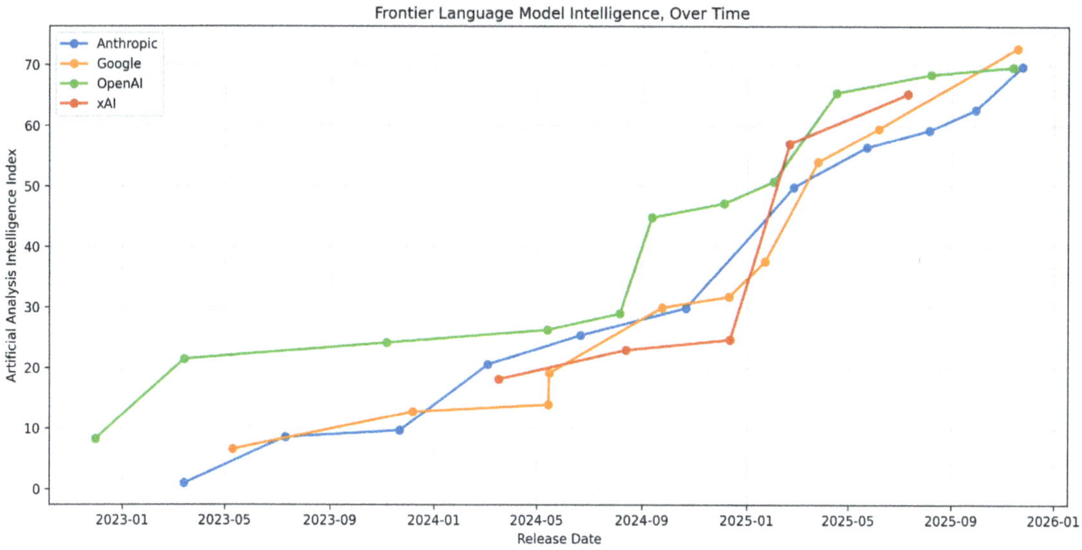

Is 2025 also the year that LLM progress started to slow down? That's less clear, but there are some indicators. If we look at that same chart, but only show the current leading model, we can see a potential slowdown in the second half of 2025, to go along with the convergence of the top model providers shown above.

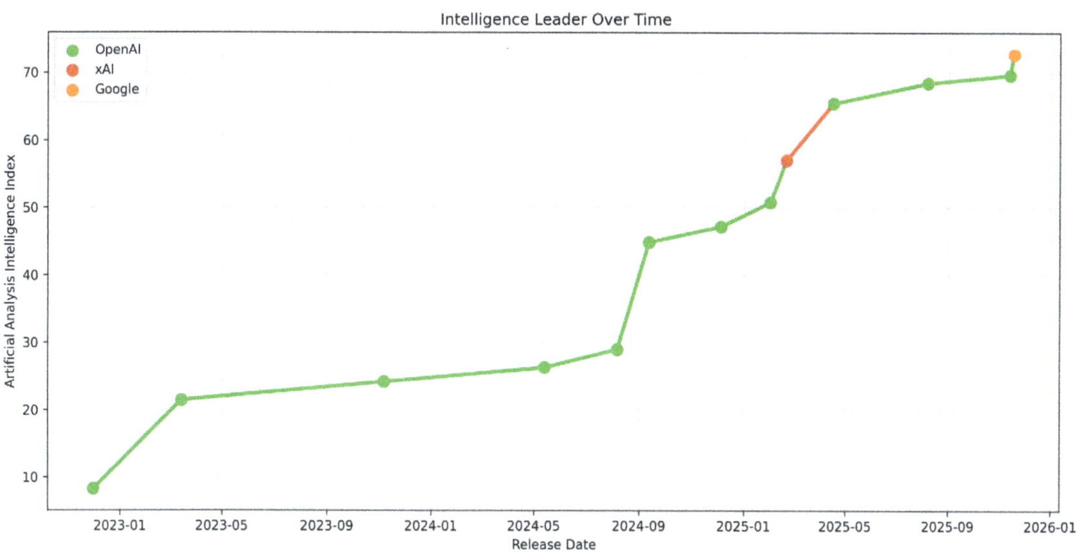

The idea that LLM scaling is starting to show diminishing returns is based upon a lot more than that graph I just made. It's something that even former scaling advocates, like OpenAI co-founder Ilya Sutskever, have started to say (https://www.businessinsider.com/openai-cofounder-ilya-sutskever-scaling-ai-age-of-research-dwarkesh-2025-11).

Of course, LLMs are not the only AI technology out there, and in fact, many of the improvements in 2025 have been with how LLMs interact with and use other systems via tool use. In other words, even if LLMs don't get much smarter internally, they are getting better at doing things like utilizing external APIs and databases, web search, and browser use. This makes them more useful, but also more disruptive and more dangerous.

Practically, what does that mean to our tool selection process? On one end of the spectrum, we've got tools like PostHog and Amplitude that are all-in on AI, deeply integrating it across their product suites. At the other end, we've got a bunch of tools with no AI features at all.

Let's split up the levels of AI integration into three levels:

Level 0: No AI
Many tools, especially those in the simplified category and those that are more focused on privacy, have avoided adding AI features.

Level 1: Some AI
This level includes more modular features like AI-powered help systems, AI or machine learning (ML)-based anomaly detection, or an MCP service. These features are more like add-ons, rather than changes to the core product and how it's used.

Level 2: Substantial AI
These tools are embedding AI across their products. Agentic AI assistants, AI-generated reporting or dashboards, AI-generated insights. Much of the line between levels 1 and 2 is whether or not the AI is ever acting as an analyst or in an agentic, self-directed way.

Level of Generative AI Integration

Level 0: No Integrated AI	Level 1: Some AI	Level 2: Substantial AI
Matomo Piwik PRO Cloudflare Web Analytics Plausible Statcounter Clicky Fathom Analytics Umami	Piano Analytics Mixpanel Heap GA4	Adobe CJA PostHog Amplitude

Given the speed at which AI is being integrated into software, this chart may change quickly—but this is at least a snapshot of where we are at right now. In fact, GA4 is currently in the process of rolling out its "Analytics Advisor," which, depending on how it works, could move it from level 1 to 2 in this table. That doesn't mean that level 2 is superior to 1; in fact, I personally prefer level 1, where AI is used more sparingly.

Also, to clarify: this is about AI being integrated into the tool itself, not about whether the tool can identify traffic coming *from* AI sources like ChatGPT or Perplexity (which many can, regardless of their AI integration level).

Whether or not these AI features influence your decision is based on how much you yourself expect to use those kinds of features, specifically within the tools. As I laid out in my table above, I do find AI very useful for code generation and help. However, I don't typically do those things inside an analytics tool, so it doesn't matter to me if a tool has them integrated or not.

I would also consider the potential privacy issues involved with having deeply integrated AI. If there is an agent baked into the product at a low level, then that agent will inherently be able to access your data. This may help explain why EU-based tools like Piwik PRO or Plausible have avoided this kind of integration.

That doesn't mean tools at level 0 don't play well with AI. In order to check up on the live data for all 15 tools we're evaluating, I used Claude in the Cursor AI code editor to help me write Python code that uses the tools' APIs to return the data. The tools that Claude was able to write code for most cleanly were the ones that had the most logical and best-documented APIs. For example, the Plausible API worked on the first try, even though that tool has no AI features itself. The Adobe and Piano APIs required a lot of back-and-forth and manual code tweaking to work, even though both of those tools (especially Adobe) have more focus on AI.

I also identified "help and research" to be something AI is very useful for. For the tools that had AI-based help assistants, I asked those assistants questions about the tool. For the tools that didn't, I asked ChatGPT. For the most part, the tools' internal help systems did *not* seem significantly better than just asking ChatGPT. Again, the tools that had the most clear documentation and straightforward usability were the ones where AI-based help worked best, regardless of whether it was in ChatGPT or the tool's own (typically retrieval-augmented generation (RAG) assisted) help.

For my usage patterns, AI features *within* an analytics tool have not proved particularly useful for me. Perhaps because I use a wide variety of analytics platforms, I've been sticking with AI tools outside of platforms that are a part of my normal workflow. Your workflow may be different, and if it is, perhaps analytics tools with integrated AI are more valuable to you.

The Future of AI and Analytics

With as fast as technology changes, how can we best choose something that will continue to work well for us in the future? In the first part of this chapter, I've covered a number of details that will be outdated (but hopefully still helpful and instructive) before the first copy of this book is ever printed.

Nobody can predict the future, but via flexibility and adaptability, we can try to be as well prepared as we can for whatever happens next. Things will end up way different than we expect, yet when we look back it will seem as though it all *should* have been predictable.

Many people talk about "future-proofing" their analytics. This is a worthy goal, but when thinking about this, I suggest framing it as focusing on the current, existing issues that we know about, rather than trying to predict where technology and the market are going. Having a solid but flexible foundation now that addresses today's problems will prepare you for the future better than trying to preventatively deal with future issues that may not even happen.

We face plenty of analytics challenges today, so let's get ready for the future by solving what's in front of us now, rather than worrying too much about what may come. The so-called "death of cookies" is a good example of how uncertainty and fear about the future can lead people down the wrong track. As we discussed in Chapter 13 - Tracking Methods, analytics tools don't use 3P cookies, and the hype about the removal of those kinds of cookies was not relevant to most people outside of advertising networks.

When the first edition of this book was released in the fall of 2022, third-party cookies were on their way out, and ChatGPT had yet to be released. Three years later,

Google has about-faced on 3P cookies and privacy sandboxing, while AI is showing up everywhere from the Google home page to Coca-Cola's holiday polar bears.

We can't predict the future, but we can work on creating a robust analytics practice that gets us as ready as we can be for whatever is next. This means working on things like the following:

- Clear documentation of what we're doing, who owns it, and why we're doing it
- Avoiding brittle implementation practices that may lead to future breakage
- Monitoring of what we're doing, so when things do break, we know
- Data portability, so when vendors change things, we aren't in danger of losing data
- Understanding how new methods (e.g., server-side analytics) are relevant to solving our issues, and not just following the hype cycle

- Next, let's consider some specific questions.

Will the Vendor and Tool We Pick Still Be Around in the Future?

By reviewing only popular options, I've focused on established tools that are more likely to stick around. I'm not saying you need to limit your options to those that are already near the top of the market, but it's a factor to consider.

When weighing your options here, you should also consider how much effort it would be to move platforms if your platform disappears. If you're using a simplified tool and all you've done is drop the tag on a site, that's a much easier migration than if you've got a whole data engineering team that implemented custom instrumentation and data flows.

Will the Things We Like About a Particular Tool Stick Around?

As the genesis of this book was the UA sunset, it's obvious how this can be a sensitive issue. Based on our first question, very few would say that Google Analytics would cease to exist any time soon, but Google is not afraid to end-of-life tools and switch things up. Vendors like Adobe or Piano that offer paid-only tools focused on larger enterprises value consistency much more than vendors like PostHog or Umami that focus more on startups and moving quickly. The right vendor fit can depend on your organization's own culture and expectations.

Will We Still Be Able to Afford the Tool We Pick if Things Change?

Pricing model changes are common. Since 2023, when I first started working on this book, there's been a lot of change: Mixpanel and Amplitude swapped pricing plans, Piwik PRO discontinued its freemium plan, PostHog cut cloud-hosted prices enough to make self-hosting unattractive, Umami introduced its free cloud-hosted version, etc.

Planning for these changes might mean the following:

- Picking a tool that still leaves a lot of headroom in your budget
- Giving preference to tools with pricing transparency, so you can understand what happens if traffic grows unexpectedly
- Working with vendors that have shown contractual flexibility—meaning that they have been willing to work with you on price and features (which sometimes is in conflict with the second consideration!)

Having now considered the past, present, and future of analytics, let's move on to the individual tool reviews!

Part Two

Product Evaluations

EVALUATION METHOLOGY

In the first part of this guide, we covered a lot of background and created a framework to help our tool selection process. In Part Two, we'll apply this framework to evaluate 15 different products. Rather than scrutinize every detail of each tool, I'll focus on what makes a particular product unique and how it compares to similar alternatives.

To gain a better feel for these products, I installed them all on websites with real traffic. I believe the only way to really understand a product is to see it in action with real-world data. Walk-throughs and product demos highlight what the vendor wants you to see. Usable demo accounts are better, and provide first-hand experience with the product, but force you to use the data the vendor has selected, with all of the setup and instrumentation already completed. In the cases where the vendor does offer a demo account, I've linked to those in the tables at the top of the chapters.

In addition to my test websites, I have used a number of these tools on production websites as part of my job as an analytics consultant. Tools I've used in production outside of these tests include GA4, Piwik PRO, Matomo, Cloudflare Web Analytics, Clicky, Plausible, and Amplitude. I mention this to highlight and prevent familiarity bias on my part. For the tools I do not have production experience with, and that are more complex (Adobe, Piano, PostHog), I've asked experts whose opinions I trust and who have used those tools in production to review those chapters for errors. I greatly appreciate their help, and any remaining mistakes are mine alone.

Reviewers
Fosca Fimiani (https://www.linkedin.com/in/foscafimiani/)
Bogdan Nazaruk (https://www.linkedin.com/in/nazaruk/)
Mehdi Oudjida (https://www.withlookerstudio.com)

The two websites I used for testing had very modest levels of traffic (approximately 300 sessions per month for one, and 1,200 for the other in 2022, and even fewer in my 2025 testing). These lower levels of traffic and relatively simple site functionality made it impossible to delve deeply into some of the more sophisticated tools, but they still provide enough information to point us in the right direction.

In an attempt to further reduce bias, I have avoided discussion of the tools with vendor reps from these products in the process of doing these evaluations. Vendor reps are obviously an excellent source of information about their products, and I recommend you talk to them as part of your product evaluation, but to make these comparisons as fair as possible, I did my best to work only with data that was publicly available.

I have no current paid relationships with any of the vendors, but have in the past contracted for Plausible and Amplitude. Piwik PRO is a current sponsor of Columbus Data & Analytics Wednesday, of which I am an organizer.

Evaluations for the first edition of the book were done from July through September of 2022.

Evaluations for the second edition were done from June through November of 2025.

Tools Index

The following is a list of all the tools we'll evaluate. Each chapter concentrates on one tool, and they are grouped by category (comprehensive and simplified web analytics, and product analytics). Within each category, tools are listed alphabetically.

See the full chart with additional details at https://gaalternatives.guide/sheet.

Tool	Category	Default Tracking Method
Chapter 18 - Adobe Analytics	Comprehensive	Cookies
Chapter 19 - Google Analytics 4	Comprehensive	Cookies
Chapter 20 - Matomo Cloud	Comprehensive	Cookies
Chapter 21 - Piano Analytics	Comprehensive	Cookies
Chapter 22 - Piwik PRO	Comprehensive	Cookies
Chapter 23 - Clicky	Simplified	IP + User-Agent
Chapter 24 - Cloudflare Web Analytics	Simplified	Referrer
Chapter 25 - Fathom	Simplified	IP + User-Agent
Chapter 26 - Plausible Analytics	Simplified	IP + User-Agent
Chapter 27 - Statcounter	Simplified	Cookies
Chapter 28 - Umami	Simplified	IP + User-Agent
Chapter 29 - Amplitude Analytics	Product Analytics	Cookies
Chapter 30 - Heap	Product Analytics	Cookies
Chapter 31 - Mixpanel	Product Analytics	Cookies
Chapter 32 - PostHog	Product Analytics	Cookies

Comprehensive Web Analytics

CHAPTER 18 - ADOBE ANALYTICS

Type	Comprehensive Web Analytics
Default tracking method	Cookies
Price	Reportedly starting at ~$3,000/mo.
Home page	https://analytics.adobe.com
Demo	https://business.adobe.com/resources/adobe-analytics-sandbox.html#roll-up-your-sleeves-and-explore-analysis-workspace (requires form fill)
Similar tool(s)	Piano

Pros: Robust, mature product, reporting tools
Cons: Learning curve, pricing model, question of AA vs. CJA

Someone once said that GA vs. Adobe was the "Coke vs. Pepsi" of digital analytics. Ok, that someone was me, in Chapter Two of this book—but I think it bears repeating. Both products have long tenures in the industry, and seasoned practitioners in the field are typically steeped in the practices of one paradigm or the other. While the products themselves are very different and largely target two different markets, Adobe Analytics has historically been in the "challenger" position from a market share position.

The histories of the two products have many parallels. Google Analytics has its roots in Urchin, which was purchased by Google in 2005. Adobe Analytics has its roots in Omniture, purchased by Adobe in 2009. Urchin started as a logfile analysis tool in 1997. Omniture SiteCatalyst started as a JavaScript image hit counter called SuperStats, also in 1997.

Another parallel between GA and Adobe is the changes the platforms have experienced in the last few years. In 2019, both Google and Adobe launched next-generation versions of their classic web analytics tools. Google with App+Web (which became GA4), and Adobe with Customer Journey Analytics. While Google shut down UA in favor of GA4, Adobe chose to continue both platforms: Adobe Analytics (AA) and Adobe Customer Journey Analytics (CJA).

	Adobe	**Google**
Early days	SuperStats (1997)	Urchin logfile analysis (1997)
Acquisition	Omniture SiteCatalyst -> AA (2009)	Urchin -> Universal Analytics (2005)
Next-gen shift	Customer Journey Analytics (2019)	App+Web -> GA4 (2019)

Much as Pepsi would rankle at being referred to as a "Coke alternative," Adobe likely feels similarly about being called a "Google Analytics alternative." While many other products in this book can lay claim to being their own thing and not just following Google, Adobe has been in that lane for decades. Google has always been far more popular, but that's not because it inherently ~~tastes~~ works better.

I posit that GA's historical market share vs. Adobe has much more to do with price and distribution than the tool itself. If 20 years ago, fortunes were reversed, such that Google had purchased Omniture and Adobe had purchased Urchin, I expect that the market share today would *not* be significantly different. In that alternate history, an Omniture SiteCatalyst-based Google Analytics would still have been the dominant tool.

Speculative histories aside, as someone steeped in the Google Analytics tradition rather than the Adobe tradition, my ability to do a fair and comprehensive evaluation of Adobe Analytics may be limited. This, and the difficulty of getting access to the product, are the main reasons I didn't include Adobe in the first edition of this book. While Adobe is still hard to get access to, there is now a sandbox account that potential users can request access to: https://business.adobe.com/resources/adobe-analytics-sandbox.html.

Another complexity in reviewing Adobe is that Adobe Analytics and Adobe Customer Journey Analytics are both active tools in the marketplace. So let's first try to better understand their differences.

This book is framed as a series of alternatives to Google's Universal Analytics, and through that lens, AA is more directly comparable to UA than it is to CJA. AA was designed for web analytics specifically, whereas CJA is a broader tool with both more aspects of product analytics and a much more flexible data model and schema. As a core part of the broader Adobe Experience Platform, CJA is the product that Adobe is more actively developing and marketing, though AA is also continuing to receive software updates.

Adobe deserves praise for continuing to support AA and not doing a forced migration like Google did with GA4, even though it increases complexity to have two tools being actively supported.

While Adobe Analytics is the legacy product, there have been no announcements about its sunset. The old AA Report Builder is being end-of-lifed in June 2026, but nothing will be removed in the core platform. Still, unless you are already familiar with AA or have a particular feature need, it may make more sense to adopt the current state-of-the-art platform, CJA. Price is also a consideration, though, as CJA is widely reported by practitioners to be the more expensive product.

This can put mid-sized companies with more modest budgets who may be good fits for AA in a difficult position. CJA and the larger Adobe Experience Platform (AEP) overall position Adobe as even more of an enterprise-oriented suite than it previously was. Those organizations may also want to investigate Piano or Piwik PRO, while larger orgs with more data engineering resources may appreciate AEP more.

As with many enterprise products, Adobe has a complex pricing model with little to no pricing transparency. In addition to the difficulty this adds to budgeting, it makes figuring out the overall structure of the platform harder. Tools like Amplitude and PostHog also have large, sprawling suites, but having a free tier and being able to easily access the many different parts of the suite helps greatly with understanding and learning. With Adobe Experience Platform, there are some helpful architecture diagrams like the one at https://experienceleague.adobe.com/en/docs/blueprints-learn/architecture/architecture-overview/platform-applications, but when it comes to learning, nothing beats actually getting your hands on the tool!

Beyond having two different analytics products, Adobe also has different product levels within AA and CJA: Foundation, Select, Prime, and Ultimate.

In AA, all levels are metered based upon server calls (meaning it charges per hit), and beyond that, there can be additional charges for add-ons: (https://helpx.adobe.com/legal/product-descriptions/adobe-analytics.html). While many products are metered by hits, AA has drawn some complaints due to how charges can spike based on unexpected increases in traffic, including but not limited to bot traffic. Google and Adobe scored similarly in my bot filtering test in Chapter 16 - Bot Filtering, meaning bot traffic was equally likely to appear in the two platforms. In other words, I'm not saying that AA is more susceptible to bot traffic, just that bot traffic is more likely to drive extra costs in AA than in GA4.

When it comes to pricing, CJA has the same plan levels as AA (https://helpx.adobe.com/legal/product-descriptions/customer-journey-analytics.html), but meters based on the number of rows stored rather than server calls. This change has the advantage that data filtering or pruning can happen before charges are incurred. These rows are saved objects in the Adobe Experience Data Model (XDM). In other words, usage in CJA is charged based on database rows, more so than on hits.

Let's walk through an example of how these differences between AA and CJA might affect your bill. Say you were in the process of building a new version of your site and had Adobe installed. Your QA team was running an automated test that spidered your entire site every time there was an update released, leading to millions of extra hits. With AA, you'd likely have incurred a significant unexpected cost. With CJA, you have a chance remove those hits to avoid additional cost. This new pricing model is not without its tradeoffs, however, as *retaining* data can cost more. With AA, you pay once for the hit during the standard retention period (25 months). With CJA, you pay for every month you retain the row within Adobe Experience Platform.

Just as GA4 is better integrated than UA was into the wider Google Marketing Platform and GCP, CJA is much more integrated into the Adobe Experience Platform than AA is.

Whether we are talking CJA or AA, Adobe is an extremely powerful and customizable tool. Like many powerful tools, there is a learning curve to climb before becoming proficient and gaining access to all that power. To those who have already climbed that hill, the slope might not look very steep from the top, but to those at the bottom, it can feel quite daunting.

Both tools are made to be implemented and managed by experts, without a lot of accommodation for casual users. AA in particular contains a lot of legacy functionality, and is less strong when it comes to usability. AA is designed for power, not ease of use. In Plausible, it takes three steps to add a new site. In AA, I counted 13. Looking at the creation of the report suite, which is part of the setup, we see a lot of strange or seemingly unnecessary questions:

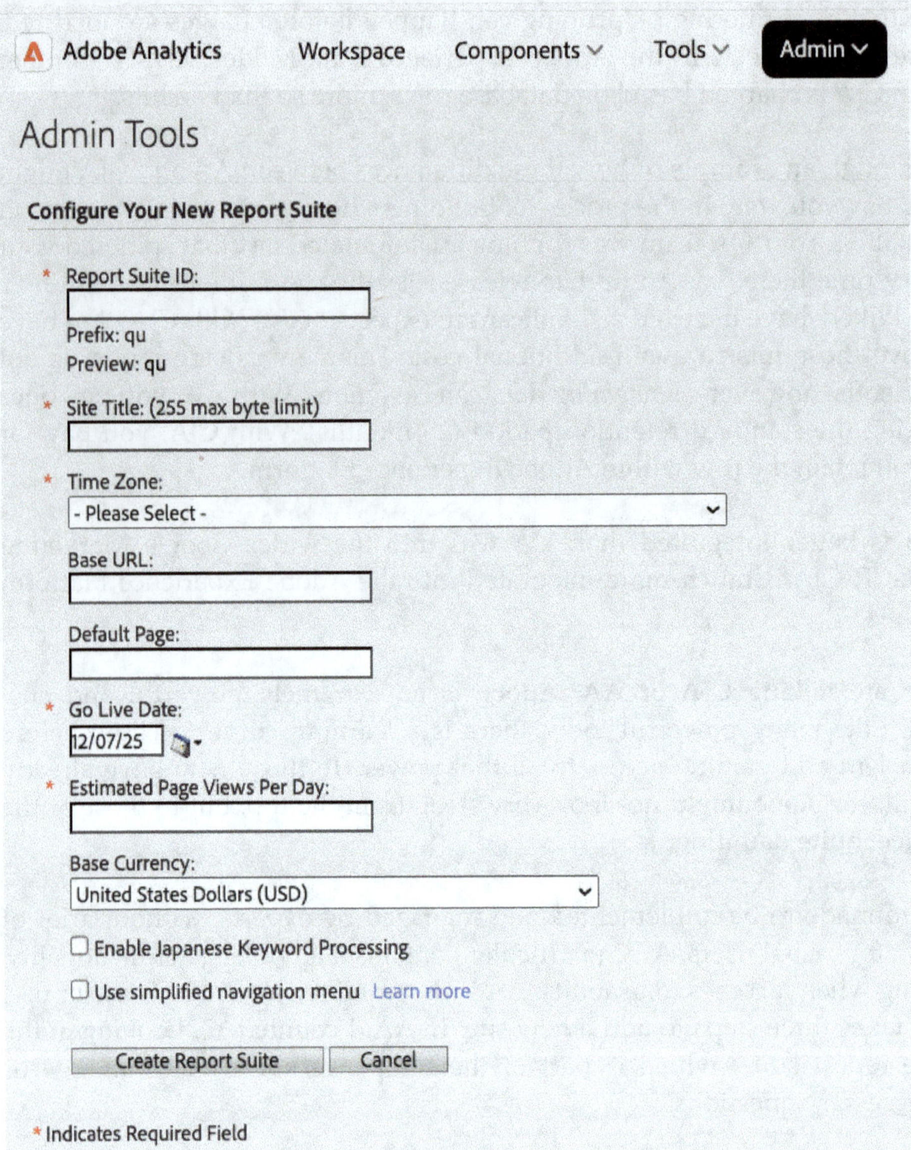

The setup form requires entering a "Go Live Date" and "Estimated Page Views Per Day" and asks if you want to "Enable Japanese Keyword Processing." The first two are to help Adobe do resource planning, and the second is to enable UTF-8 character encoding. In the mid-2020s, we expect cloud services to scale and handle resource planning for us automatically. As far as character encoding—whether it's Japanese, Cyrillic, or Emoji—we expect characters beyond those in the western standard ISO-8859-1 to be transparently handled for us, どもありがと (*thank you very much*).

While some of these options seem unnecessary or outdated, many are the result of treating the product as a power-user tool right from the start. More than GA, Adobe is designed to be run via its platform's tag manager as part of the larger Adobe Experience Platform. Until recently, its tag manager was called "Launch," but it's no longer branded separately and is just labelled as "Tags" as part of data collection within AEP. If you are familiar with Adobe's Dynamic Tag Manager (DTM), that was Adobe's legacy tag manager and has now been fully replaced by AEP Tags.

As proper instrumentation for Adobe is more involved than dropping a pre-generated tag on a page and collecting data, I would definitely recommend working within AEP Tags. Because I was running all tests in this book via the Google Tag Manager, this made things more difficult than it could have been if I were working solely within AEP.

Once we are collecting and reporting on data, we can see one of the real strengths of the product, Analysis Workspace. Workspace is Adobe's report builder for both AA and CJA, and it is excellent. Highly flexible, no sampling, fast, and endlessly customizable. If you are familiar with GA4's Explore reports, it's similar to that, but actually good. If you enjoy slicing and dicing your data by visually navigating dimensions and metrics rather than building SQL, Analysis Workspace is built for you.

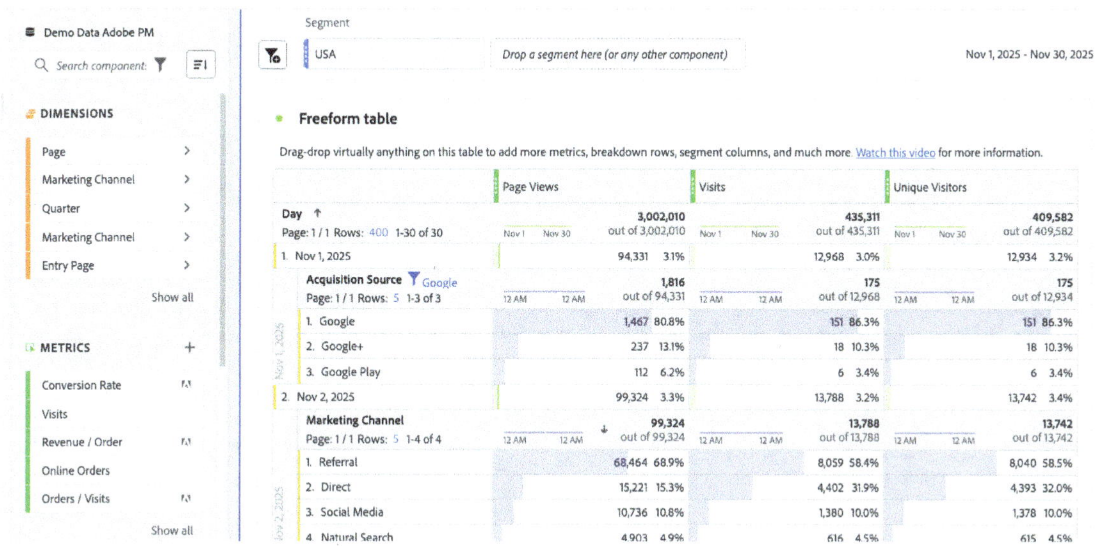

You want a table with a different (filtered) dimension breakdown for each individual day? You want a treemap of all the different marketing sources that drove purchases? You want a Venn diagram of first-time users, users in Norway, and mobile users who didn't experience a crash? Workspace has you covered (whether those particular reports are a good idea or not).

As an American company, Adobe is less focused on privacy and compliance than its competitors with European roots, like Piano and Piwik PRO. That said, Adobe is certainly much better on those items than Google is, for reasons we have discussed in the first half of this book.

Take Health Insurance Portability and Accountability Act (HIPAA) compliance, for example. The Business Associate Agreement (BAA) that HIPAA mandates is not an option for GA4 at all. With Adobe, it is possible with CJA, but not AA. Meanwhile, Piano and Piwik PRO will both sign a BAA and, in fact, make easy HIPAA compliance a big part of their marketing. As a true enterprise option, CJA does offer the data residency and governance frameworks you would expect.

Overall, for companies willing to invest the time and money to learn and implement it, Adobe can be a powerful and highly useful platform. With CJA, even more than ever it remains not for the faint of heart or light of wallet.

Chapter 19 - Google Analytics 4

Type	Comprehensive Web Analytics
Default tracking method	Cookies
Price	Free with minimal limitations Reportedly starts at $4,167/mo.
Home page	https://marketingplatform.google.com
Demo	https://analytics.google.com/analytics/web/#/a54516992p213025502 (requires Google account)
Similar tool(s)	Amplitude, Piwik PRO

Pros: Price, Google stack integration, community, underlying technology
Cons: Privacy, usability, data caveats

People love to hate GA4. Some of this hate is well-deserved: it can be very frustrating to work with, and was a disappointing update to Universal Analytics.

Here's my hot take—GA4 is ok, but not the right tool for most of the websites that have it installed. GA4 is a very good data collection platform with an incredibly generous free plan. It also has an aggressively user-unfriendly interface that assumes a high level of familiarity with analytics.

When GA4 was moved out of beta in October 2020 and became the default for new GA properties, it was highly deficient in functionality and usability, especially for non-technical users. By July 2023, when UA was shut down, and GA4 became the sole option, things had improved, though many users remained dissatisfied. Post-sunset, the rate of GA4 feature releases increased, though there remain many highly requested updates, and GA4 still receives mixed reviews at best from the community.

We can see the rate of change by looking at the public "What's new" pages from Google (https://support.google.com/analytics/answer/9164320), which shows the following number of changes per quarter since launch:

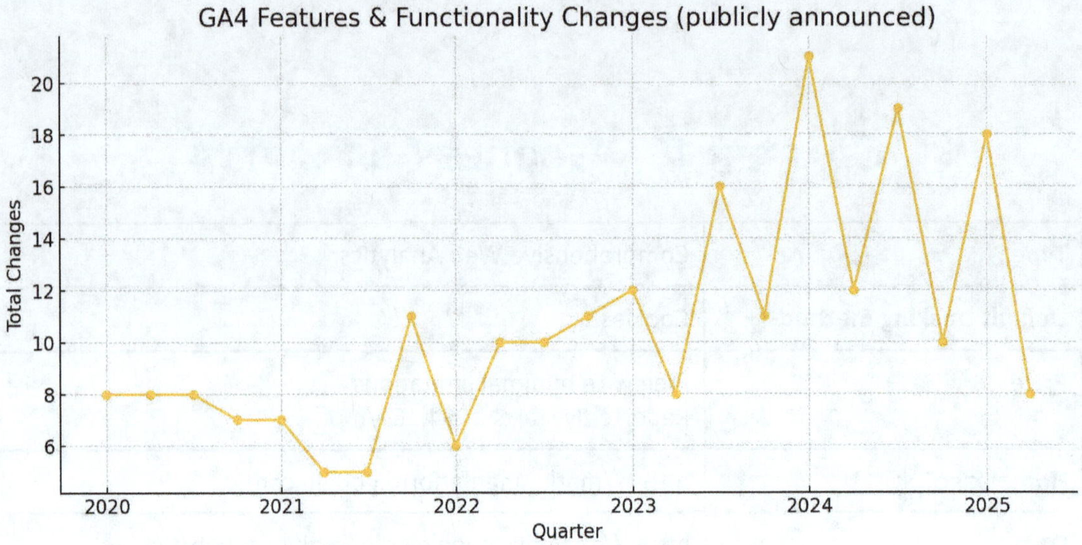

The time that it has taken Google to release simple, yet highly requested, features, such as annotations or on-page percentages, gives the impression that Google is not listening to the community and lacks commitment to the product. Annotations were a widely used part of UA, and yet it took until March 2025 for them to be added to GA4. Other well-known annoyances, like the inability to use Control+C to copy numeric values, persist.

It should not take five years to release improvements such as these. That said, if Google made an offer to restore Universal Analytics as it was at the time of its sunset in 2023 instead of GA4, I would no longer take that offer.

Much of what is frustrating about GA4 is clearly Google's fault. However, much is also attributable to the increased complexity in practicing analytics since the heyday of UA. For example, users may gripe about the default "blended" user identity, which considers user ids, cookies, and modeled data. Circa 2010, we could rely on cookies existing and being relatively stable, but this is no longer true, so all tools have had to adapt.

Google chose to rely on modeling, but it frequently doesn't work well, and doesn't work at all for small sites. Yet without this feature, there would be no ability to estimate usage by users that decline consent at all. This industry-wide rise in data collection complexity has been a challenge that all platforms have to deal with.

One of the biggest upsides of GA4 is its free export to BigQuery. Free accounts are allowed up to export up to 1M events a day per property to BigQuery. Standard UA did not have any export to BigQuery at all, it was a paid GA360-only feature. GA4 also has no stated hit limit, whereas UA had a 10M/mo. hit limit (though that was lightly enforced). The paid version of GA4, 360, reportedly includes 25M hits/mo. and charges starting at *$17.50*/M beyond that.

This full data export to BigQuery allows an amazing level of customization and data integration. However, there's a good reason that this feature was previously only in the paid enterprise version of the product—which is that it's something typically only used in enterprise-level installations. Many best-practice guides for using GA4 suggest turning on this export, but outside of organizations with more advanced analytics practices, this export is not typically well-utilized. BigQuery storage is very cheap (and free for the first 10GB/mo.), but leaving that export on indefinitely or running careless, unoptimized queries can cause unexpected charges to pile up. Ultimately, this is a great feature that most installations don't need.

As an analytics consultant, perhaps I should appreciate that GA4 is a robust source of consulting work as organizations seek to better understand reporting or "fix" their data.

Common Data Issues

Issue	GA4-Specific Notes
Bot traffic	- GA4 bot filtering has limited effectiveness and is always enabled. - Lack of ISP details like hostname makes this traffic difficult to filter within GA. - GA claims to use the user agent-driven Interactive Advertising Bureau (IAB) bot list and Google-specific research, but the latter seems very limited.
Sampling	- In free GA, reports that access over 10M data points may be subject to sampling (paid limit is 100M). - Sampling primarily affects reports that use granular data like Explore reports, vs. pre-aggregated reports such as standard reports.
Spam	- GA has been a frequent target for spammers. With GA4, this has been less of an issue than with UA, but it still happens and pollutes data.
Data retention	- For event-level reporting as used in Explore reports, there is a very limited default of 2 months, and the max is only 14 months for free accounts.
Cardinality limits, HyperLogLog++	- Beyond sampling, GA uses HLL++ to estimate distinct counts for metrics like users and sessions. Using BigQuery can frequently be the only way to get "actual" numbers.
Consent modeling	- Google consent mode "cookieless pings" drive behavior modeling, but it requires around 1,000 users/day granting consent to work and is a questionable privacy practice.
Ad blocking	- GA is susceptible to ad blockers, just as most tools are, but Google has largely avoided addressing the issue.

None of these technical challenges are exclusive to GA4. However, GA4 does a poor job of protecting its users from these issues. In some cases, like sampling and HyperLogLog++, the issues result from Google prioritizing server resources over end-user experience (with the free product in particular, this is an understandable, if frustrating, choice). Paid GA improves some of these issues, but doesn't totally solve any of them.

As doing analytics gets more complex, I would like to see analytics tools innovating to help solve and simplify these issues. I'd like to see tools reducing caveats, reporting gotchas, and lowering cognitive load—but Google has done poorly at this with GA4.

GA4 also makes things more difficult for analysts with slow data processing. Comparing GA4 to Piwik PRO, we see that GA is far slower at every step. Other platforms in this category like Adobe show processing times more similar to Piwik PRO than GA4, making GA4 the outlier in slowness.

Data Freshness

	GA4	Piwik PRO
Debug report	~30 seconds	~5 seconds
Real-time re-port	a few minutes	~30 seconds
"Intraday"*	2–6 hours (1 hour for GA360)	30 minutes
Full report	12–24 hours+ (up to 48h)	< 2 hours

*Intraday here means the in-process data for the current day; final numbers may change when processing is completed.

By "freshness," I mean the amount of time that it takes for data to be processed and show up in reports, based on vendor claims and my own ad hoc observations. Neither platform provides any service-level agreements or obligations that guarantee data processing within a set amount of time.

Paid GA does have faster processing times compared with the free version for the incremental intraday reports, and may have prioritized processing over free GA in general, but the official documentation only mentions a different level for those intraday reports.

You can read Google's full list of limits in free vs. paid GA4 here: https://support.-google.com/analytics/answer/11202874. The free versions of GA4 and UA are similar in that a few paid features are withheld in the "freemium" offerings. GA's free tier remains the most generous of all similar products.

One major advantage the paid GA4 360 has over the older Universal Analytics is a much lower starting cost, at *$50,000* vs. *$150,000* annually. The GA4 pricing structure differs significantly from UA's, although it's still opaque and subject to individual agreements with your GA reseller (https://www.cardinalpath.com/blog/ua-360-vs-ga4-360-pricing-model has more details on the pricing model).

The data models of UA and GA4 are also starkly different. Here's a helpful comparison of the two: https://support.google.com/analytics/answer/9964640

For many consumers of GA reports, the biggest issue with GA4 is the user experience of the reports themselves. GA4 reports don't leave any users happy:

- Less sophisticated users have trouble finding what they need in the standard reports. Customized reporting libraries can actually make things more confusing, as this means "standard" may vary from account to account and change over time.

- More sophisticated users rely on the Explore reports. Explore reports have a shorter time range and more sampling issues. Explore reports also can't be easily shared and managed (e.g., shared Explore reports need to be duplicated by the non-owner user to change date ranges).
- These factors push more reporting in Looker Studio dashboards, which require significant time and effort to maintain, but this also prevents those less sophisticated users from learning the core GA4 reports, decreasing overall GA4 proficiency.

We have yet to talk in this chapter about privacy and compliance, which, in my experience, has been the top reason that organizations move away from Google. We discussed this in Part One, but let's spell things out again here. GA4 is not a privacy-focused platform and has many problematic features for those concerned about compliance, particularly within the EU. With the correct setup, it can be sufficient for most applications and jurisdictions, but (along with Facebook) it will remain a top target for compliance actions and lawsuits.

A few eagle-eyed readers may notice that I have moved GA4 from the "product analytics" category in the first edition of this book to the "comprehensive web analytics" category in this edition. Part of this is a general blurring of the lines between categories. GA4 has also added more features that move it back towards UA and the web/digital/marketing analytics realm. Tools like Amplitude and PostHog have also added these types of features, but I believe those tools' overall perspective remains that of a product analytics tool. Ultimately, the categories I've assigned here are a basic guidepost rather than anything highly rigorous.

Before GA4, it was relatively common to run UA alongside a product analytics tool. These days, does it make sense to run both GA4 and another tool, like Amplitude, when there's so much more overlap? The answer to that should be led by reporting needs. It's highly preferable to have everyone in the same tool, but that's not always practically possible. Anecdotally, I have also seen a growing number of cases where organizations continue to run GA for the additional Google-specific data and integrations it can provide, but no longer treat it as their primary tool.

If your marketing team wants to use GA4 while your product team wants to use a product analytics tool, and neither team's critical reporting needs can be serviced from just one tool, then running both tools is a reasonable solution. Working in different tools means those teams won't have identical answers to the same questions, and it also means they aren't as likely to collaborate. This is why defining what is "critical" in your reporting is so important. If the marketing team can get what they need out of Amplitude, or the product team can be satisfied with GA4, then a single tool will be a better outcome. However, this sort of compromise is not always possible. Using multiple tools can indeed work well, especially in larger organizations that have dedicated analytics teams.

While you shouldn't pick GA4 by default, you also shouldn't choose an alternative just because GA4 isn't Universal Analytics.

Chapter 20 - Matomo Cloud

Type	Comprehensive Web Analytics
Default tracking method	Cookies
Price	$39/mo. for 100k hits $369/mo. for 2M $4,390/mo. for 25M
Home page	https://matomo.org
Demo	https://demo.matomo.cloud
Similar tool(s)	Piwik PRO

Pros: Mature product, full suite of tools, open source, similar to UA in functionality
Cons: Expensive and slow at large scale, limited ability for ad hoc analysis, interface can be clunky

Within the world of web analytics, Matomo (originally known as Piwik) has long been one of the most well-known and most popular alternatives to GA.

Matomo's popularity is well-earned: It's been around since 2007, is open source, and has an extensive feature set similar to Google's Universal Analytics in terms of design and functionality. *If you're looking for something that most closely matches UA, then Matomo or Piwik PRO is likely your best option.* Matomo and Piwik PRO both resemble UA more than GA4 does.

This similarity to UA makes for a straightforward migration to Matomo, assuming you were familiar with the old version of Google Analytics.

The downside of this similarity is that some of the drawbacks of UA also exist in Matomo. Google dealt with this legacy problem by abandoning UA and then re-introducing some of its lost features back in GA4 over time. Matomo has been much more consistent, slowly introducing features and making adjustments.

This consistency is good in some ways, but it also carries baggage in the form of technical legacy that newer platforms do not. For example, Matomo uses PHP and MySQL, a classic combo used by WordPress and many others—but one that lacks many of the technical advantages of more modern architectures.

In particular, MySQL does not compare favorably at scale to databases like Google Bigtable or ClickHouse, which were designed with analytics in mind. As a result, if you're looking for a solution for sites that get more than 10 million hits a month or have large amounts of historical data actively used in reports, you may want to look elsewhere. If you have lower traffic levels, this will be less of an issue.

While being MySQL-based is a downside for performance, it's an upside for self-hosting. MySQL is much more widely available and is simpler to set up and use. Self-hosted Matomo works as expected and is not difficult to set up. Matomo is even included as part of many shared hosting plans. For example, many budget hosting providers like Bluehost or Hosting.com include one-click install of Matomo via the Softaculous software library, which can be found in cPanel-type hosting plans. For example, Hosting.com includes an easy Matomo install in its $11.99/mo. Starter plan, which is much less than the $26/mo. starting price for Matomo Cloud. Notably, this *would not* include any of the Matomo paid add-ons like Funnels, Heatmaps, and Session Recordings, which do come included in Matomo Cloud. Still, this can be a great bargain for small sites that don't need any of the add-ons, though there would be a risk of performance issues for both Matomo and your hosted site itself, depending on volume.

My critique of MySQL might make you think, "Why doesn't Matomo support multiple databases, then? MySQL for the self-hosted small sites and ClickHouse for the big installs?" This has long been something requested from Matomo, but it would add so much complexity that the maintainers have chosen to stick with MySQL only. PostgreSQL was requested in 2009 and ClickHouse in 2021, and both remain open GitHub issues.

Matomo is pageview-based rather than event-based like GA4, which can be a drawback when dealing with mobile app data. While it does have a mobile SDK, it doesn't provide the level of seamless integration between different platforms that other event-based tools in the product analytics category can.

I mentioned Piwik PRO at the start of this chapter, so let's clear up the Matomo vs. Piwik confusion. Piwik started as an open source project in 2007 and was renamed "Matomo" in 2018.

There's no longer a product called Piwik, but there is "Piwik PRO," which began as a part of the Piwik project in 2013 before splitting off in 2016. This can be quite confusing since Matomo is the direct continuation of the Piwik project, but Piwik PRO is the only project using the Piwik name.

Matomo and Piwik PRO are fully separate products that share the same historical foundation. Piwik PRO is not open source and no longer contributes back to the core Matomo project, and they've significantly diverged. We'll evaluate Matomo and Piwik PRO individually, though much of what I say will actually apply to both.

Choosing Between Matomo and Piwik PRO

Feature / Concern	**Recommendation**
Open source, self-hosting	Matomo
Performance at scale	Piwik PRO
Built-in Heatmaps or session recording	Matomo
Built-in consent management (CMP) or customer data platform (CDP)	Piwik PRO
Sites with significant traffic, but high price-sensitivity	Matomo
Sites with serious privacy and compliance concerns	Piwik PRO

Matomo also offers automated data imports from GA4, which Piwik PRO does not. Historical data import is a very helpful bonus feature, but full of caveats. The biggest one to watch out for is that data imported from GA is aggregated data only, not reprocessed raw data. This means there will be no detail available on this imported data beyond standard reports, and all the raw data was originally processed according to GA's rules, not Matomo's (https://matomo.org/faq/general/limitations-when-importing-google-analytics-data/). The result is that you'll inherently be comparing different types of data. If you do this import, I suggest doing it into a separate historical website property rather than into your current product website property (you also can't import into a pre-existing property).

Like GA, Matomo is a comprehensive tool with a myriad of customization options. It might be more appropriate to compare Matomo to the Google Marketing Platform as a whole rather than GA alone, since Matomo includes the following features:

- Analytics
- Tag manager
- A/B testing
- Heatmaps
- Session recording

Quite a few of the alternatives we evaluate are components of suites that include functionality beyond basic analytics. I'll mention those additional functions when relevant, but we aren't explicitly evaluating other suite components like session recording. I will say that these additional components are typically not as high-quality or robust as the best-of-breed options. This is certainly true with Matomo, where its built-in session recording tool is quite rudimentary compared to industry leaders like Fullstory or Hotjar.

The core reporting functionality of Matomo is classic web analytics that any long-time practitioner will recognize from its roots in UA. While the main dashboard may at first seem more akin to some of the simplified analytics tools, its reporting goes much deeper than anything from that category.

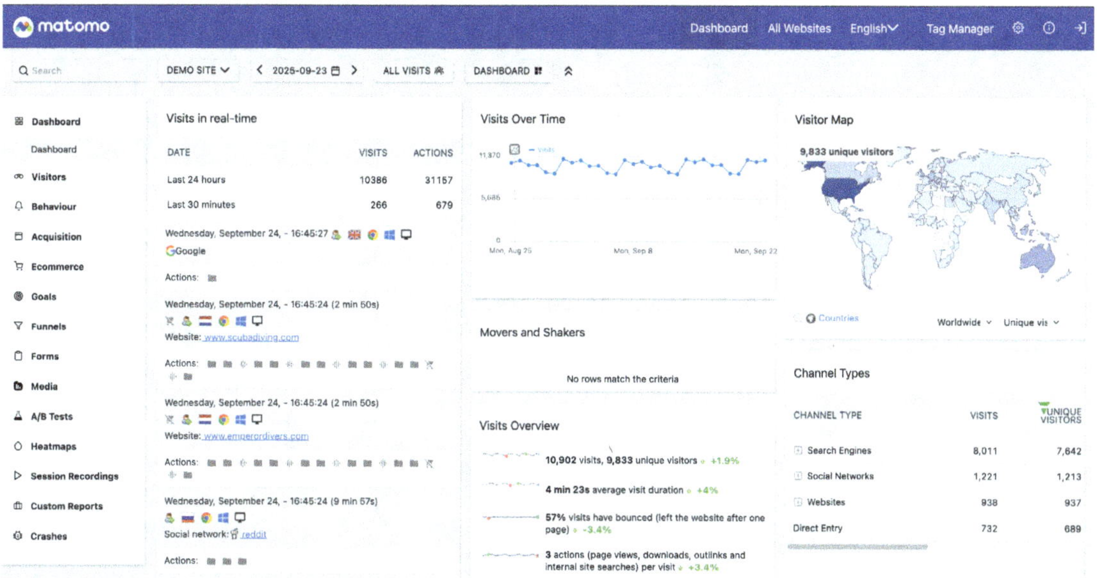

When you look at the left-hand navigation, you can see the similarities to Universal Analytics: Visitors, Behaviour, Acquisition, etc., with submenus underneath. This isn't to say Matomo is a clone of UA—on the contrary, it's substantially different, but it works within the same paradigm and is UA-like by design.

Where Matomo falls short is its lack of efficient ad hoc analysis. In other words, it can become slow and frustrating when you want to move beyond the standard reports. This likely stems from the product's technical underpinnings, specifically what we talked about in regard to the database.

Matomo has a powerful segment builder:

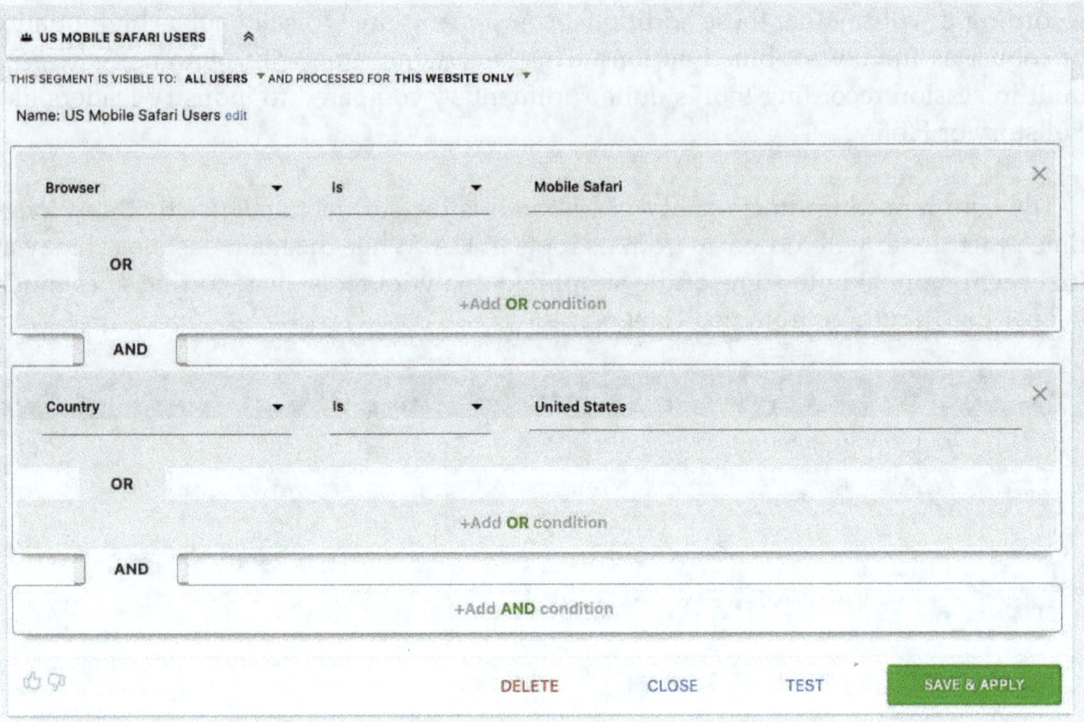

but segments are not immediately available, as they need to be processed first:

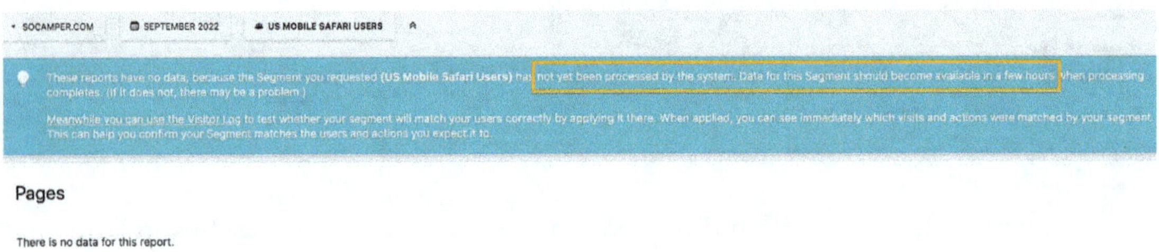

So, *once you create a segment, you may have to wait a few hours to view its data.* With my smaller testing dataset, segments tended to be available within a few minutes of creation—so if you have a site with less traffic, this may only be a slight annoyance. However, for a site that has significant amounts of data, this drawback could be incredibly frustrating.

Another of Matomo's ad hoc analysis limitations is evident in default reporting.

Compare the pages report in Matomo:

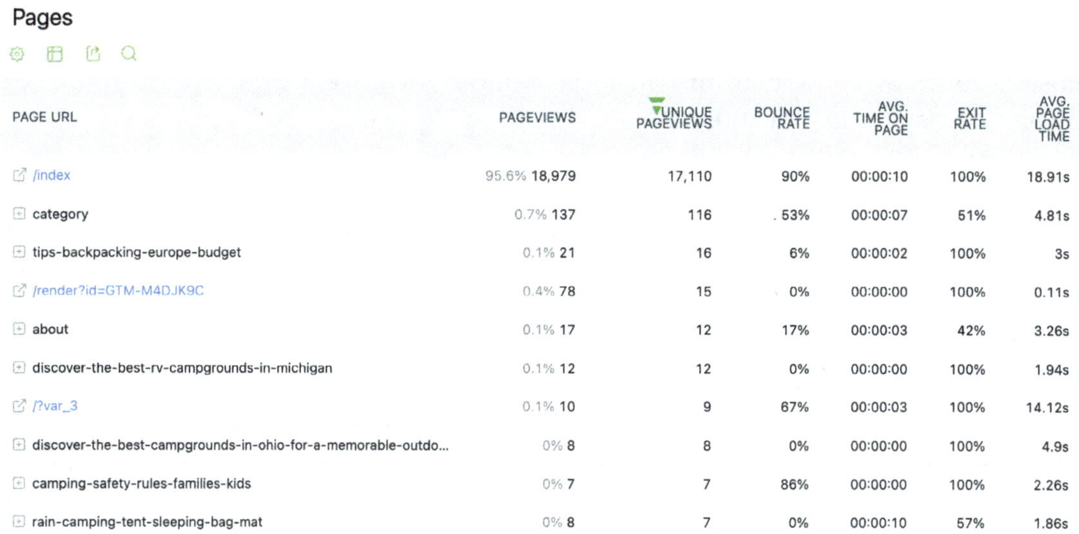

to the equivalent in Piwik PRO:

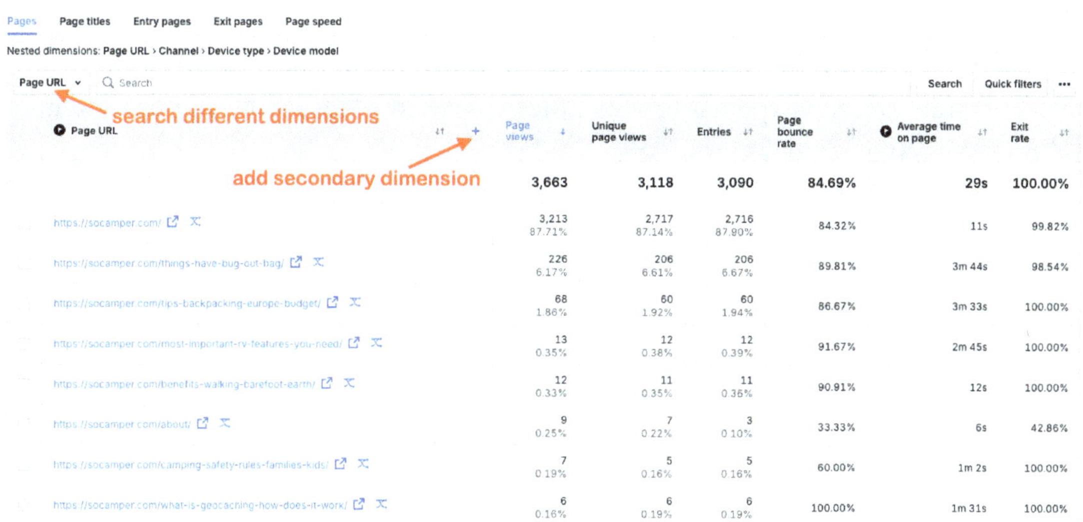

Although fundamentally similar, Piwik PRO allows substantially greater ability to filter dynamically. We can use the search box to include or exclude by dimension, leverage secondary dimensions, and even change primary dimensions within the same report. Matomo can't do this because of its limitations in dynamic reporting; rather, it has to generate its reports ahead of time.

When compared to newer tools in the product analytics category, Matomo's user interface can feel slow, clunky, and outdated. I have no issues with older user interfaces per se; sometimes they're well-tuned, easy to use, and bulletproof from so many years of testing and customer feedback. In Matomo's case, it tends to slow down when dealing with lots of data or doing filtering. This could particularly be an issue if you are self-hosting but on a server with limited resources. Going back to that example of Hosting.com's $12/mo. plan that includes Matomo, you will get the level of performance you pay for in that situation.

Another site speed issue I had with Matomo Cloud is that everything is hosted in the EU. Even though I'm in the US, every request was sent to AWS in Germany. We discussed how tracker speed can be an issue in Chapter 12, and how a US-based company like Amazon has limits for data sovereignty in Chapter 10.

There's also a large number of different reports, and it can be confusing and require a lot of clicks to find what you're looking for. Sometimes reports that you expect to be there are not (e.g., a basic source/medium acquisition report), and sometimes reports that seem useless or outdated are (e.g., a per-search engine report on keywords when essentially no search engines pass that data).

UA had similar issues with complexity, though we became less of aware of them after many years of use.

Overall, Matomo is a solid replacement for many current UA users. It can be underwhelming if you expect it to be all that you wish GA4 had been, but it's a good fit for the majority of smaller GA installations.

Chapter 21 - Piano Analytics

Type	Comprehensive Web Analytics
Default tracking method	Cookies
Price	None disclosed
Home page	https://www.piano.io
Similar tool(s)	Adobe, Piwik PRO

Pros: Privacy & compliance, powerful data tooling, broad overall platform
Cons: No pricing transparency, UI can be confusing, non-trivial migration from GA

Piano Analytics is another tool with a long history in the world of analytics. It was previously known as AT Internet, which, as a company, dates back to 1997 and the early days of web analytics. AT Internet ran a free web analytics tool called XiTi from 2000 until it was sunset in 2023, beating UA's more well-known sunset to the punch by a couple of months (https://web.archive.org/web/20230919211450/https://blog.atinternet.com/en/xiti-its-over/).

While AT Internet's Analytics Suite never reached high levels of market penetration within the United States, it was relatively popular in Germany as well as its home country of France. In 2021, AT Internet was acquired by Piano Software, itself a combination of companies with a history in the US and Slovakia. Piano is now based in Amsterdam, with its US HQ in Philadelphia.

Perhaps due in part to this cosmopolitan history, Piano has a strong focus on privacy and compliance. When the French data protection authority CNIL listed tools that could be configured to use cookies *without* needing consent, its original list only included Piano (as AT Internet) and Matomo. CNIL no longer explicitly names tools, but being on that list from the start highlights those tools' long-term commitment to privacy and compliance. Piwik PRO and Adobe were also added to CNIL's tool list before it was discontinued.

Piano Analytics is also part of a much larger data product ecosystem from Piano Software. Piano has four product lines (Analytics, Audience, Activation, Amplifier), and then within those product lines, there's a total of eight different tool modules. I am only evaluating Piano Analytics, but it's important to know what all these other tools are, since their availability in the overall suite could be a major reason to select Piano.

The breadth of these tools available from Piano likens it much more to a full enterprise marketing suite like Adobe Experience Cloud, rather than just an analytics tool provider. Product lines like Piano Audience (CDP) or Piano Activation (personalization) are separate from Piano Analytics and not necessarily purchased together, yet they are part of the same overall suite of tools. As a comparison, this structure is much different from that of Piwik PRO, where all product packages come with every module it offers: analytics, tag manager, CDP, and CMP.

Complete Piano Platform

Product Line	Module	Description	Similar Products
Analytics	**Piano Analytics**	Digital Analytics Platform	Adobe Analytics, Piwik PRO
	Ad Revenue Insights	Ad Revenue Dashboarding	?
Audience	**Audience**	Customer Data Platform (CDP), Data Management Platform (DMP)	Segment, Treasure Data, Adobe Audience, Oracle BlueKai
Activation	**Composer**	User personalization, A/B testing	Braze, Zuora
	ID	Identity management	Okta, Auth0
	VX	Premium content paywalls, subscription management	Recurly, Zuora
Amplifier	**Socialflow**	Social publishing	Hootsuite, Buffer
	ESP	Email automation	Marigold, Braze

There's a lot to digest here! Like many enterprise software suites, it can be hard to get a handle on what all these different products *actually* do just from reading the marketing website.

I'm listing a few similar products to help give you a general idea of the realm a particular module works within, but as we know, these comparisons get messy and complicated. In other words, while I can say that both Piano ID and Okta are both tools that help manage user identities and logins, I am not saying that Piano ID could necessarily replace your Okta setup.

Despite all of its different tools, it's worth noting here that Piano does not offer a tag manager or CMP. There is an official Piano Analytics tag in the GTM community gallery.

Now that we've covered the history and larger suite of products, let's start digging into the analytics tool itself. From here on, when I refer to "Piano," I will be referring to Piano Analytics specifically unless otherwise indicated.

Piano is a full-featured, comprehensive tool with extensive functionality, as befits a long-standing enterprise-level tool. There's a powerful reporting interface with a lot of options to customize each report.

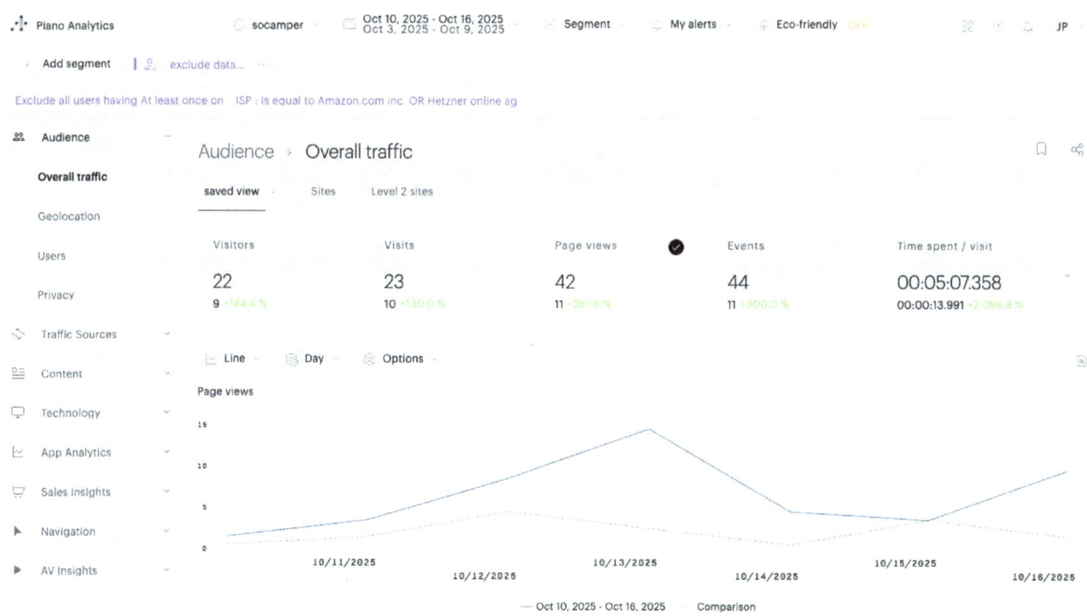

In this sample comparison report above, we can add anomaly detection, predicted ranges, additional segments, labels for min/max, or several other options. For more customization, we could click the share icon in the upper-right to open this report in the data query editor to fully control every property and metric used. Then, once in the data query editor, we could click the copy icon to get an API query that we could use programmatically. This functionality isn't always totally intuitive (e.g., the share icon to enter the data query editor), and you can easily create unreadable graphs.

For longtime users of GA, there will be a learning curve, though probably not as much as switching from GA to Adobe. Users switching from GA to Piwik PRO or Matomo feel at home more quickly because those products historically were designed as GA alternatives. Like Adobe, Piano is a case of parallel evolution with GA.

One of the most powerful features in Piano is the fully customizable data model. GA users are, of course, familiar with custom dimensions and metrics. In Piano, this kind of customization is done in the data model editor.

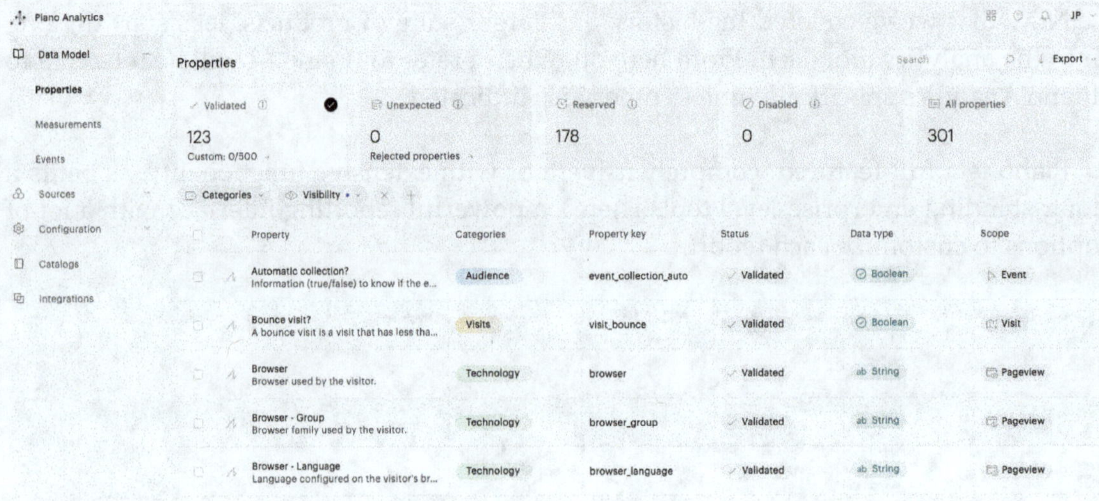

You can easily add new properties, which are similar in functionality to custom dimensions in GA, except in Piano, they:

- are treated more like built-in dimensions than in GA.
- have more configuration options.
- allow up to 500 custom properties, much higher than GA4's base limits (which have a total of 85 custom dimensions in free and 250 in paid, and are effectively much lower).

As Piano was not designed to be a drop-in replacement for GA, it lacks connections to Google. For example, Piano does not support UTMs without customization. Piano has its own type of built-in URL parameter tagging that is similar but uses "at" instead of "utm" as a prefix, e.g., `yoursite.com/landing-page?at_medium=email&at_campaign=newsletter`, and if you want to support UTMs, you'll need to do a little setup work, including creating properties in the data model editor we just discussed. This lack of UTM support by default could be improved, as even Piano's own email platform, Piano ESP, talks about doing UTM tagging. Piano also doesn't offer integrations with Google Search Console or Google Ads, though there is a Looker Studio connector.

More than most of the tools we review, Piano highlights the database that powers much of its platform: Snowflake. In Chapter 10 - Self-Hosting, we listed the database engines behind the analytics tools. Many tools do not highlight what tech they use behind the scenes, as they may not see it as relevant to the end user of the product or feel it has no particular value in marketing the product. For example, Adobe Analytics uses Apache HBase, yet there are no webpages on the business.adobe.com marketing site that I could find that mention that fact. Piano mentions Snowflake multiple times on the product home page for Piano Analytics (https://www.piano.io/product/analytics).

If you asked most people (or LLMs), "What is the most highly regarded enterprise data warehouse product?", the top answer would likely be "Snowflake." In fact, I did ask Gemini, ChatGPT, Claude, and Grok, and they all said Snowflake.

Does that really mean Snowflake is the best tool? Or, more precisely, does it mean that it's the best database to power a web analytics tool? I couldn't say, but certainly, Piano believes being "powered by Snowflake" is a benefit, and based on the processing speed and schema flexibility of Piano, it has a good argument to make. We talked about the data model editor, and indeed Piano processes data extremely quickly. There is no need for a "real-time" section at all because data appears in the standard explorer reports within two minutes. Raw data can also be exported to Snowflake or BigQuery.

The downside to Snowflake is likely the price, or at least that is my assumption, not based upon any specific info from either vendor. Snowflake can be very expensive at a large scale, and we must assume those big bills that Snowflake sends to Piano are baked into what Piano will charge you. Piano itself does not reveal any pricing information. Piano did inform me that its primary fees are tied to the platform and it is working to "reduce reliance on traffic volumes driving pricing." This is good information to know, and my interpretation is that this means the features and modules you select as part of your plan should drive the cost more than just traffic volume alone, despite how Snowflake may bill Piano.

Piano has an option called "Eco Mode," which is turned on by default in reports and dashboards like the following:

When you turn on the "Eco-friendly" mode, Piano switches to HyperLogLog cardinality estimation to make counts return more quickly with a small amount of added error (usually < 2%). GA4 uses HyperLogLog++ for this same reason, though you can't turn it off in GA! Piano gives you the option to turn it off, and when you turn it off, it seems to stay off.

The user interface of Piano is clean; however, it feels like it could use a careful user interface design review. Here's the home page of the data collection configuration section:

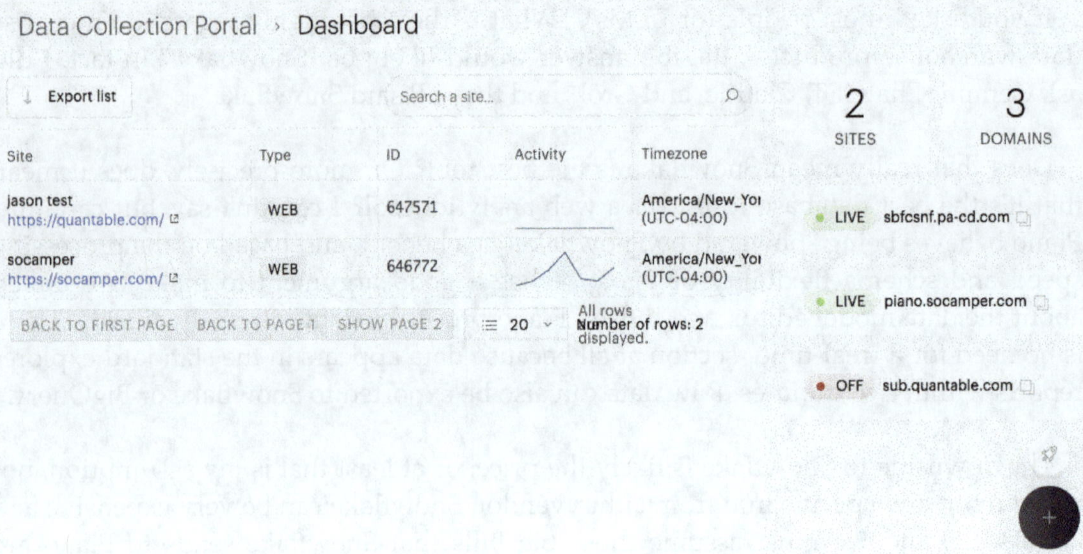

It's ok, but there are a lot of UI details that could be improved to make it feel smoother and more immediately understandable. For example:

- Why is there pagination (e.g., "SHOW PAGE 2" and "BACK TO PAGE 1") when there isn't more than one page's worth of items? Yes, those links are greyed out, but they are still there as big, all-caps text and make you read more on the page.
- The "↓ Export list" with that down arrow and its position above the table makes it easily mistaken for a table sort icon.
- Why is the "+" icon that adds a new site on the far lower right rather than more clearly grouped with the list of sites? And what's the rocket-ship icon above it for? Neither have tooltips that pop up on mouse-over, so you have to click to find out.

While this is surely nitpicking, and once you learn the product you won't even notice this kind of thing, it can make the tool feel less polished and a bit confusing when learning the platform.

Even if there may be some clunkiness and sprawl in the platform, it is highly functional and made for analysts. For example, segments can be scoped a whopping seven different ways and easily shared with others on your team. If you wanted to create a segment containing just carts where users had added items to the cart over a month ago, and set that as public within the property, you can do that.

If you're looking for a robust, enterprise-level analytics tool with strong privacy and compliance that plugs into a wider marketing data platform, Piano should definitely be on your shortlist.

Chapter 22 - Piwik PRO

Type	Comprehensive Web Analytics
Default tracking method	Cookies (default), IP+UA
Price	$128/mo. for 100k hits (Business) $430/mo. for 1M hits (Enterprise) $598/mo. for 2M hits (Business)
Home page	https://piwik.pro
Similar tool(s)	Matomo, GA4

Pros: Closest to UA, includes CMP & tag manager, privacy features
Cons: Relatively high entry price, no dedicated support or non-EU hosting until enterprise plans

If you put a bunch of engineers and seasoned web analysts in a room to create a new, privacy-friendly version of Universal Analytics before its sunset, what they'd have come up with might have looked a lot like Piwik PRO. As an engineer and old-school web analyst myself, that's a compliment, though one with perhaps a caveat or two.

Piwik PRO was founded in 2013 and has its origin in enterprise consulting for open source Piwik (Piwik is now called Matomo, please read the Matomo chapter (Chapter 20) for the naming history). With these enterprise roots, Piwik PRO has long targeted enterprise installations much more than Matomo has. In 2023, Piwik PRO merged with consent management company Cookie Information, and its CMP is now a core part of the Piwik PRO offering.

Piwik PRO Pricing Plans

Level	Starting Price	Features
Business	Starts at €35/mo. for 25k events	Max of 2M events/mo., public cloud hosted in Sweden only, max 25 months of data retention
Enterprise	Starts at €366/mo. for 1M events	Yearly contracts only, HIPAA compliance, raw data exports, Microsoft Azure hosting worldwide

Piwik PRO previously offered a free plan named "Core," but as of 2025, the plan is no longer offered and has been replaced with the "Business" plan.

While many will miss the Core plan, the Business plan can be an affordable way to get started with much of what Piwik PRO offers. Unfortunately, the Business plan's pricing does not scale up with traffic in a highly customer-friendly way, and also excludes a number of features that some sites may consider crucial. This still leaves Piwik PRO as an excellent option for many sites, but somewhat limits its target audience.

Piwik PRO has excellent documentation, including which features come with what plan (https://piwik.pro/pricing/#plan-overview). When looking at pricing, consider that all Piwik PRO plans also include its Tag Manager, CDP, and Consent Manager. So if you are already paying for a CMP like OneTrust, Cookiebot, etc., you may be able to drop that expense with a switch to Piwik PRO.

Let's compare pricing for Matomo Cloud and Piwik PRO. Note that Piwik PRO's pricing is currently set in euros only, which I have converted to US dollars.

Monthly Hits	Matomo Cloud Business (Monthly)	Piwik PRO Business (Monthly)
50k	$26	$64
100k	$42	$92
1M	$204	$443
2M	$399	$595
10M	$1,900	?

As with all pricing in this guide, this is a snapshot taken in fall 2025 and subject to change.

Piwik PRO maintains a detailed comparison versus Matomo: https://piwik.pro/piwik-pro-vs-matomo-comparison/.

Matomo also publishes a comparison: https://matomo.org/piwik-pro-vs-matomo, which doesn't go into quite the same depth but is still quite comprehensive.

We, of course, need to take vendor-published comparisons with a grain of salt—especially checklists without deeper context. For example, Matomo's comparison indicates Piwik PRO doesn't have real-time reporting (it does) and that Piwik PRO doesn't allow SQL access to the raw data (technically true, but the Piwik PRO BigQuery export provides effectively the same thing).

Conversely, Piwik PRO's comparison gives Matomo only one star out of three for privacy compliance features, even though Matomo's ability to self-host and privacy-friendly design make it one of the best tools available for compliance. In that regard, either are far better than Google Analytics, where a privacy comparison is much more distinct.

To make the distinction clear, let's compare Piwik PRO's privacy to GA:

Privacy & Compliance Comparison

	Piwik PRO	**GA**
GDPR compliance	Supported	"It's complicated"
HIPAA compliance	Supported, will sign the required BAA (with Enterprise plan)	No
Built-in CMP	Yes	No
Data sovereignty	Choose your data center (with Enterprise plan)	Can be collected in the EU, but processing may happen elsewhere
Cookieless support	Configurable, choose method according to your own legal advice and risk tolerance	Google Consent mode "cookieless pings" form basis of modeled data, but are still reliant on cookies

Piwik PRO is EU-based and most actively targets that market, but its privacy features can also be a critical feature in other locales, like the United States with regard to HIPAA compliance. To illustrate the difference in market approach, most of the world (including the EU) has the following hero text on the home page: "Turn behavioral insights into actions that grow your revenue." In the US it says, "HIPAA-compliant analytics suite: Collect and activate patient data for better marketing results."

This comparison table is just a start of the differences between GA4 and Piwik PRO. One thing that you'll also notice about Piwik PRO is that it offers a high degree of customization in most things, including privacy and compliance. For example, when it comes to collecting visitors' IP addresses, there are many different options:

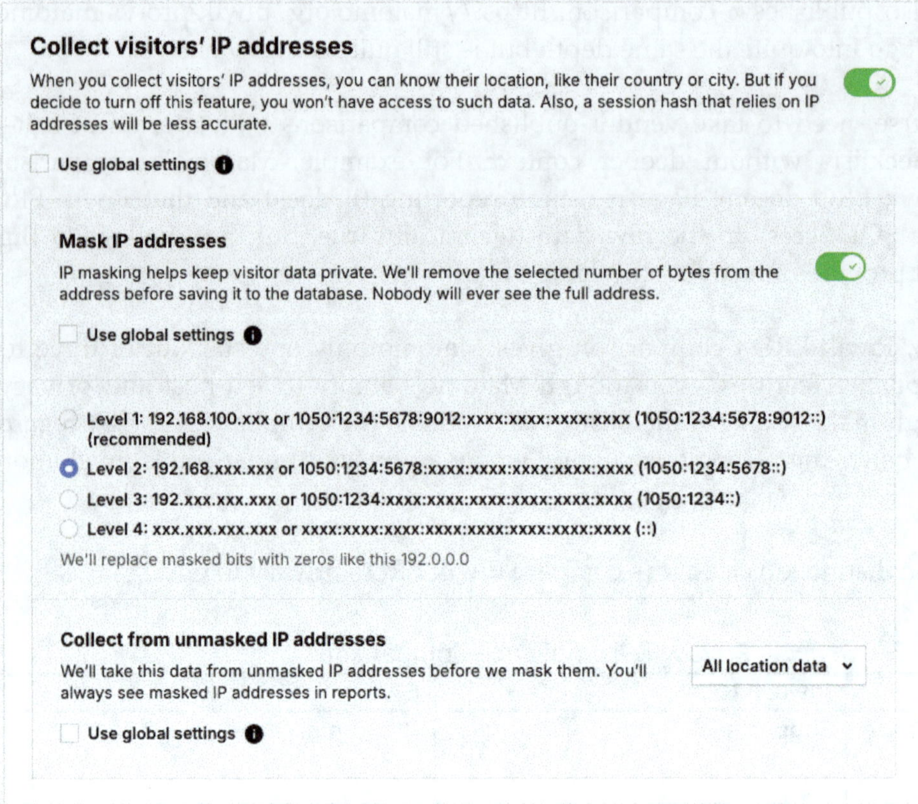

This is very comprehensive. In GA4, there are no options for IP masking at all (it defaults to Piwik PRO's equivalent of Level 1), with no customization available. In GA4, IPs aren't ever stored, but they are used for things like exclusion filters and geographic information. This means we could actually set Piwik PRO to be *less* compliance-friendly than GA4 and store every user's full IP if we wanted (though in that case, I would still consider Piwik PRO to be more privacy-friendly, since it does not share that information with an ads platform, as Google does).

The large selection of options is great as a power user, though it can sometimes feel like choice overload. Not just in the UI itself, but also just determining which option is right for you.

Take the following privacy options from that same page:

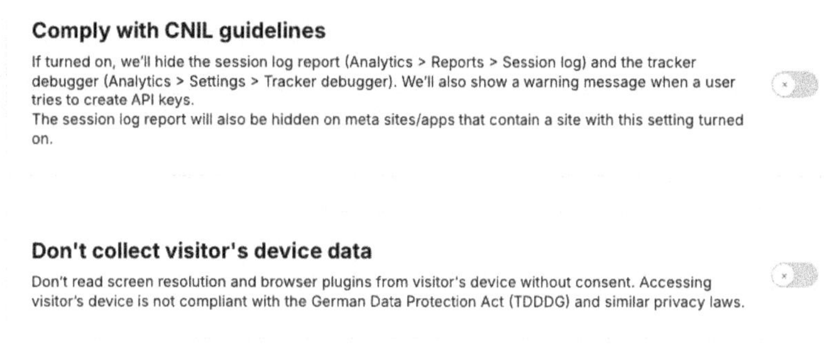

CNIL is France's data protection authority, and if your company is based in France, you may appreciate this option and understand what it does and why it's an option here. Outside the EU, it can seem like just one more confusing checkbox. The same goes for the TDDDG (the German Telecommunications Digital Services Data Protection Act). This proliferation of options is ultimately a function of the complex regulatory environment we find ourselves in, but Piwik PRO's choice to offer all these configuration options does add complexity.

In the GA4 chapter (Chapter 19), I said that I hoped to see platforms innovate to help ease this kind of complexity. As analytics has become more complex, we need help from vendors to simplify things rather than simply passing along that complexity to us.

Piwik PRO does much better than GA in many of the data caveats I list in the GA4 chapter (e.g., reducing sampling, introducing bot filtering, and better CMP integration). Where Piwik PRO doesn't fully succeed is in easing complexity. Whether it's privacy settings, a complicated segment builder, the clunky heatmap functionality, or the outmoded multi-channel Funnels attribution reports, Piwik PRO takes the approach that what users want is more and more powerful features.

If you're thinking that complaints about having "too many features" don't seem like the worst thing, I would tend to agree with you! Once you learn the product, having a toolset that is both deep and wide is great, but it does make for a harder learning process. However, those of us with backgrounds in UA will find that hill much easier to climb due to Piwik PRO's similarity to that now-defunct product, as you can see in the screenshot below.

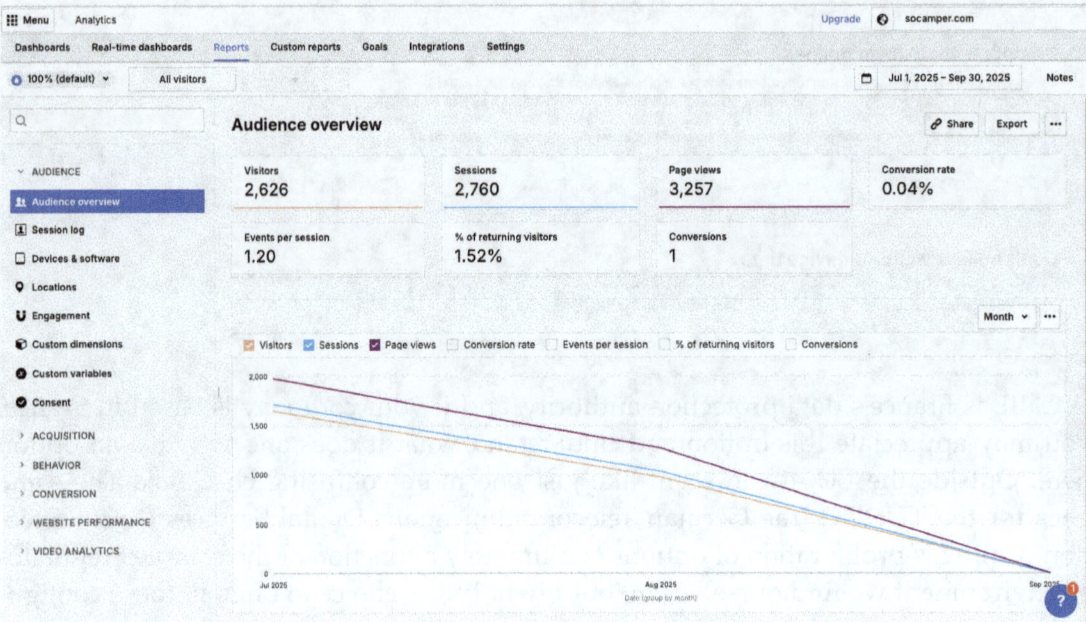

Piwik PRO also has some of the best Google Ads and Google Search Console integrations of any GA alternative. Like Matomo, Piwik PRO is designed to fully replace GA, including offering Google integrations when possible. The Google Ads integration is incredibly easy to set up. The GSC integration takes a little more work and requires using the Google Cloud Platform to set up API access, not just a simple click-through via OAuth.

Piwik PRO is also currently beta testing an integration with the bot detection platform fraud0. This integration has the potential to be a much-needed and unique feature to help mitigate bots, as discussed in Chapter 16 - Bot Filtering. This is potentially a game-changing feature for many sites with bot issues.

I didn't evaluate the Piwik PRO tag manager or consent manager. As with all the alternatives we're evaluating, I used Google Tag Manager to deploy the tags. Piwik PRO's tag manager is quite similar to GTM, though not as full-featured. One common source of confusion with Piwik PRO is that the tags it generates by default are Piwik PRO tag manager tags, which include analytics, not the bare Piwik PRO analytics tags.

If you see `containers.piwik.pro` in the tag, that means it is calling the tag manager, and it is the tag manager that deploys the Piwik PRO analytics tag. If you are deploying Piwik PRO analytics only and using another tag manager (like GTM), then you may want to use just the analytics tracking code (https://help.piwik.pro/support/getting-started/no-piwik-pro-tag-manager-install-a-tracking-code/) or use the GTM Community Template Gallery tag template (which also is just the analytics tracking code).

Piwik PRO remains the closest thing to a successor that Universal Analytics has, both in terms of approach and feature set. It's highly configurable, with robust privacy and compliance features. Like UA, it can be a lot to handle for smaller teams who may be better off in a simpler product. At the opposite end of the spectrum, its focus on web analytics might not make it the right fit for large enterprises looking for the user journey tracking that is more associated with the product analytics category.

Simplified Web Analytics

Chapter 23 - Clicky

Type	Simplified Web Analytics
Default tracking method	IP + User-Agent (also supports cookies)
Price	Free for 3k *daily* pageviews (with 31 days data retention) $10/mo. 30k $20 for 100k $88 for 400k
Home page	https://clicky.com
Demo	https://clicky.com/stats/?site_id=32020
Similar tool(s)	Statcounter

Pros: Mature product, white-labeling, price scales very well
Cons: Outdated UI, legacy reports, rudimentary add-on features

Clicky is another long-standing GA alternative. It launched in 2006, predating everything else in the category aside from Statcounter. I first used the product in 2011 and felt it was a market leader at that time. Reviewing the product in 2025, little has changed. The upside of this approach is that Clicky has remained consistent and slowly introduced new features and add-ons over time. Its core design has experienced few fundamental changes since its creation, even when those changes might be needed.

Per BuiltWith, Clicky's market share plateaued in 2015 and has decreased in recent years. BuiltWith still tracks it as being installed on 2.3% of the top 1M sites, however, so despite its relatively low profile, it retains decent popularity. This popularity in the install base does not translate to any sort of online community around the product. At the time of writing, Clicky's own help forums have had only two questions asked in the last month, and neither were answered. While market share loss alone is not a reason to pass over a particular tool, it does raise concerns about the continued stability and pace of improvement of the product.

That said, Clicky's pricing model is one of the most attractive of any tool, and it scales up with traffic and number of sites extremely well. For a site with 400,000 daily pageviews (12M pageviews a month), it's only $88 per month. This makes Clicky a very low-priced option for larger sites. Clicky also supports a selectable number of sites, so you could run 100 different websites all under that same $88 monthly plan, as long as they add up to fewer than 400,000 daily pageviews combined. A per-day usage cap is disadvantageous in comparison to a monthly limit (since it doesn't allow for traffic spikes to be averaged out over a full month's usage), but with prices as low as they are, that's not much of a concern.

Pairing this advantageous price model with Clicky's white-labeling ability makes it a great option for running analytics on a large number of smaller sites. I used Clicky for that exact scenario in the early 2010s—white-labeled for hundreds of similar but unrelated sites, all under one umbrella, and it proved very effective. This ability to be white-labeled and run cheaply at scale is likely the reason that it has a wide installation base, implying that there are a lot of individual sites running the tool, if perhaps not a lot of individual customers of the product.

Clicky's reporting is similar to Statcounter and others in this category, though it breaks the reporting up across multiple screens rather than a single dashboard. It also has more features available than most simplified category options, including basic uptime monitoring, integration with an SEO search engine results page (SERP) ranking service, A/B testing integration, and heatmaps. Even more than other tools we've talked about that integrate things like heatmaps, Clicky's versions of these additional features are very rudimentary in comparison to industry leaders.

Here's what Clicky's main dashboard page looks like:

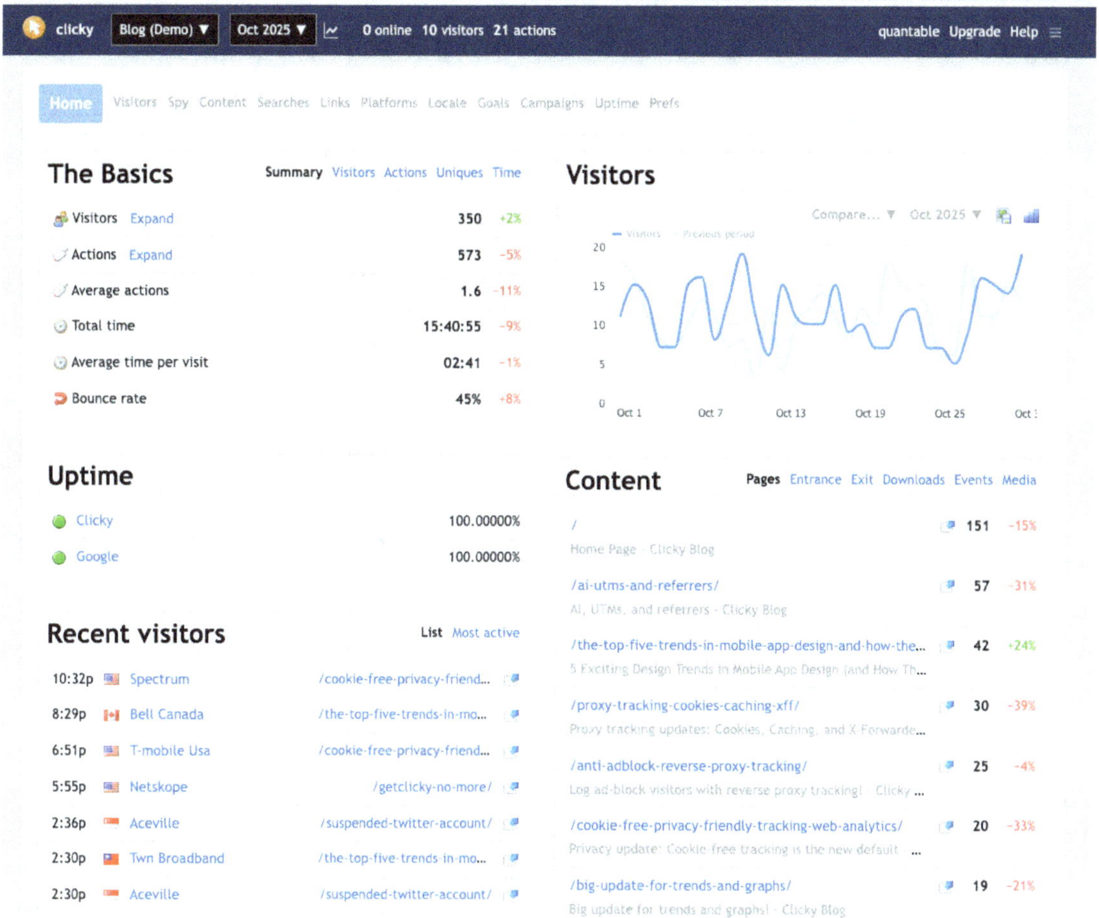

In addition to the outdated look of the UI, it also contains reports that have long outlived their relevance. For example, Clicky still includes reporting on search engine keywords—except almost all of the data is marked as "[secure search]," making the report effectively useless. Google has not provided that keyword data since 2011. That report isn't about Google Search Console data (which Clicky also does not support), but rather about pulling the keywords directly from the HTTP referrer data, which is no longer feasible. This feature is both outdated and adds confusion.

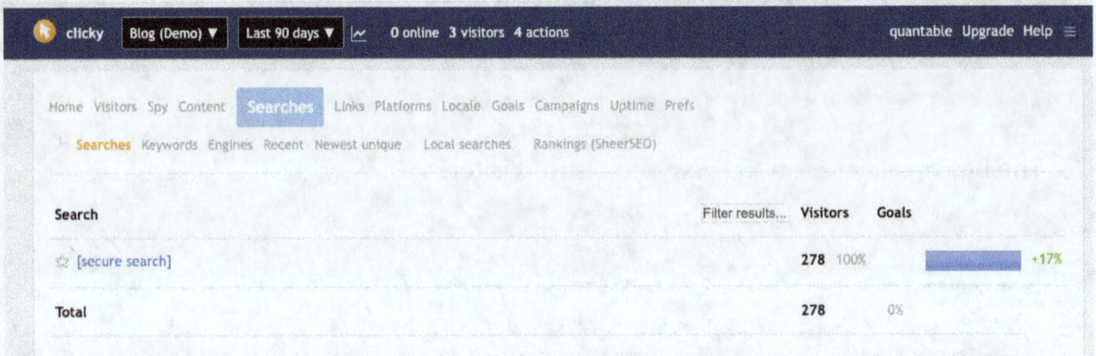

Most top-level nav items (Content, Searches, Links, etc.) have sub-reports, overall providing a higher level of reporting detail than we get from most of the simplified category tools. For example, Clicky reports individual browser version numbers (e.g., "Chrome 142" vs. just "Chrome") and ISP organizations (e.g., Comcast, T-Mobile, etc.), which most simplified tools do not.

You may look at the top-level navigation and think that "Spy" sounds privacy-unfriendly, but it's just its real-time stats page. Overall, Clicky is privacy-friendly and uses IP + User-Agent to identify a visitor rather than cookies by default, though it supports both. Clicky wasn't designed with privacy in mind the way Cloudflare, Fathom, and Plausible were, but it's been retrofitted with privacy features. If EU hosting is part of your requirements, Clicky does not appear to offer such an option, and always routes requests through Cloudflare's network. Clicky's privacy practices are, however, preferrable to Statcounter, its closest competitor in this guide.

Clicky also has additional features like uptime monitoring and SEO rank tracking integration via the third-party service sheerseo.com. In most cases, I recommend separate tools for uptime monitoring and SEO rank tracking, but for simpler sites, it can be nice to have them all in the same place.

As mentioned, Clicky's implementations of these additional features are very limited. For example, its split testing feature only counts which variation drove a conversion. It provides no ability to manage experiments or their content. This feature would be similar to using a session-scoped custom dimension on a goal in GA to count which variation is the winner (https://clicky.com/help/faq/features/split-tests/how). Clicky's heatmap feature is slightly more complex, but still very limited—heatmaps are not even captured for visitors on mobile devices.

If you choose Clicky, planning to run robust A/B testing or do involved uptime monitoring, you will likely find its implementations insufficient. In Clicky's defense, it doesn't try to sell these solutions as more than what they are. It also offers A/B testing integrations with Visual Website Optimizer (VWO) and Convert. Some of the much bigger platforms like PostHog, offer features like session capture or A/B testing that can legitimately considered as competitors for packages like Hotjar or VWO, but Clicky does not offer that.

While Clicky overall remains a solid tool, its use case is fairly limited. It is a good match for organizations with multiple sites, a lot of traffic, a low budget, and limited reporting needs. Other simplified tools like Fathom, Plausible, and Umami have caught up with or passed Clicky in terms of usability and privacy.

Chapter 24 - Cloudflare Web Analytics

Type	Simplified Web Analytics
Default tracking method	Referrer
Price	Free
Home page	https://www.cloudflare.com/web-analytics/
Similar tool(s)	none

Pros: Free, robust privacy, strong technical underpinning, unsampled site speed monitoring

Cons: Limited tracking abilities, no events, tied to complex platform, no reporting API

Cloudflare's analytics offerings can be confusing. We're evaluating its web analytics offering, which launched in 2020, but there are other Cloudflare solutions that look similar and are frequently mistaken for its web analytics tool.

Cloudflare Web Analytics is free, with no volume restrictions, although there are a couple of feature limits if you aren't on a regular Cloudflare plan (restrictions are described here: https://developers.cloudflare.com/web-analytics/limits/).

You can deploy Cloudflare Web Analytics as a JavaScript snippet on your site like any other analytics tag. Alternatively, you can deploy it automatically via the Cloudflare proxy if your site uses the regular Cloudflare service. The standard Cloudflare service is a CDN and reverse proxy service that sits in front of your website and provides a full suite of tools, from caching and security to image optimization.

Tens of millions of sites use the standard Cloudflare service, though the standard service does not enable the web analytics tool by default. The web analytics tool can be incorporated either as part of its regular service or as a separate *à la carte* offering.

The main point of confusion is that the regular Cloudflare service does include a "traffic analytics" offering available under the individual website options in its nav:

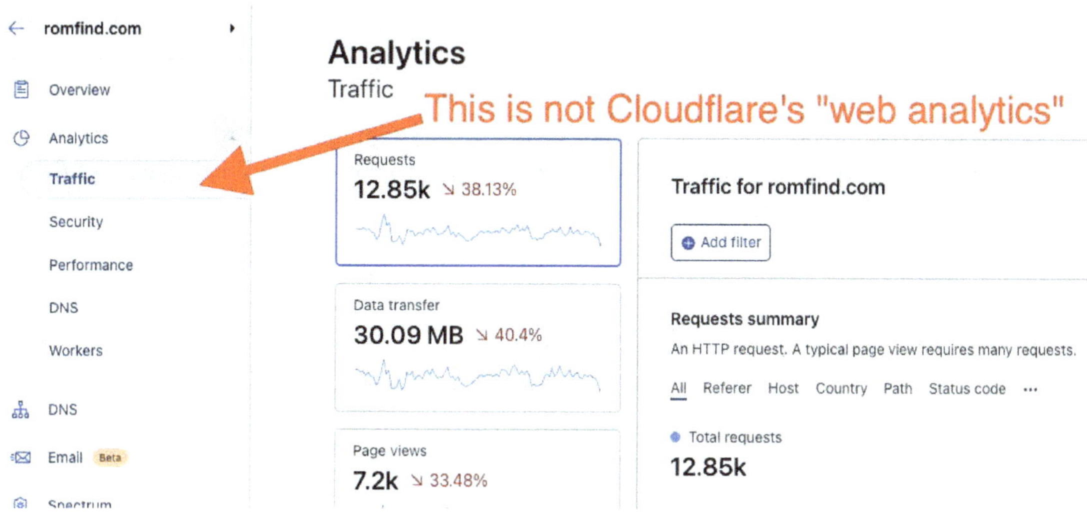

Traffic analytics reports metrics we associate with web analytics, like pageviews, but it's not its official "web analytics" tool. This traffic analytics tool is run automatically on all requests that come through the Cloudflare reverse proxy, so it intentionally includes lots of bot and other types of traffic that a web analytics platform generally wouldn't report. On our test site (which has significant bot traffic), the traffic analytics reported *100 times* the number of users GA did. Also, these numbers are *not* free; you need to be on the $20 monthly pro plan or higher to see them, compared to the web analytics numbers, which are free.

We can't talk about Cloudflare without mentioning bot blocking. Cloudflare has some of the best anti-bot technology out there, though its Web Analytics package represents only a small portion of that. Full Cloudflare bot detection involves being on "regular" Cloudflare behind the proxy, and the full Bot Management tool is only available on Enterprise plans. Cloudflare Web Analytics wasn't included in our bot test in Chapter 16 because the platform does not report in comparable ways to the other platforms and does not contain a reporting API. While Cloudflare overall is excellent at blocking bots, this has a modest effect on Cloudflare Web Analytics.

Cloudflare's supporting documentation doesn't do much to clear up the confusion between different Cloudflare services. Under the "About Cloudflare Analytics" section, it says, "It is possible that your Cloudflare metrics do not fully align with data for the same site as reported by other analytics sources, such as Google Analytics and web server logs." (https://developers.cloudflare.com/fundamentals/data-products/about-analytics/.)

I'd say a hundred-fold traffic increase counts as "not fully aligned." There is information about the web analytics product under the "Types of analytics" link on that page, but it seems odd to mention data discrepancies with GA on its main analytics documentation page and yet not mention its tool that actually will line up reasonably well with GA.

I've spent a fair amount of this chapter telling you what Cloudflare Web Analytics is not, because it's a common point of confusion. I was flummoxed by this the first time I tried to use Cloudflare Web Analytics, and I've seen multiple online reviews that claim to be about Cloudflare ***Web*** Analytics but actually cover Cloudflare ***Traffic*** Analytics.

Let's look at the correct feature:

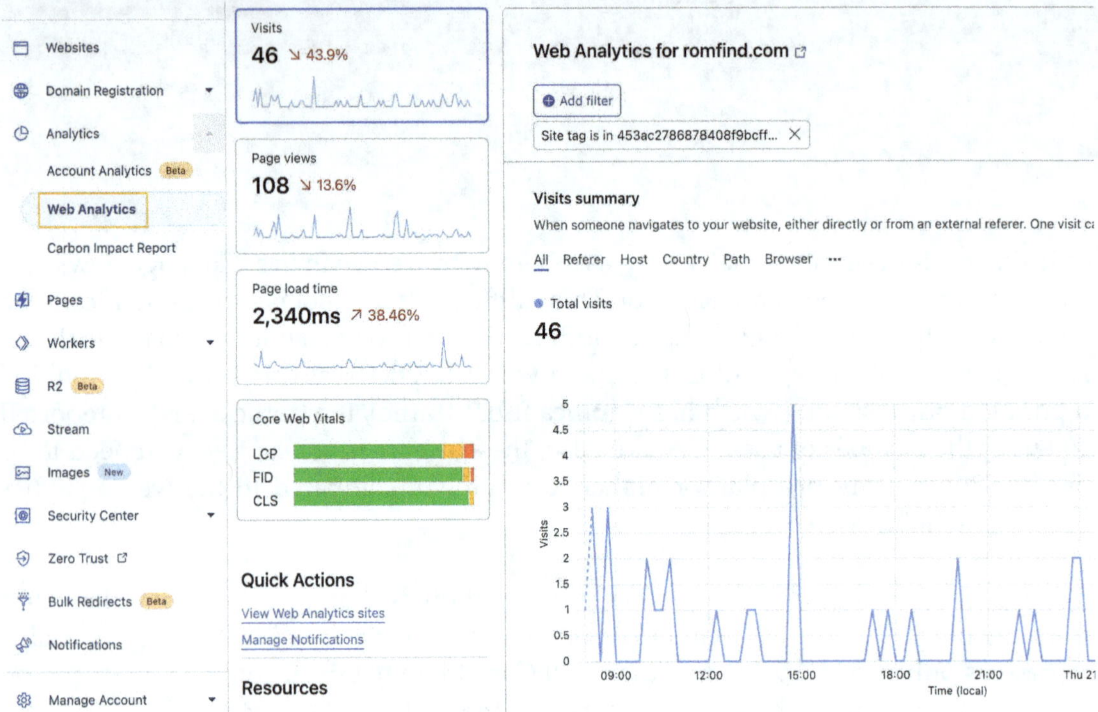

This is its web analytics tool. It looks and functions like its traffic analytics, but is located at the account level rather than inside a particular website.

Similar to the other tools in the simplified category, this tool is limited by design. It doesn't use cookies or any session tracking technology at all, so it's incapable of tracking visitor paths through the site—no flow tracking, no goal tracking, no UTMs, not even events. Cloudflare is the simplest of the simplified; in fact, it's too simple for most use cases.

Unlike Plausible, Fathom, etc., which employ hashed IP + User-Agent, Cloudflare uses *no session identifier.* It tracks visitors by looking at HTTP referrer headers. So, any time it sees a request without an outside referrer, it counts it as a new visitor:

- Arrive from google.com: new visitor
- Arrive directly (no referrer): new visitor
- Click from home page to about page: *not* a new visitor (internal referrer)

This method was discussed in more detail in Chapter 13 - Tracking Methods.

In my testing, Cloudflare over-reported visitors by about 30% vs. GA. This is vastly more accurate than the one hundred-fold over-report from Cloudflare traffic analytics, but it's still less accurate than the IP + User-Agent method, which itself is less accurate than cookies. The upside of this method is that it's great for privacy and compliance. There's no cookie set, no IPs tracked, and no ability to identify individual users. For better or worse, these restrictions make it hard to learn much about your site visitors.

I consider this method to be superior to the method of IP + User-Agent from a privacy perspective. A potential privacy drawback, though, is that you send traffic through Cloudflare, one of the largest collectors of data on the internet.

Cloudflare is US-based and sees over *20% of all traffic on the internet* route through its systems (https://developers.cloudflare.com/reference-architecture/architectures/security/). Cloudflare Web Analytics offers no choice for data location, which could potentially be a compliance issue for EU-based companies, based on the data transfers. There's no personally identifiable info tracked within Cloudflare, but the company does see the user's IP.

Another Cloudflare feature that's unique among our evaluated alternatives is that it performs its web analytics measurement through the browser performance API (https://developer.mozilla.org/en-US/docs/Web/API/Performance) rather than a traditional web beacon. This is a smart move because it allows it to provide detailed website speed data without additional calls on 100% of the data (i.e., no sampling of page speed tracking like in UA, Piwik PRO, and others).

Here's an example of Cloudflare's web performance reporting, based on real user monitoring (RUM, field-based) rather than automated testing (lab-based). As previously discussed, RUM is important for SEO as that's what Google uses for Core Web Vitals. A more detailed description of the differences between field-based and lab-based measurements is available from Google here: https://web.dev/lab-and-field-data-differences.

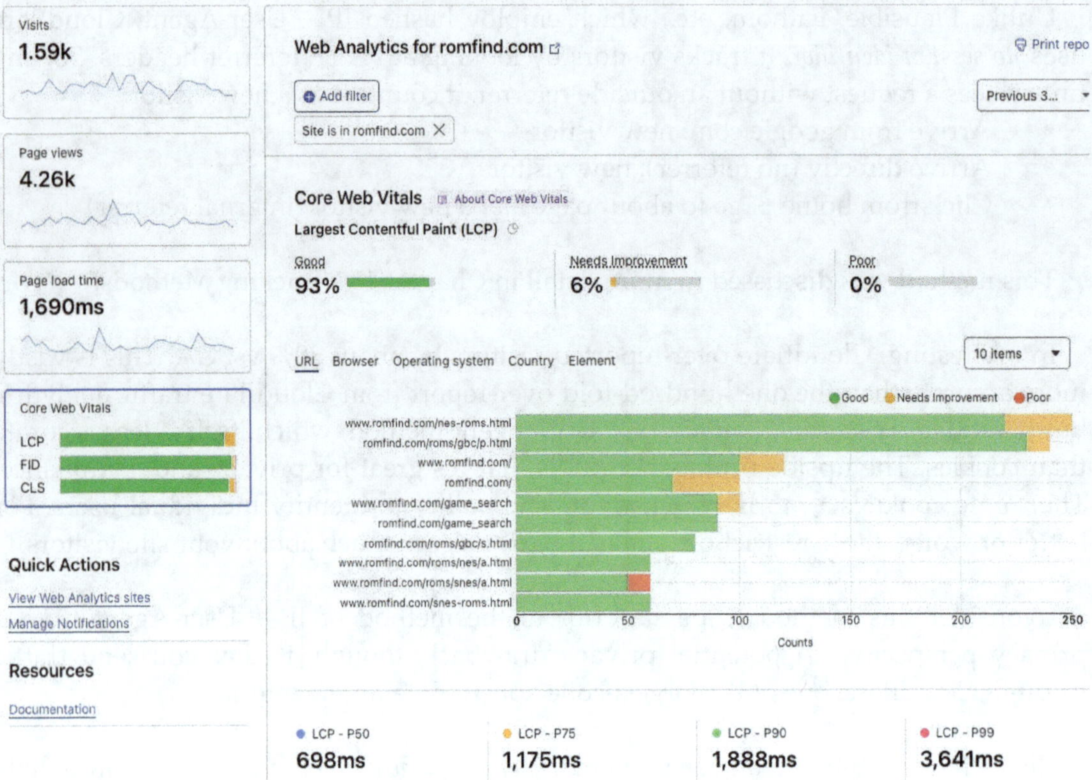

With Cloudflare, you can drill down into LCP, INP (previously FID), and CLS in detail (see Chapter 12 for definitions of these). Because Cloudflare currently has no limits on the volume of traffic, this could be a great free option versus tools like Pingdom that charge significant amounts of money at scale for RUM data.

Cloudflare's depth and reporting flexibility are far less sophisticated than more robust paid RUM tools like SpeedCurve or Calibre, but it's a simple, free option to monitor Core Web Vitals numbers. Many sites are dependent upon the free Core Web Vitals monitoring that's part of the Google CrUX dataset, which is an excellent source of data, but is delayed (released for the previous month on the second Tuesday of the month) and only includes data from Chrome. It is also possible to track RUM via GA4 (https://www.simoahava.com/analytics/track-core-web-vitals-in-ga4-with-google-tag-manager/), but it lacks the easy usability that Cloudflare provides here.

If you already use Cloudflare for some other purpose, turning on its web analytics tool as well could be a fruitful supplement, especially if you want to monitor Core Web Vitals. However, as a standalone product, it's too basic to replace GA for most use cases.

Additionally, Cloudflare does not seem to be doing much to actively maintain or improve this product. The lone substantive change in the product since my 2022 review is to update the FID metric to INP, following the change that Google made in its definition of Core Web Vitals metrics. Cloudflare doesn't make these stats available in any API that I was able to discover. Cloudflare has very extensive APIs, and the lack of a reporting endpoint in this set of APIs shows its lack of commitment to this particular product. I don't recommend this tool outside of the limited use case of simple, no-cost Core Web Vitals monitoring.

Chapter 25 - Fathom

Type	Simplified Web Analytics
Default tracking method	IP + User-Agent
Price	$15/mo. for 100k pageviews $74/mo. for 2M pageviews $470/mo. for 25M pageviews
Home page	https://usefathom.com
Demo	https://app.usefathom.com/share/deasaicp/hilarious+platypus
Similar tool(s)	Plausible, Umami

Pros: Privacy, data retention, good for multiple sites
Cons: Limited reporting and filtering

While there are now many web analytics tools focused on privacy with simplified dashboards, Fathom may have been the first to kick off this trend. Paul Jarvis, one of the founders of Fathom, posted the following tweet in 2018, including an early screenshot of what would become the first version of Fathom.

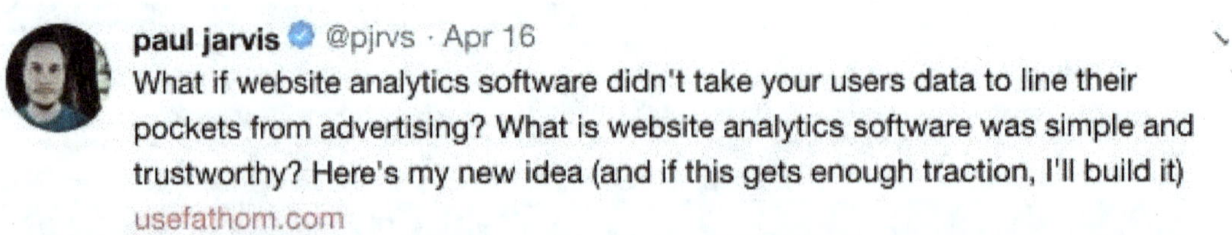

The reception to this and the number of simplified tools that have since followed shows that this is an idea whose time had come. As illustrated by Statcounter and Clicky being much older tools, simpler web analytics tools are not a new idea; however, Fathom was the first in the newer generation of tools that were both purposely simple and privacy-first. Or at least the first to gain traction, as others (including Fathom co-founder Danny van Kooten) had worked on similar projects before Fathom.

Fathom was shortly followed by similar tools such as Simple Analytics (2018), Plausible (2019), and Umami (2020), showing that Fathom had indeed tapped into a growing trend. This trend was headed the opposite way from Google Analytics. In July 2019, when Google launched the beta of what would become GA4, this resurgence of simplified web analytics had already begun, though clearly the switch to GA4 provided more space for these tools to grow.

Fathom was originally launched as an open source project, but switched to closed source in 2019 to focus on its hosted service and paid customers. There still exists the original open version, renamed "Fathom Lite," but that version is now effectively defunct, with no significant updates since 2022.

As with many of the offerings in this category of Simplified Web Analytics tools, you can see most of what the product can do from the main dashboard.

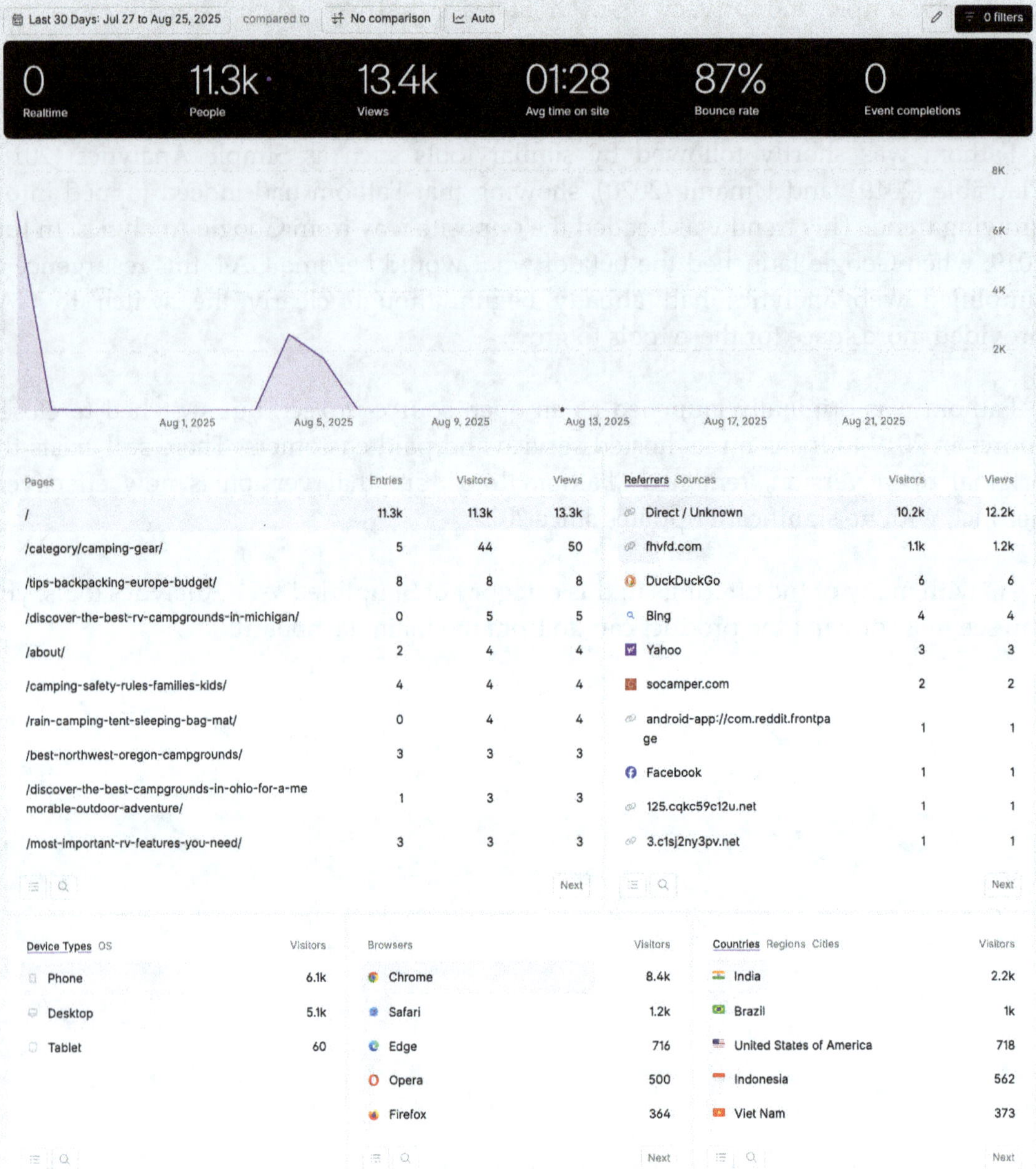

There's no navigation to drill down into, nor any hidden reports. Fathom is at the opposite end of the spectrum from GA4's myriad reports and customization options. Fathom lacks custom report building, and there are no secondary metrics to add to our reports. The main action we can perform from the dashboard is filter to a particular metric.

For example, if we wanted to see only the mobile Chrome users from Brazil, we'd click on each of those in the dashboard to add them as reporting filters.

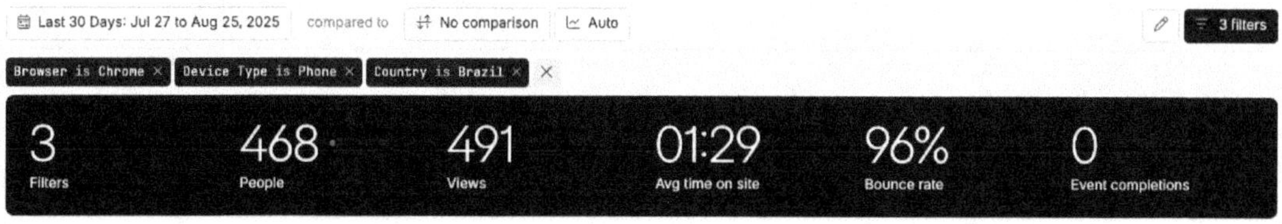

If you're wondering why there is so little information about attribution, consider that Fathom (as with Plausible and Cloudflare) also has *no concept of returning visitors across multiple days.* As discussed in Chapter 13 - Tracking Methods, Fathom's user identification method hashes IP addresses in such a way that the same user returning the next day from the same IP would receive a different hash. New day, new user, as described here: https://usefathom.com/blog/anonymization. Meaning if you had a Google Ads campaign and someone clicked but didn't convert until the following day after their initial click, that goal in Fathom would *not* be attributed to Google Ads.

This is the world of consentless analytics: significantly reduced detail on users and a lack of attribution beyond the initial user session or day.

While there aren't a lot of features in Fathom, the features that are there are simple and easy to use. As an example, let's say you want to block an internal IP. In GA4, you'll need to:

1. Go to web stream > configure tag settings (click on show more) > define internal traffic.
2. Create a rule set.
3. Add IPs to block, note that the default match type is Classless Inter-Domain Routing (CIDR) notation (e.g., 192.168.1.0/24).
4. If there are more than 10 IP match rules, create a new rule set for each group.
5. Go to property settings > data collection > data filters.
6. Enable the Internal Traffic filter.
7. Wait 24–36 hours to see if the filter is working correctly.

Whereas in Fathom, you would:

1. Go to the site firewall settings.
2. Add IPs to block under "Blocked IPs" (note that matches use wildcards, e.g., 192.168.1.*).
3. Wait 60 seconds to see if the filter is working correctly

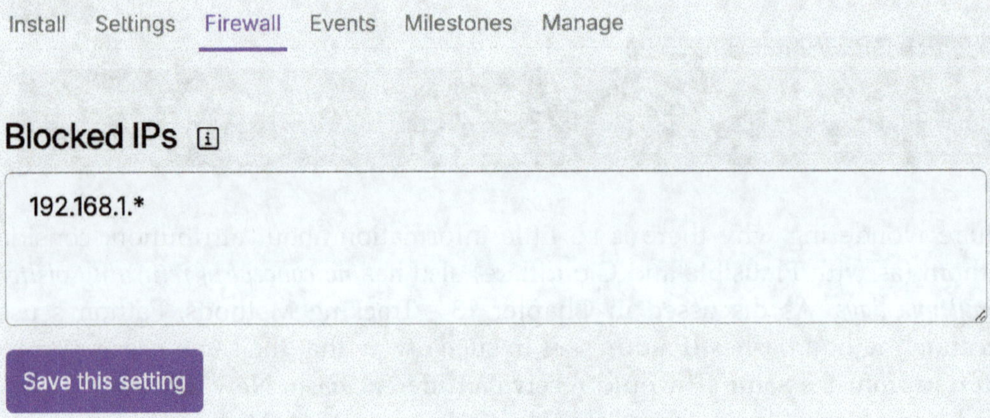

Fathom's IP blocking is quick and easy. GA4's is hard to find, complex, and error-prone (mostly due to users forgetting to activate the filter). However, GA4's implementation is also more powerful, as it allows CIDR and regex on the IP rules, naming rulesets (so you can know what IPs were from your Ohio office vs. your London office), and being able to test rules without actually excluding the traffic. This difference is emblematic of the two tools' different approaches, and should be expected when comparing a comprehensive tool like GA with a simplified tool like Fathom.

Fathom has much of the most commonly used functionality, and it will be easier to use, but it's lacking in more comprehensive functionality that larger organizations could need.

Fathom and Plausible are very similar. Here's a comparison of a few of their functionality differences:

Fathom has...	**whereas Plausible has...**
Annotations (called "milestones")	User-based access to reports (teams)
Regex search in filters	Saved segments
Combined multi-site reporting	Custom dimensions

As with any tool comparison, this kind of "feature matrix" can be problematic. Maybe you don't care about a particular feature, or perhaps you do, but the vendor is planning to launch it next week. Having watched both of these tools for a few years, my judgement is that Plausible has maintained a slight edge in functionality. Fathom does still include all functionality under one plan level, however; Plausible does not. For example, Plausible has single sign-on (SSO) and Fathom does not, but Plausible has restricted this feature to the Enterprise tier only.

Fathom also has unlimited data retention and 50 sites included in all plans, whereas the Plausible starter plan only has one site and three years of data retention.

One difficulty I ran into was that Fathom's default tag didn't work in Google Tag Manager. It provides a different tag in the documentation that *does* work with GTM, but this was unclear from the script settings page and caused me confusion during installation.

In addition to the privacy inherent to its simplified design, Fathom (which is based in Canada) also has an "EU isolation" mode (https://usefathom.com/features/eu-isolation) that keeps data away from US-based servers, if that is a feature you desire. It does use AWS, however, so if you are looking to steer clear of all US-based companies, you should look to fully EU-based Plausible instead (which is hosted with Hetzner).

Like most of the tools in the "simplified" category, Fathom Analytics is a very small company. LinkedIn lists only two employees, and the company has talked about its "Company of One" philosophy, including a book by that name written by its co-founder, Paul Jarvis (who is no longer at the company). For Fathom, having a small number of employees is by design.

Is picking a tool from a tiny company a risk? That is a risk, but there is also a risk that a large company decides to divest itself of its tool or completely change it. All of the other tools we are talking about in this book have reached a level of adoption that makes it likely they will continue to exist.

In many ways, it's strange to compare products by tiny companies like Fathom, Clicky, Umami, etc., to offerings from giant organizations like Google, Adobe, or Cloudflare. Google has around 180,000 employees. If we combine every tool in the simplified category aside from Cloudflare (Clicky + Fathom + Plausible + Statcounter + Umami), that would be roughly 20–30 people. Certainly, Google only has a tiny percentage of its company working on GA, but the resources it has overall are many orders of magnitude different.

The small team size behind these successful products says a lot:

- It's a testament to the efficiency and quality of the work that small teams can put out.
- It shows how modern tooling and platforms can enable small companies to compete at high levels. Fathom uses the analytics database SingleStore and hosts on AWS, allowing a "Company of One" to have performance and reliability comparable to what Google can achieve.
- It highlights how simple the "simplified" category tools really are. The smallest company outside this category is likely Matomo, with a head count of roughly 50—making it also larger than all of the dedicated simplified vendors com-

bined. This isn't just about the software development or DevOps challenges; it's also about the sales and support required to offer a more complicated product.

When choosing between Fathom, Plausible, and Umami, in addition to reading all three of their reviews in this book, you should try the live demos that each one offers. While there are certainly differences between each of them, in many use cases any of these three may work, and the decision could come down to things like small feature differences, pricing differences, or the feel you get for the product yourself.

Chapter 26 - Plausible Analytics

Type	Simplified Web Analytics
Default tracking method	IP + User-Agent
Price	$19/mo. for 100k pageviews $89/mo. for 2M pageviews
Home page	https://plausible.io
Demo	https://plausible.io/plausible.io
Similar tool(s)	Fathom, Umami

Pros: Open source, privacy, easy GA data import
Cons: Limited reporting, some basic features withheld for higher-level plans

Plausible and Fathom are, to my mind, the quintessential representations of the "simplified web analytics" category. These two products are also the most similar of any of our alternatives.

Why is Plausible so emblematic of the category?

- It prioritizes privacy over reporting detail.
- It offers streamlined user interfaces that focus on popular pageview-oriented metrics.
- It's produced by a small team and targets smaller sites.
- It has an intentionally limited feature set.

Plausible is simple, with minimal capacity for customization. Yet what's included is very well-considered. Depending on your use case, this simplicity could be incredibly frustrating, or exactly what you need. Non-specialists will also find it easy to use, which is great for that frequently mythical idea of "self-service analytics." Unlike GA4 and many other complex platforms, you can hand over a Plausible login to a wide variety of users, and they will be able to use it effectively.

If you are in the market for a simplified tool like Plausible, it can be difficult to select one, since they can all seem fairly similar. We talked about how Matomo and Piwik PRO both came from the same open source project, but even those two tools with the same origin are further apart in functionality than tools like Plausible and Fathom.

This simplicity has also led to a minimal barrier to entry, where many variants on this general theme have entered the space. In addition to those I am reviewing in this book, there are tools like Pirsch, Beam, Ahrefs Web Analytics, and many more, which all have followed this general template of using an IP + User-Agent identifier (i.e., no cookies) and very simple reporting. As one of the most popular and most mature of these offerings, I recommend looking at Plausible first.

Many of these offerings have lower prices than Plausible, so if you are highly price sensitive, you may end up elsewhere with products like Umami or Beam, which have free tiers.

Plausible has different plan levels (Starter, Growth, Business, and Enterprise) versus only one plan level with most of the others. From the vendor's perspective, this makes sense as a way to charge businesses that can afford to pay for more advanced features to do so. Plausible has long publicly focused on being a sustainable and independent small company supported by subscriptions alone, so it's easy to believe some amount of price discrimination is necessary to support the business.

Yet with a product so simple, many of the features withheld from lower-tier plans are things small sites may still need. For example, funnel reporting and the Plausible Looker Studio connector are withheld until the "Business" tier. Also built into the tiers are data retention rules, where the lowest-level plans have three years, and the highest plans are five years or more.

This can make Fathom (or others) significantly cheaper, depending on what features you need. For example, if you had 500k pageviews split between 10 sites, Fathom would be $45/mo. with unlimited data retention vs. Plausible's $99/mo. with five years of data retention on the "Business" plan.

Here's the main reporting view:

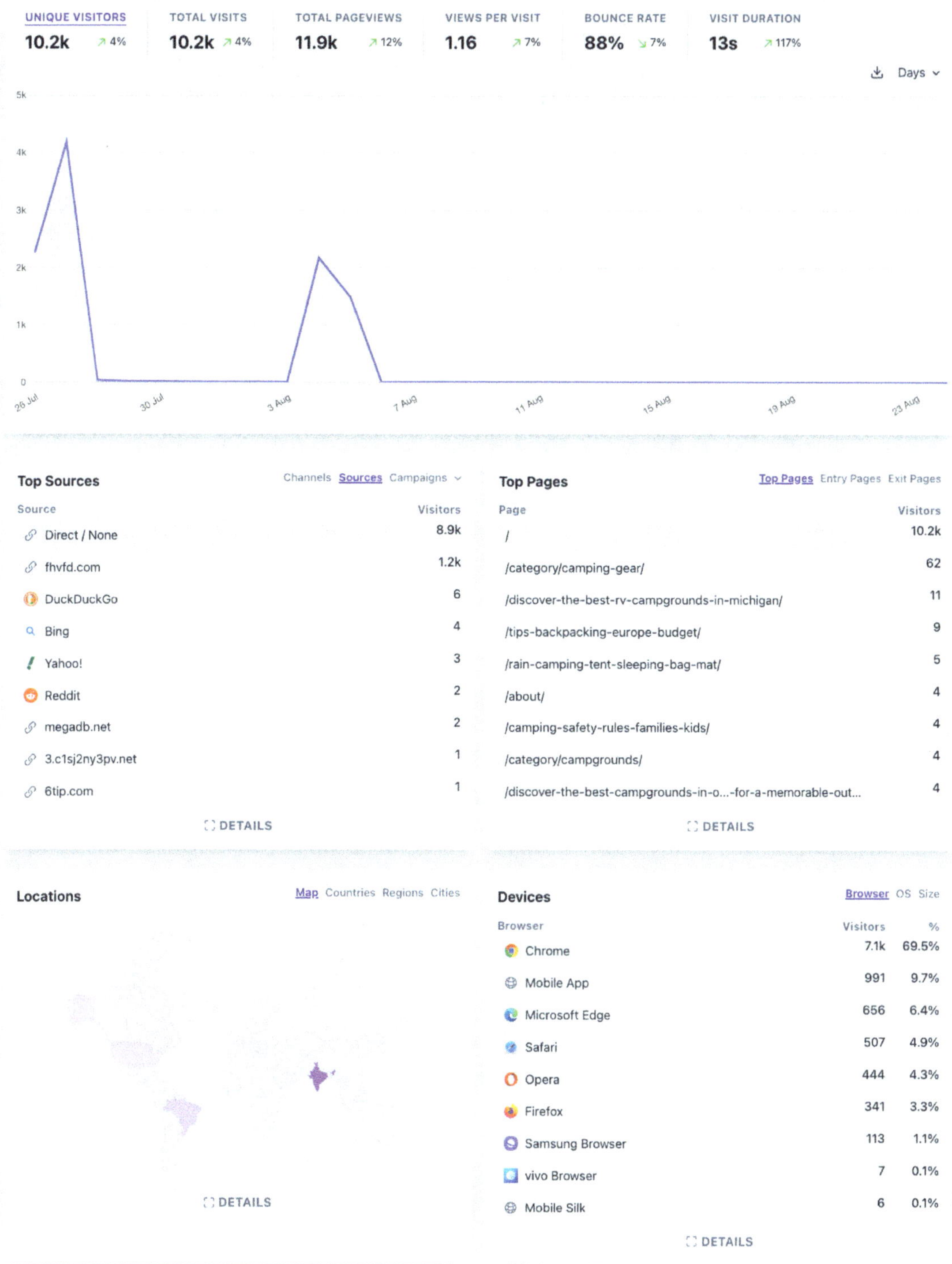

That's basically the whole interface! As you can see, Plausible provides a very limited number of metrics and dimensions. Unlike GA, there are limited ways to perform a task, making reporting much more intuitive.

As we talked about in Chapter 14 - Consent, many of these tools—including Plausible—are intended by the vendors to be run without consent. It's not just their lack of cookies; it's their overall approach of minimizing and simplifying that bolsters their claims to be able to run without consent.

Plausible has claimed its IP + User-Agent approach to visitor counting is reasonably close to Google Analytics' method of long-lived cookie ids (visitor counts are within 10%, according to https://plausible.io/blog/google-analytics-cookies). I was skeptical of this assertion, but in my test site, it came within 5% of the GA number, with only a slight undercount. However, this accuracy will vary significantly depending on the type of traffic you receive.

One such case where Plausible et al. might significantly under-report would be if much of your traffic comes from shared IPs or VPNs. For example, if you ran a B2B website where many of your corporate customers had the same browser installed company-wide and the corporate network only had a few outgoing IPs, then hundreds of different users might show in Plausible as only one or two.

Plausible also offers an excellent WordPress plugin. Besides "enhanced measurement" options that give you some additional tracking functionality, it also offers an ingeniously simple way to bypass ad blockers. Although Plausible is very privacy-friendly, ad blockers, including those that use the EasyPrivacy list (such as Brave or uBlock Origin), still block it. The keepers of such lists have broad definitions of what a "tracker" is and are disinclined to make exceptions. Here's how to bypass that blocking in one click from the Plausible WordPress plugin:

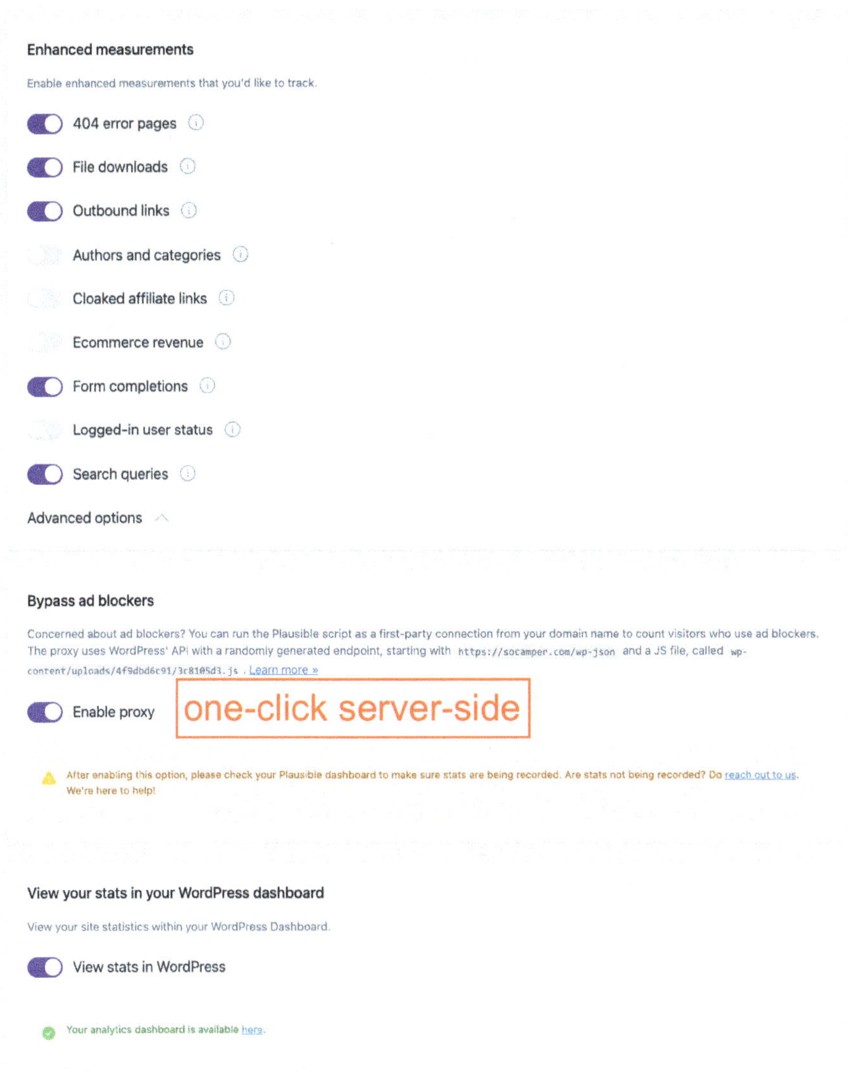

If you turn on "Enable proxy" in the Plausible WordPress plugin, it will load its JavaScript from a random file on your own WordPress site, like this: `yoursite.com/wp-content/uploads/dfa9f0/d2c5b.js` (instead of `plausible.io/js/plausible.js`). Then, it'll proxy the measurement request via a random endpoint like this: `yoursite.com/wp-json/bdcdbb/v1/bba0/6bc77f3c` (instead of `plausible.io/api/event`).

This is server-side deployed with one option toggle, or at least the ad block avoidance part of it. Technically, it's a web proxy that relays client-side tracking data, but that's what most things called "server-side tracking" start with—changing what URLs the browser uses so they are harder to detect and block. Please see Chapter 15 - Server-Side for a deeper discussion of server-side. While it'd be possible to replicate this same functionality for GA4 in WordPress (and perhaps some plugins have done so), the privacy-invasive nature of GA4 makes that something to avoid blindly doing.

Plausible's Google Analytics data importer also works smoothly (although it would be nice if you could easily search through the dropdown that lists the views to import from). Unlike Matomo's importer, you do not need to set up a GCP project and credentials—it can be done with basic OAuth alone in seconds. The data you import from GA functions no differently than if the data had been collected by Plausible directly. The additional data fields that GA has that Plausible does not support are not migrated. As with all GA data imports we talk about, this imports from the GA data reporting API, which has aggregated data that has already been processed by GA, not raw data. The import is also subject to the data retention settings on your GA property.

As we talked about in the case study in Chapter 11 - Open Source, Plausible is indeed open source, though not as open as some others like Umami. If you're looking to self-host, then this is a consideration, but for most users, I would recommend cloud-hosting and not spending too much time researching things like which open source license a particular tool uses.

If you're looking for basic visitor counting, a reasonable price at scale, and easy compliance, then Plausible is an excellent option. Even at 10 million monthly pageviews, it's just $169 a month. On the other hand, there's no free tier, so if you run a low-traffic site (fewer than 10,000 pageviews), the base $9 plan may seem like a high price to pay each month if you're used to free GA.

Chapter 27 - Statcounter

Type	Simplified Web Analytics
Default tracking method	Cookies
Price	\$9/mo. for 100k pageviews \$49 for 2M \$249 for 50M
Home page	https://statcounter.com
Demo	https://statcounter.com/demo/summary/
Similar tool(s)	Clicky

Pros: Mature product, affordable, full-featured (within its category)
Cons: Weak on privacy and data ownership

Statcounter is the longest-running option we are evaluating. It was established in 1999, well before Google Analytics existed. Like the other options we look at in the simplified category, it doesn't have an extensive feature set.

Unlike the other options in this chapter, this more basic reporting isn't part of a strategic tradeoff for improved privacy. Meaning Statcounter has significantly less reporting functionality than GA, but we haven't gained user privacy features in exchange.

Statcounter uses cookies by default (though they can be disabled), and full IP addresses are stored and available in reports (though they can be configured to be masked, with the last octet removed). In comparison, GA doesn't make IPs available in the product at all and forbids the storage of IPs in custom fields. IPs are available in many of the product analytics tools we review, but only Statcounter and Clicky support IP storage in the simplified category.

Here's an example of the level of detail provided to an individual user in Statcounter:

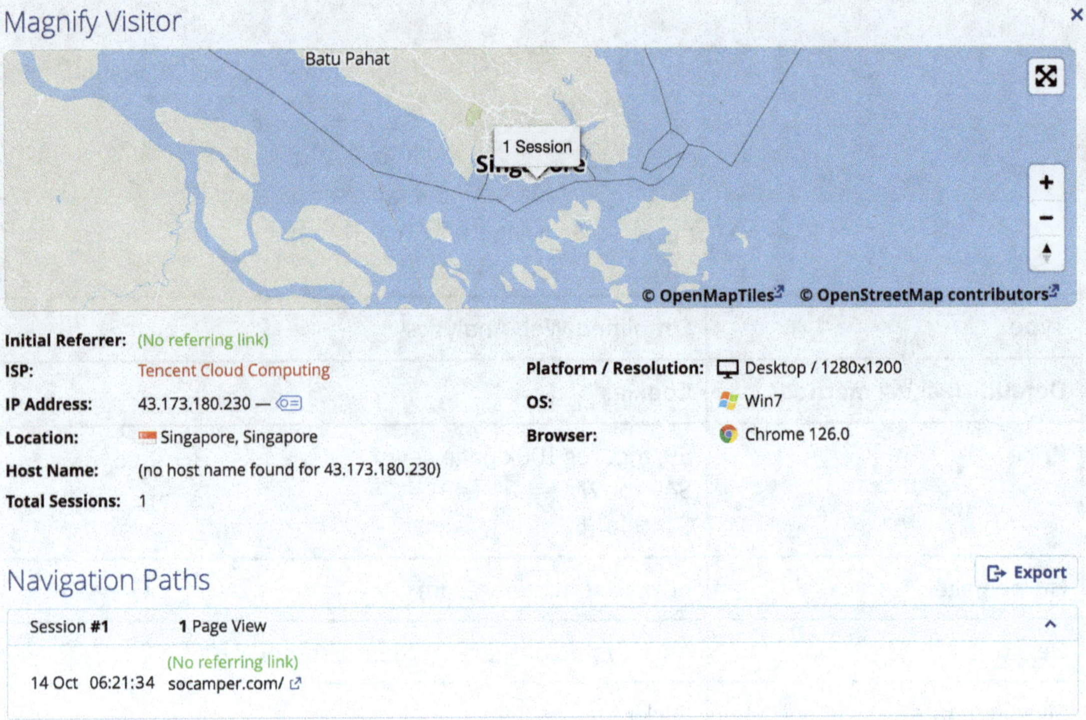

This is much more information than GA4 provides: it includes the IP of the visit, other IPs that the same visitor came from, and the ISP information. (Note: for privacy reasons, this screenshot is of bot traffic, not a real user.)

On the plus side, Statcounter's pricing is attractive and scales well. It charges only $249 per month for a site with 50 million monthly pageviews. This makes it one of the cheaper options available for large-volume sites.

For a modest additional fee (starting at another $9 a month), Statcounter also includes a session recording tool, similar to products like Hotjar or Clarity. This session recording tool is integrated into Statcounter's standard reporting, meaning once you identify a visitor to investigate, you can see their session recordings attached to their regular analytics reporting. The functionality available in the session recording tool is minimal compared to tools like Hotjar, but it's much cheaper and delivered via the same existing tag, so there's nothing additional to install. While the features like session replay and heatmaps are limited, they are more full-featured than what Clicky offers. In a comparison between Clicky and Statcounter, I found Statcounter to be more user-friendly, but Clicky's privacy features were much better. Both tools were created well before modern privacy standards and expectations arose, but Clicky has done more to update the product to those standards. Both tools have otherwise had minimal changes and new features added in recent years.

The pageview-based reporting will be familiar to users of any traditional web analytics product and has the basic reporting you'd expect:

Then there are standard reports for each section as well:

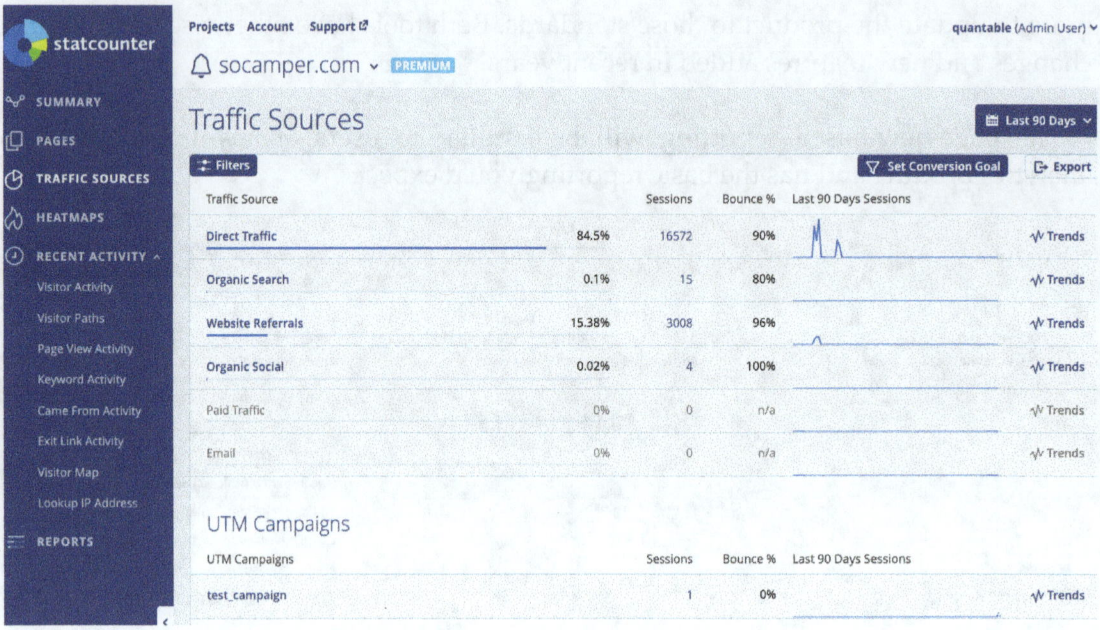

Additionally, "custom tags" are free-form key–value pairs that can be used to tag and segment traffic. Though not as flexible as a custom dimension in GA for reporting purposes, Statcounter's version is easier to set up, since it's fully free-form (meaning you don't have to pre-define custom dimension slots, like in GA).

Statcounter is perhaps best known for its browser and search engine industry stat numbers (https://gs.statcounter.com). These stats are widely cited; in fact, I referenced them myself in the first edition of this book. The stats come from the sites that run Statcounter, and, unlike Google Analytics benchmarking, there's no obvious way to opt out. This means that when you run Statcounter, your users contribute to those industry benchmarking numbers whether you like it or not. According to Statcounter, the stats come from 1.5 million sites, which is good for the quality of the benchmark data but problematic for the users of the analytics service who lack an opt-out.

In addition to the weak privacy features, there are also concerns about data ownership. The following statement appears in the Statcounter terms (https://statcounter.com/about/legal/):

> 12. We both own the data regarding visitors to your Web site that we collect. You can use the data we provide for any legal purposes. We will use the data in compliance with our privacy policy.

My interpretation of that somewhat paradoxical statement is that Statcounter claims joint ownership of the data collected, which I find highly problematic.

This is a more laissez-faire approach to data ownership than Google's. Some claims (including one from Matomo here: https://matomo.org/google-owns-your-data/) assert Google owns your site's analytics data, but that's incorrect; in GA's terms (https://marketingplatform.google.com/about/analytics/terms/us/), Google says it's allowed to "retain and use" your data, but it doesn't claim ownership. It explicitly states that you retain ownership here: https://blog.google/around-the-globe/google-europe/google-analytics-facts/.

> [Organizations] retain ownership of the data they collect using Google Analytics

These issues make me hesitant to recommend Statcounter for any site concerned about data privacy. I think the price and functionality are solid and appropriate for many content-oriented websites, but its privacy stance needs to be updated to reflect current standards.

Chapter 28 - Umami

Type	Simplified Web Analytics
Default tracking method	IP + User-Agent
Price	$0/mo. for 100k events $20 for 1M
Home page	https://umami.is
Demo	https://eu.umami.is/share/LGazGOecbDtaIwDr/umami.is
Similar tool(s)	Fathom, Plausible

Pros: Fully open source, low price, clean and simple interface
Cons: Limited feature-set and integrations, privacy missteps

Umami is a relatively new entrant into the market (version 1.0 was released in October 2020), but its popularity has increased enough since the first edition of this book to now merit inclusion.

Umami's growth is likely due to the following reasons:

- It's open source.
- It's simple to use.
- It's free for up to 100k events/mo.

Umami is quite similar to Plausible and Fathom, which we covered in previous chapters (26 and 25, respectively). Unlike those two products, Umami offers a zero-cost cloud-hosted plan. Whereas 100k pageviews would cost $19/mo. in Plausible and $15 in Fathom, in Umami, that level of traffic is totally free. At that price, it's not hard to see how it has grown its market share.

A lot of users will choose based upon pricing, and Umami is significantly cheaper than its two most direct competitors.

Umami, Fathom, and Plausible Price Comparison

Monthly Events	Fathom	Plausible Starter Plan	Umami Cloud
10k	$15	$9	$0
100k	$15	$19	$0
2M	$74	$89	$40

Note: Fathom and Plausible's pricing plans are both listed in pageviews, but custom events are charged the same as pageviews.

Users love free tiers, and it's a great way for a tool to gain traction in a crowded market. However, as illustrated by the recent removal of Piwik PRO's free tier, there's no guarantee a free tier will continue indefinitely, as it may not prove to be a successful business model. I would expect that a free tier could be difficult to maintain in a tool like Umami that is more targeted at small sites. This pricing strategy sets up a free-rider problem, where it's possible that too many users end up on free plans for the product to remain viable in the long term. Unlike Plausible and Fathom, which are purely bootstrapped companies funded only by their customers, Umami raised $1.5M in pre-seed venture capital in 2022. This VC money likely helped accelerate development and allowed for the generous free tier, but it does place Umami on a different path than the other two bootstrapped companies.

As we saw in Chapter 11 - Open Source, Umami has quickly grown to be one of the most popular GA alternatives on GitHub. It is considerably more popular than Plausible among open source developers, despite Plausible's much larger installation base.

While Plausible is also open source, it is not as fully open as Umami. Umami has a more permissive license (MIT vs AGPL) and releases all of its code. Plausible's open source version is its "Community Edition," which withholds some features and isn't updated as frequently as the cloud-hosted version. Additionally, Plausible requires ClickHouse to run, whereas Umami can run on Postgres or MySQL. The latter two tend to be easier databases to run, and may already be part of your shared hosting platform. Umami v3—released in November 2025—drops support for MySQL in favor of Postgres only, and also adds a significant number of features. This review covers version 2 only.

If you are primarily interested in self-hosting, these items may be enough to make Umami more appealing than Plausible.

Though Plausible has only been around for a year or two longer than Umami, Plausible's cloud-hosted edition is a significantly more mature platform than Umami's. As mentioned in its chapter, Plausible has an excellent official WordPress plugin, whereas Umami has only a minimally-featured third party plugin. Plausible also has a

Looker Studio connector, a GA4 data importer, a Google Search Console connector, and the ability to send emails on big traffic spikes or drops. I also found the Plausible data reporting API to work more cleanly. Plausible is generally a more polished product, yet Umami does have some features that Plausible doesn't and is overall more ambitious in its reporting feature set, as you can see in the left-side menu bar in the image below.

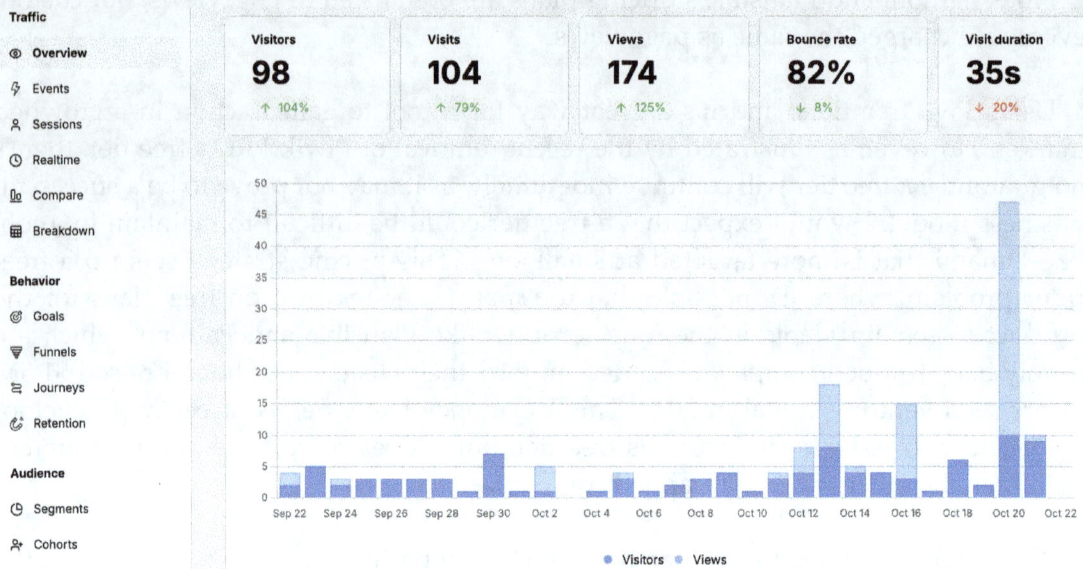

One of those features that Umami has and Plausible does not is the ability to create custom reports. Plausible adheres quite strictly to its "one-page reporting" system. In Plausible, you can add filters, select different sub-tabs (like for custom properties or funnels) within that one page, but it's always just one page. Umami has multiple reports and even lets you generate custom reports, so that, if you want to save an attribution report with a first-click model over the last 30 days, you can do so.

Wait, did I just say "attribution"? How can we have attribution without cookies that can identify a returning user?

Here we find one of the biggest differences between Umami and the other IP + User-Agent cookieless platforms we review.

Umami creates its identifier in essentially the same way as the other platforms:

```
visitor_id = hash(salt + website id+ hostname + ip_address + user_a-
gent)
```

But the hash is rotated *monthly*, not daily. Meaning that users may have the same id for up to a month, as opposed to a day or less for Plausible, Fathom, cookieless Matomo, cookieless Piwik PRO, etc.

This means if someone came in from Google organic on day 1 and completed a goal on day 5, of the list above, only Umami would be able to attribute that goal completion back to Google. While helpful for our attribution practice, this undermines the rationale for being able to use this tool without consent. A pseudonymous visitor identifier that can last up to a month under some circumstances can still be used without consent, but Umami provides no guidance or details other than that you don't need a "cookie notice" because it doesn't use cookies.

In Chapter 14 - Consent, we talk in more detail about the IP + User-Agent method and its relation to consent, including Umami's minimal statement about consent and compliance.

This being an open source project, you could, in theory, submit a pull request back to Umami with a configuration option that allows this salt rotation to be configurable. In fact, there is an open discussion on this issue in Umami's GitHub page (https://github.com/umami-software/umami/issues/3427). Or you could fork your own version. Then you could set whatever salt rotation you are comfortable with. The current monthly rotation does seem problematic to me, though, not just because of privacy, but because a fixed monthly cycle of rotation means different users have different maximum visitor id retention lengths. In other words, since the salt rotates on the first day of the month, a visitor that comes on June 2nd could have 28 days of being identified as a return visitor, while a visitor that comes on June 29th would only have 2 days.

Another example of Umami's less stringent approach to privacy is its "Distinct ID" feature, which optionally allows different sessions to be unified, if they are tagged with an identifier. The example Umami uses in its documentation (https://umami.is/docs/distinct-ids) is sending a user's email to allow reporting on multiple sessions from this same user on different devices.

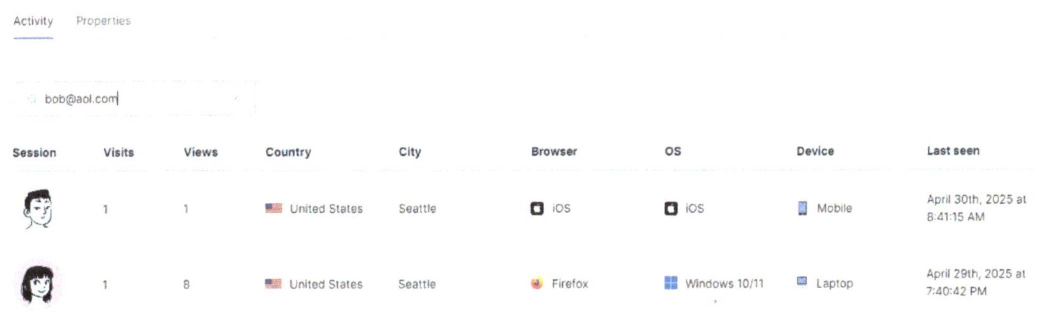

This is clearly a useful feature, but encouraging users to upload personal information like email to unify sessions does not align with what should be expected from a privacy-by-design tool.

While I may have some issues with Umami's approach to privacy, it's clear that it is a strong competitor in the simplified web analytics space. It's great to see so many viable options enter this area, filling the clear market demand for simple, easy-to-use tools. Over time, I hope that some of these tools will add enough functionality to make the leap out of the simplified category into the comprehensive category, and Umami is a candidate to do so.

Product Analytics

CHAPTER 29 - AMPLITUDE ANALYTICS

Type	Product Analytics
Default tracking method	Cookies
Price	Free plan for up to 10k users/mo. $61/mo. for 1k users (basic "Plus" plan) $561/mo. for 50k $3,150/mo. for 300k
Home page	https://amplitude.com
Demo	https://app.amplitude.com/analytics/demo/home (requires giving your email)
Similar tool(s)	Mixpanel, PostHog

Pros: Sophisticated and broad tool set, flexibility
Cons: Complexity, pricing for some sites

Amplitude started in 2014 as an app analytics company, then shortly thereafter pivoted to cover product analytics more broadly. The company went public in 2021 and has continued to grow and expand its product offerings since. Today, it has one of the broadest suites of tools of any of the products we review in this book. These tools are all included in the same suite, rather than being sold and activated separately.

According to BuiltWith, Amplitude is currently installed on <1% of the top 1M sites (6,600 of 1M). This places it as our fourth most popular tool behind GA, Cloudflare, and Matomo. Amplitude is in a cluster of tools that each hold around .5% of the market share, including Mixpanel, PostHog, Statcounter, Plausible, and Adobe. As we talked about way back in Chapter 2, these market share numbers are not highly accurate, but the tools in this tier of popularity do show the kind of traction that makes them contenders for growth to the next level.

While no tool is coming for GA's #1 most popular status, in particular, Amplitude and PostHog both seem poised to grow into widely popular all-in-one digital data platform suites. That they both have useful free tiers as well, so you can start getting familiar with the platform without having to commit to anything.

Since my first review of Amplitude in 2022, it has added a lot of new features. This is what the home page for a newly created Amplitude project looked like in 2022:

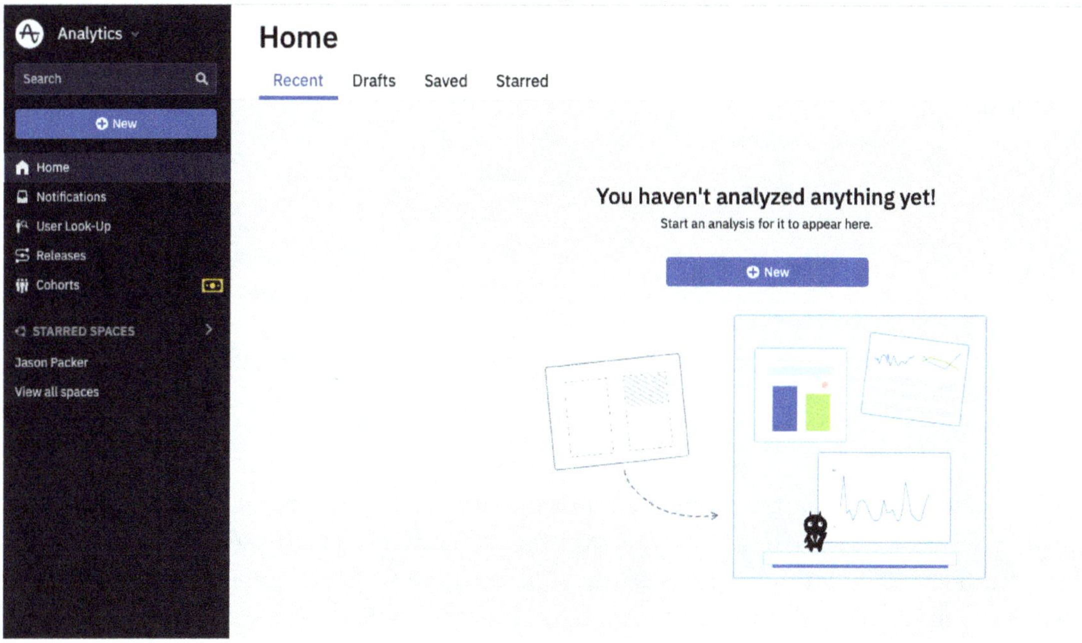

And this is what it looked like in 2025:

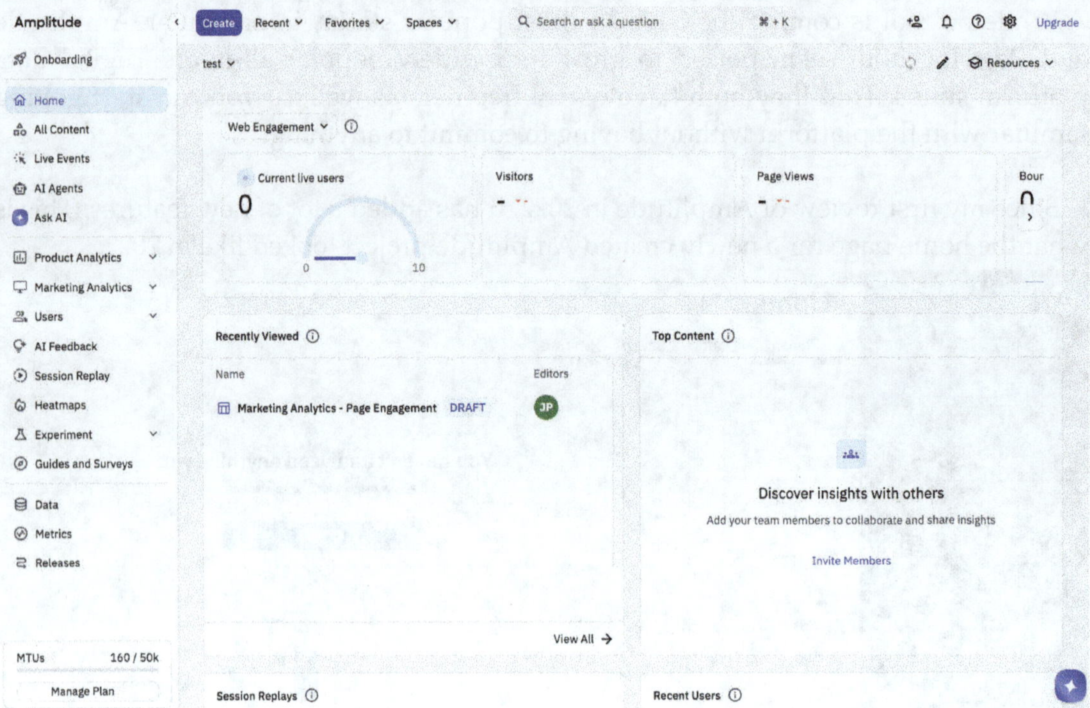

One of my complaints about the product in 2022 was around the difficulty of starting with that blank page, even if you had already collected plenty of data. While Amplitude still encourages generating your own reports, it comes with more pre-installed reporting and can be easier to get started with. While it comes from the tradition of explicit tracking, meaning you had to instrument events manually (Amplitude refers to this as "precision tracking"), it now also has an implicit "Autocapture" option similar to Heap's auto-tracking, and will capture most events automatically. Having the ability to support both methodologies together is a nice improvement.

While Amplitude has also added "Marketing Analytics" to the top-level navigation, it does not automatically include all of the functionality we'd expect to see from something with that name. This is in line with its overall approach as a product analytics tool, but may come as a surprise to users switching from platforms like GA. Things like UTM, `gclids`, and referrers are not tracked by default in Amplitude. Additionally, while there is a default "Traffic by Campaign" report under the Marketing Analytics section, there are no default channels set up. Neither of these things are difficult to set up; for example, you can start to capture UTMs just by adding `includeUtm: true` to your amplitude.js SDK setup.

By our definitions of types of tools in Chapter 5, Amplitude most cleanly fits in the product analytics category, even though it now has more marketing analytics features. It is focused on users (and pricing is metered upon monthly tracked users), it does not offer any tag management tools (unlike four of the five comprehensive web analytics tools we review, which do), and it does not focus at all on things like cookieless tracking or user modeling.

This wide-ranging functionality and the tasks we might need to do to get it to work the way we prefer can make the platform feel a bit overwhelming. It is generally well-organized, but having so much functionality under one roof adds a certain amount of unavoidable complexity.

Most functionality is available even at the lower tiers of the product. The free "Starter" tier has a 50k MTU limit, but includes most features. The "Plus" level, which is the basic paid plan, starts at $61/mo. for 1k MTUs.

Amplitude Pricing Plan Features

Available in Basic "Plus" Plan	Requires Add-on, or Higher-Level Plans
Session replay (up to 10k monthly)	Heatmaps
Experiments	Session replay AI summaries
Core Web Vitals reporting	Guides & surveys
AI tools	Traffic volume > 300k MTUs

One of the complaints in my 2022 review was that Amplitude had held back a number of key features from lower-level plans, but it has largely rectified that. I would still like to see heatmaps and AI summaries of session replays available in the Plus plan.

As with most enterprise products, once you get into the higher tiers of the product, it is not cheap. Amplitude's most recent financial disclosures, which we referenced in Chapter 2, counted 653 customers who pay it more than $100k a year. If you consider that Google's Universal Analytics 360 started at $150k/year, that still may make Amplitude sound like a bargain for some, considering how much you get, but it does mean you will need to plan for how you would grow within the product's price tiering.

Amplitude switched in January 2023 from a hit-based pricing meter to counting monthly tracked users (MTUs). This makes Amplitude the only product we are evaluating that bases its pricing on user counts, though Heap's is based on sessions, which can effectively be similar. If you are using Amplitude on a site with significant engagement per user, this could be great for you, but if the opposite is true, then the pricing model can be a poor fit.

It all depends on what your monthly events per active user are. PostHog has released some data on this and found that most of its customers were in the range of 50–100 tracked events per user per month (https://posthog.com/blog/calculating-events-from-users). If you are on the high end of that, > 100 events per user, then MTU-based pricing is probably a good deal for you.

At plans higher than the Plus level, Amplitude does offer pricing metered by event instead. This is excellent flexibility, but it leaves a hole in the pricing structure for sites that have significant traffic but don't have the budget for a higher-level plan. In other words, if you are a company with a modest budget and 300k+ users a month, yet a low number of events per user, it may be hard to find a plan that fits your budget. Content sites, utility sites, non-recurring ecommerce sites, and anything where users aren't highly engaged could fit into that pattern.

In Chapter 17 - AI & The Future, we identified Amplitude (along with PostHog and Adobe CJA) as the tools that were the most "all-in" with AI. Some of the AI-driven tools in Amplitude currently include the following:

- AI Feedback (AI-powered summaries of online feedback)
- AI chat-based interface
- AI Agents
- AI Visibility (i.e., how much your brand shows up inside major LLMs)

While many of these features have potential, there's a limited degree to which I'd be willing to put most into production workflows at the moment. This would be true with similar functionality in any tool we review, but as Amplitude's home page now highlights it as an "AI analytics platform," we'll delve into those features in this chapter.

For example, I like the idea of integrating a social listening tool, what Amplitude calls "AI Feedback," into a product analytics platform. With this feature, Amplitude can connect to your support desk software (e.g., Zendesk), pull reviews from the Apple App Store, or third-party sites like Trustpilot, and then summarize all this feedback, and even extract things like feature requests. Here's a trivial example that pulls feedback from the Apple App Store for a guitar tuner app I created:

It's automatically fetching the reviews from the app store and summarizing them. This could be very useful, updated feedback from multiple sources in one place to reference against actual product usage. But when I used the AI chat interface and asked it to build a dashboard based on this feedback, what it gave me was not at all helpful:

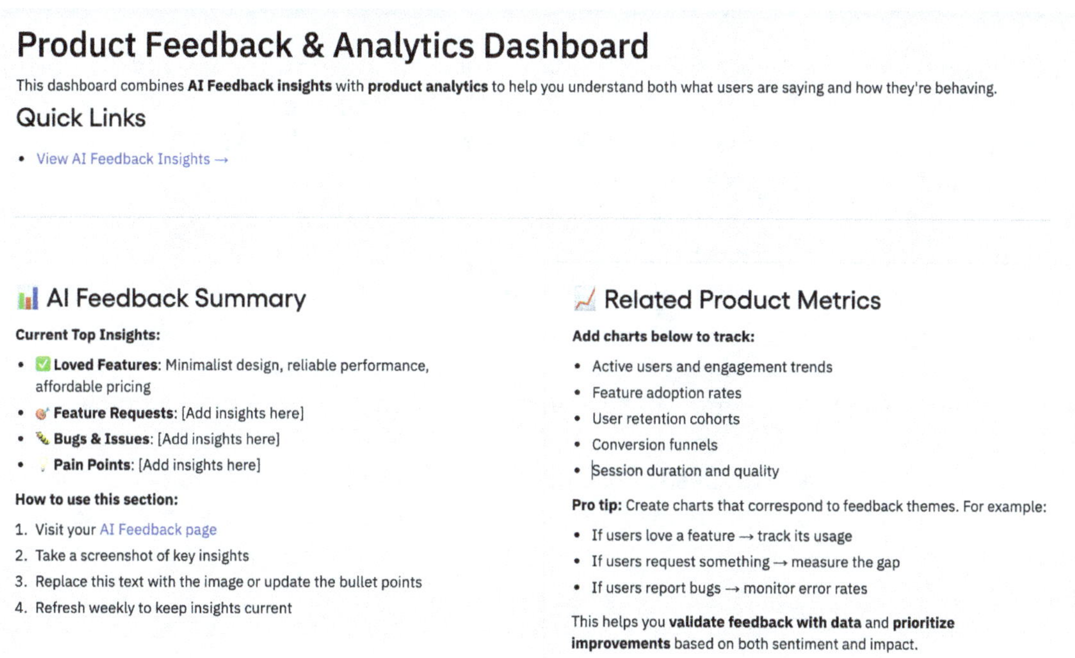

Since Amplitude can't yet automatically connect AI Feedback to a dashboard, what the chatbot created suggests I manually update the dashboard with weekly screenshots from the first report above. Additionally, while AI Feedback does currently offer

13 different data sources (including things like Discord and pulling in a whole subreddit without search terms), this is very limited compared to dedicated brand management tools like Brandwatch. So potentially very useful, but not yet full-featured or totally integrated.

Amplitude also has an AI visibility tool, which can track how frequently your brand appears in prompts within the major AI models. This tool works similarly to how SEO keyword ranking services work: it runs a set of prompts against OpenAI's GPT and Google AI Overviews to see if it can find your site mentioned. Like with keyword tracking, the key to doing it well is to pick good, representative search terms (in this case, prompts) to track. Even more than with keyword tracking, this tracks only a tiny fraction of the kinds of interactions that users will have with an LLM that might surface your brand. As with AI Feedback, AI Visibility felt like a beta or early release version, especially when compared with the polish in other parts of Amplitude, like the core Product Analytics reports.

What do I mean by beta quality? The dropdown for selecting "model" gave me the following choices: GPT, Google AIO, Claude, and Gemini—but only the first two actually worked. When I asked the chatbot help explain how I could enable Claude and Gemini, it told me that those options (and also Perplexity) were available as configuration options, which wasn't true.

AI Visibility is a marketing function that many digital teams are already clamoring for, so even if what Amplitude has isn't ideal, it is included automatically in all Amplitude plans, even at the free tier. In comparison, Semrush's AI visibility starts at $99/mo., and Ahrefs charges $699/mo.

Amplitude has also recently launched AI Agents (still in beta), which are fully automated agents able to do things like check dashboards or session replays for notable changes and attempt to do their own analysis and notify you. This falls clearly into what I defined as the "danger zone" of AI usage in Chapter 17. To be clear, it still could be very useful for some use cases, but it could be dangerous in others. For example, I would never recommend setting up an agent here that reviews the dashboards, does a root-cause analysis, and then emails the findings automatically to your CEO or client. Hopefully, this reads like common sense to you, but it's easy to see how this could cause issues.

If it seems like I'm being harsh on Amplitude's AI tools, that may be because I have few criticisms of the rest of the platform. Amplitude is overall an excellent suite that I expect will continue to improve. If you are only looking for a small part of the suite, it can be overkill, though. Additionally, if you are looking for web/marketing analytics alone, it's likely you will prefer one of the tools in the web analytics categories. Beyond those caveats, it has a very broad appeal.

Chapter 30 - Heap

Type	Product Analytics
Default tracking method	Cookies
Price	Free (limited features) to 10k/sessions $375/mo. for 17k sessions $938/mo. for 42k sessions
Home page	https://heap.io
Similar tool(s)	Mixpanel, PostHog

Pros: Simple auto-tracking, good usability
Cons: High price, feature limits on basic plan, no data reporting API

Heap launched in 2013 and was one of the originators of the "implicit" tracking concept I introduced in Chapter 7, which auto-captures user actions on a site. Heap doesn't automatically capture *all* interactions (for example, it does not auto-capture scroll depth), but it does track most things without any work coding events. Unlike many of its competitors in the product analytics category, Heap is designed to work in an "out of the box" fashion, with automatic tracking and more pre-built reporting, and without a lot of instrumentation and report-building work.

In 2023, Heap was acquired by Contentsquare. Contentsquare (CSQ) is a French company that has been rolling up a number of leading digital tools under one umbrella—including Hotjar and Clicktale, in addition to Heap. Heap is now also branded as "Contentsquare Product Analytics" inside the CSQ suite, but it also still exists as a standalone product. It does not appear that Heap is fully integrated into the CSQ suite yet, as a standard login to app.contentsquare.com does not currently include a product analytics option.

Heap and Hotjar both have large active user bases, and there is a lot of overlapping functionality between all the companies that CSQ has acquired, so it may be some time before there is a seamless experience across the whole suite of tools. If that full integration is completed, the CSQ suite will contain a broad selection of digital tools, including product analytics, session replay/heatmapping, web performance monitoring (RUM), and more. This review will focus on Heap alone.

Heap automatically tracks all clicks; however, those that are then labeled and named receive first-class treatment in the reporting interface. This definition takes place after the data has been recorded, either through a manual admin or through a visual overlay tool. Essentially, the auto-event capture collects everything, then you can favorite the events you're most interested in reporting on. This labeling is a manual process, but it's done with point-and-click interfaces and doesn't require custom instrumentation or coding.

The visual overlay tool to label events looks like this:

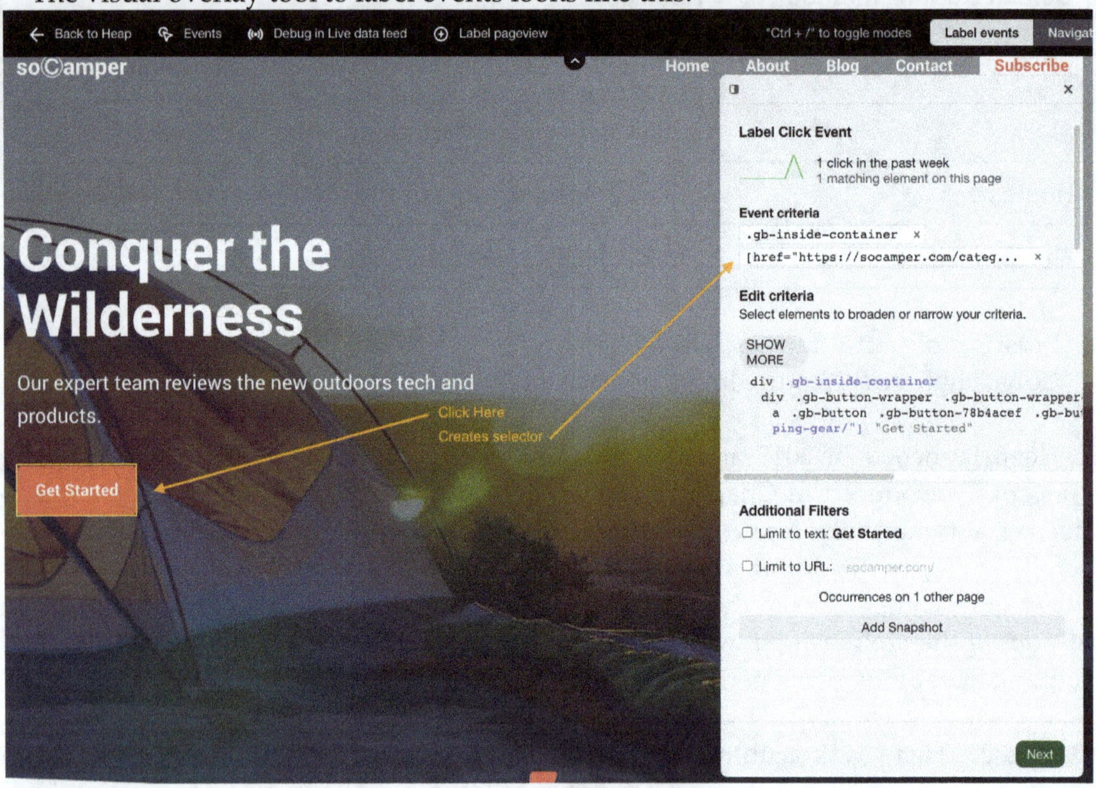

You can click on the button you want to track, and it automatically creates a CSS selector for you and shows you the amount of historical traffic to that event. You still may need to add additional event criteria to that automatically generated CSS selector. In the screenshot above, I had to add an additional selector specific to the button's div container; otherwise, it would have also counted other links to the same target URL. Another potential issue with this method is sites where these selectors might change frequently, for example, JavaScript frameworks that dynamically generate CSS ids.

In the admin, Heap has a list of labeled events that serve as a data dictionary, explicitly listing all of the events deemed important enough to get labels. While in general I do prefer events to be instrumented as data layer pushes by the app itself, done in a more systematic way, Heap has built a very usable interface for its chosen style of data collection. Overall, Heap has a friendly user interface and some good pre-built dashboards. I found it to be one of the more intuitive products in the product analytics category.

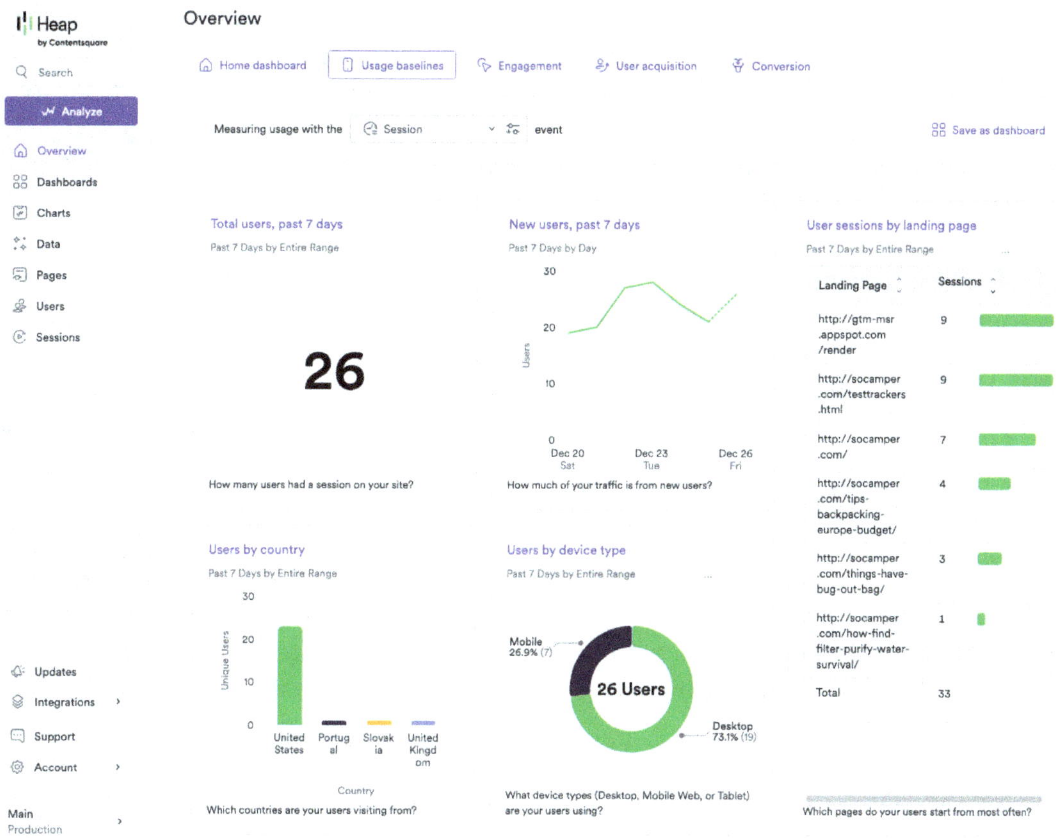

Heap currently has no reporting API available. It has client-side and server-side reporting APIs, but no data reporting API. For example, in Chapter 17, I described creating Python code to pull basic numbers across all 15 platforms I'm testing, and I was unable to do that for Heap. This makes it the only tool in this book (other than the extremely simplistic Cloudflare Web Analytics) to not have one, which feels like a big gap. There is a data warehousing feature, "Heap Connect," which allows for exports to BigQuery or other similar platforms, but this feature is not available at the basic "Growth" plan level. Meaning if you wanted to include your Heap data into a third-party dashboarding platform like Power BI or Looker Studio, you'd have to purchase a higher-level plan, export the data to a data warehouse, and then build your own SQL.

One of Heap's biggest downsides is its price. Heap is the only tool in this guide with a session-based pricing model, and the cost can be significant for a high-traffic site. The free tier of 10,000 monthly sessions could be great for a fledgling SaaS product that wants an analytics tool whose instrumentation process is simpler and less technical, but the price starts at $375/mo. and scales up pretty quickly. At 83,000 sessions per month, the cost of the "Growth" tier plan is $1,250/mo.

As we discussed in Chapter 6 - Pricing, whether this is a good match for your site or not will depend greatly upon your usage pattern. If you have a small number of highly engaged, logged-in users, then it can be a very good fit. If you have a lot of anonymous sessions and a lower number of events per session, then it will be quite expensive. Especially with auto-tracking like Heap provides, there's solid logic in having the pricing model structured around sessions rather than events, since the events themselves happen automatically.

The Growth tier is the only one with any public pricing, but that tier also lacks a lot of features. As with all of the product analytics tools that we review, Heap has session recording functionality. However, *session recording is not available until the Pro tier,* which does not have public pricing and requires interfacing with Contentsquare sales. The Growth tier also does not include heatmaps, error analysis, report alerts, or standard support. That you could be paying $1,250/mo. for Heap, and not have access to basic tech support for help, seems customer-unfriendly.

It's inevitable that there will be a certain feature that you want from a higher tier in situations where your volume and overall usage pattern don't otherwise justify that tier. I prefer pricing models where the main factors determining tiers are volume and support level, rather than picking and choosing individual features that the vendors think are more "enterprise."

If you are looking for standalone product analytics with automated tracking, and your traffic pattern matches its pricing model, then Heap can be a good choice. If Heap eventually gets smoothly integrated into the larger Contentsquare platform and this bundling allows for more value for the price, then it could become an even stronger competitor.

Chapter 31 - Mixpanel

Type	Product Analytics
Default tracking method	Cookies
Price	Free plan up to 1M events/mo. $259/mo. for 2M events $2,289/mo. for 20M events
Home page	https://mixpanel.com
Similar tool(s)	Amplitude

Pros: High-volume free tier, straightforward product analytics
Cons: Add-ons prices as % of base plan, some features require Enterprise plan, security lapses

Mixpanel launched in 2009 and is one of the originators of the product analytics methodology. In 2012, Mixpanel famously railed against traditional web analytics stats such as pageviews and unique visitors as "bullshit metrics" (https://allthingsd.com/20121217/andreessen-and-mixpanel-call-for-an-end-to-bullshit-metrics/). It advocated instead for a focus on user actions (i.e., events) and engagement. Mixpanel still operates with an emphasis on events rather than pageviews and highlights user retention, flow, and funnels.

I disagree with the idea that pageviews, unique visitors, or even bounce rate are inherently useless vanity metrics. It's how you use the metrics that determines their worth. If you measure bounce rate change over time to determine how well certain segments of users engage with what they see upon page landing, that can be highly valuable. If you report bounce rate to your investors without context, compared to benchmark sites to show how great your site is, that is indeed bullshit. An analyst declaring a metric to be passé does not affect what the business actually needs to know about in order to operate well. Over ten years later, pageviews are still the most vital measure of content success for many sites.

Mixpanel is most similar to Amplitude, but with a reduced feature set. Some of the features that Amplitude has but Mixpanel doesn't include are surveys, explicit marketing analytics, more AI/ML tools, and advanced data management tools. Amplitude is overall a broader tool, more in line with PostHog in terms of breadth of features, even though its functionality feels most similar to Mixpanel. If you don't need all those additional features, then you may prefer working in Mixpanel.

This is not to say that Mixpanel has a limited feature set; it has extensive reporting functionality, including funnels, flows, and retention reporting. It also has session recording as well as a number of features like experiments, feature flags, anomaly detection, and data pipelines that are only available at the Enterprise level or via add-ons.

In January 2023, Mixpanel switched from a user-based pricing meter model to a hit-based model. That very same month, Amplitude went the opposite direction, switching from a hit-based to a user-based model.

Currently, both have solid free tiers, but Mixpanel's is more generous. However, Mixpanel's lowest-level plan now starts at $140/mo., higher than Amplitude's. Let's take a look at what you can get at the lowest level of pricing for each:

Mixpanel vs. Amplitude Entry-level Pricing

	Mixpanel	**Amplitude**
Free tier	1M events, 20k sessions recorded	50k MTUs, 1k sessions recorded
Startup tier (1st year free)	1B events for companies with <$8M raised, <5 years old	1.2B events for companies with <$10M raised, <20 employees
Lowest price	$140/mo. for 1.5M events	$61/mo. for 1k MTUs

Both tools highlight similar "first year free" plans for startups that meet certain qualifications. While getting 1B or more events for free is very appealing, startups should also be careful that they will be able to afford to continue with the product after that first year. Both products scale reasonably well in terms of price for volume, though neither does so as well as PostHog.

As discussed in Chapter 6 - Pricing, the fit of a particular pricing model depends on your site's usage pattern. As discussed previously, sites with highly engaged users that log in may prefer Amplitude's monthly tracked user cost basis, whereas sites with less engaged or more anonymous users will prefer Mixpanel's event hit-based price.

Like other product analytics tools, Mixpanel does not focus on marketing analytics, but rather on user journeys within a product itself. Compared with GA, Mixpanel's reporting of traffic sources still leaves something to be desired, because (among other things) it treats referrals and UTMs separately.

In Mixpanel, we're forced to implement this flow chart manually if we want to recreate the same attribution logic. Additionally, the UTM source is a separate field from the referrer, and `gclid` on a URL has no meaning at all. So, if we hit Mixpanel with a URL like: `https://socamper.com/?utm_source=foo&utm_medium=bar&gclid=123`, it would look like the following:

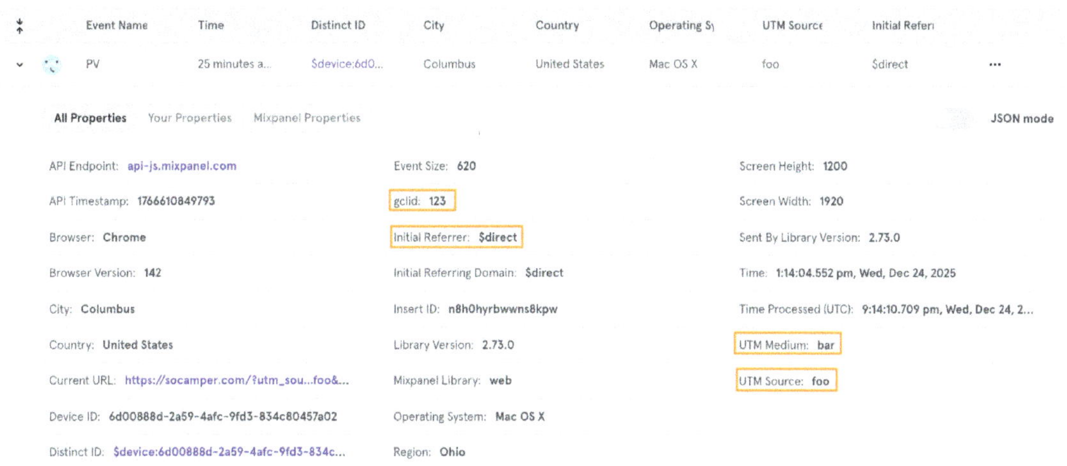

With that URL, the referrer is considered direct, and the UTMs are stored under their own fields. There can also be a "search engine" field populated by the referrer and stored associated with the user. There's no single "source" field we can use.

Since my first review in 2022, Mixpanel has added the ability to create channel rules to roll up UTMs into marketing channels. However, this channel classifier is not automatically created and applied to new properties, and when it is created, the pre-defined rules that it uses are very limited and out of date. Using the SaaS sample data set Mixpanel helpfully provides, a simple report of signups per channel appears like this:

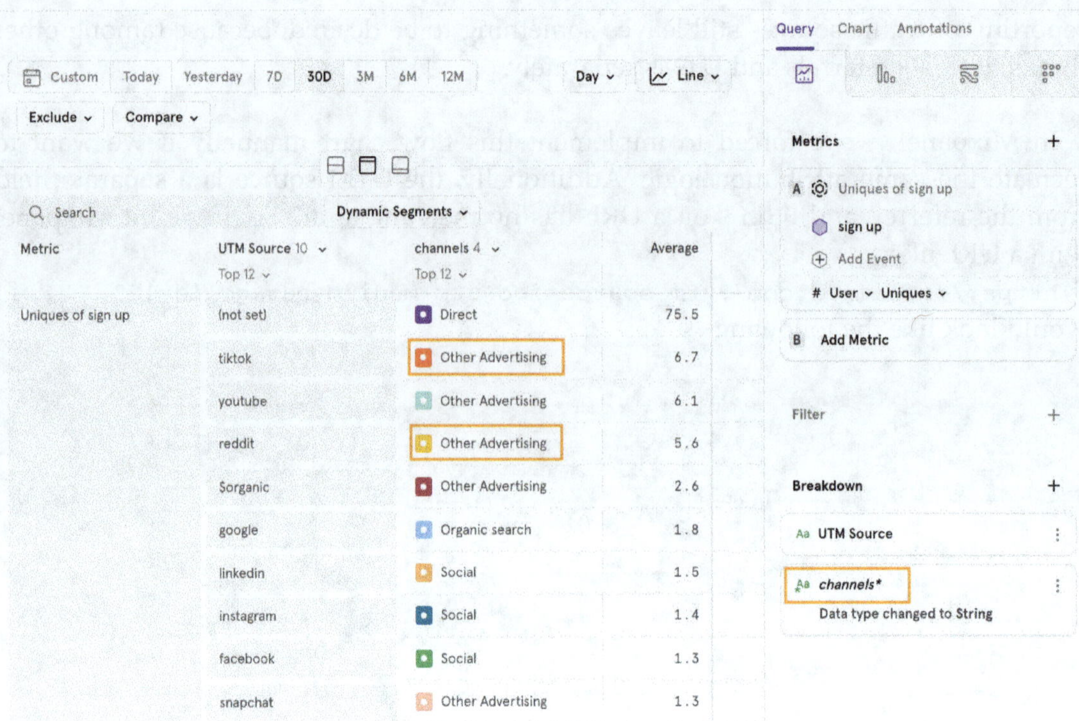

This inaccurately attributes sources like TikTok and Reddit to the fall-through "other" category rather than Social. The rules can be easily edited, but doing so requires using Mixpanel's property scripting syntax. The default rules look like this:

```
// Define variables for types of domains.
LET(
  search, ["google", "bing", "yahoo"],
LET(
  social, ["linkedin", "facebook", "twitter", "instagram"],
LET(
  shopping, ["amazon", "alibaba", "stripe", "ebay", "etsy",
"shopify", "walmart"],

IFS(
  // Defining "Paid Search"
  (@"""{"label":"UTM Source","propertyDefaultType":"string","re-
sourceType":"event","type":"string","value":"utm_source"}"""@IN search
OR @"""{"label":"Referring Domain","propertyDefaultType":"string","re-
sourceType":"event","type":"string","value":"$referring_domain"}"""@IN
search OR PARSE_URL(@"""{"label":"Referring Domain","propertyDefault-
Type":"string","resourceType":"event","type":"string","value":"$refer-
ring_domain"}"""@, "domain") IN search)
  AND @"""{"label":"UTM Medium","propertyDefaultType":"string","re-
sourceType":"event","type":"string","value":"utm_medium"}"""@IN
["cpc","ppc","paidsearch"],
  "Paid search",
```

...

There are very limited definitions, no AI channel, outdated source names, etc.

While attribution isn't one of Mixpanel's strengths, the ability to report on events sliced however you'd like is a major benefit. Like others in this category, you are encouraged to build your own reports, and the interface to do so is pretty intuitive. Here's an example drill-down report with multiple dimensions:

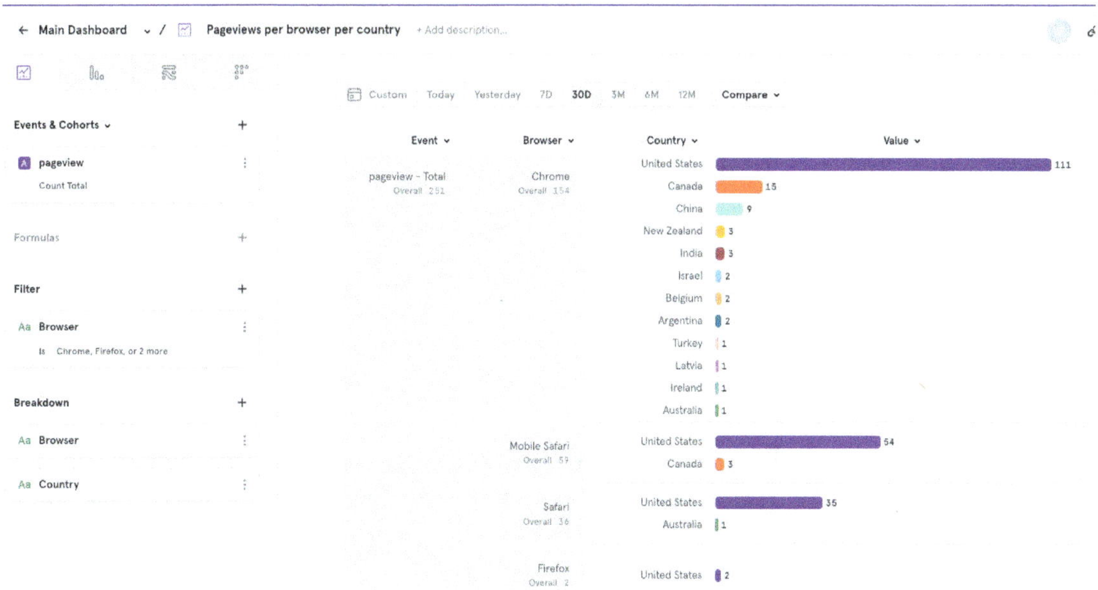

Beyond event reporting, Mixpanel also has a number of add-on "apps," such as A/B testing and auto-correlation detection (requires Enterprise plan), statistical significance measurement (any paid plan), a JavaScript-based query language called "JQL" (all plans), revenue analysis, and more.

The JQL query language is adequate, but SQL would be preferable. Here's an example of what the query builder in the product looks like:

While there are some benefits to doing this in JavaScript, such as allowing you to build more sophisticated functions into queries, the learning curve is much more significant than for SQL, which many analysts will of course be already familiar with, as it's the ubiquitous way to do this sort of analysis.

The JQL user interface does have a clear design, and comes with some examples and documentation, so you don't start from a blank page needing to learn a completely new query language.

Mixpanel also contains a data governance dictionary called "Lexicon," which keeps track of all the events being fired on your site and allows labeling with descriptions and aliases. We didn't have a "data governance" chapter in Part One, since most of the products we look at have such features, but I like Mixpanel's approach here. This is a great improvement on GA's free-for-all, and the way Mixpanel has implemented it could make Lexicon useful, even if it is only used to document some of the events.

There's no way to enforce naming, but that fits with my personal preference for soft rather than hard naming convention requirements; I prefer an approach where a naming convention is agreed upon and documented but not enforced by the tool itself.

Unfortunately, Mixpanel has had some significant data security issues. In November 2025, it had a data breach where customer data was stolen. This affected some very high-profile customers, including OpenAI and Pornhub. Pornhub reported that data from this leak, including users' search and watch history, was being used by a third party to extort money (https://www.bleepingcomputer.com/news/security/pornhub-extorted-after-hackers-steal-premium-member-activity-data/). This was one of the most serious analytics-related data breaches in recent years.

Mixpanel's auto-tracking has also gotten it in trouble in the past. In 2018, it was noticed that it was inadvertently collecting data from hidden and password fields automatically (https://techcrunch.com/2018/02/05/mixpanel-passwords/). Mixpanel recently re-introduced auto-tracking again, but it is not on by default, and appears to have better guardrails in place.

In addition to highlighting some questionable security practices from Mixpanel, these issues highlight a couple of important analytics security issues:

- The idea that web analytics data is not a significant security concern because it's all aggregated and non-identifiable. Especially when dealing with user login data that can be tied to email addresses or other PII, the realm of product analytics data requires significantly more care.
- The dangers that auto-tracking (and session capture!) can pose. When you are capturing everything and relying upon the analytics platform to redact or exclude sensitive information, things can sometimes go wrong.

Mixpanel is far from being alone in having these kinds of security issues.

Overall, Mixpanel remains a highly viable choice in its category. With the speed of improvement that PostHog and Amplitude have brought to this category space in the last couple of years, Mixpanel may no longer be the leader and innovator it was in the early days of product analytics, but it's still worth a look. In particular, teams looking for just product analytics alone and not a whole platform and the sprawl that entails, will appreciate Mixpanel.

Chapter 32 - PostHog

Type	Product Analytics
Default tracking method	Cookies
Price	Free up to 1M hits/mo. $50/mo. for 2M hits/mo. (50% identified) $1,721/mo. for 25M hits/mo. (50% identified)
Home page	https://posthog.com
Similar tool(s)	Amplitude, Mixpanel

Pros: Open source, low prices, rich feature set
Cons: Complexity, breadth over depth, limited 3P connectors

PostHog was selected as one of my favorites in the first edition of this book, and it's only gotten better since. In fact, it may well be the tool that has changed the most since then, and its popularity has grown accordingly.

PostHog bills itself as a "Product OS suite," and includes a lot more than just the web and product analytics this review is focused on. It includes 34 (!) different apps, including the following:

- Product Analytics
- Web Analytics
- LLM Analytics
- Session Replay
- Feature Flags
- Experiments
- Surveys
- Dashboarding

With such a broad product, it should not come as a surprise that each individual component is not as rich or deep as the best-of-breed tools within that category. While components like Session Replay are much improved since my first review, they still have room for improvement when compared against segment leaders like Fullstory for session recording or Qualtrics for surveys, etc. Yet while PostHog's offerings might not compare to those tools in terms of depth and polish, its advantage is that they are all part of the same suite and typically much cheaper than those top tools.

In addition to its very broad feature set, its pricing and transparency make it an attractive option. PostHog is a company operating fully in the open! A good example of this was its team's response to the first edition of this book. They read my analysis and then opened a public pull request with my feedback, and ultimately implemented many of the suggestions I had made. I definitely appreciate their responsiveness, even if it meant I had to rewrite this entire chapter.

This transparency also extends to pricing, which is both all public and among the lowest out there. PostHog is the only tool we are evaluating whose public price per event has significantly *decreased* since its first review. Since 2022, the cost of events per million at the base level has decreased by over 40%. As the cost of compute goes down in general, it seems logical that the price per event would also go down, but this has not generally been the case across the industry. PostHog has also received $182M in venture funding to date, so it's likely that the low event price and generous free tier are in part underwritten by that VC money. PostHog's strategy does not *depend* on VC money, though, so as a potential user, I don't think you should be worried about the company vanishing at the end of a startup runway.

To be clear, PostHog's pricing is not driven entirely by volume. It has add-on "Platform packages," which bundle features, creating the equivalent of different plan levels.

PostHog Pricing Levels

Package	Additional Monthly Cost	Additional Features
Free	$0	1M events, no credit card required, 1 project, 1-year data retention
Pay-as-you-go	$0	>1M events, email support, 6 projects, 7-year data retention
Boost	$250	Unlimited projects, enforced two-factor authentication (2FA) & SSO, white labeling, HIPAA BAA
Scale	$750	Priority support, SAML SSO
Enterprise	$2,000	Account manager, training, RBAC, payment via invoice

The other thing to know about PostHog pricing is that there is a big difference in price per event for anonymous events (starts at $50 per 1 million) vs. identified users ($198 per million). If you've got a website without any login, then all your events would be anonymous, charged at that low $50/M cost. My estimated prices assume a 50/50 split, e.g., at 25M events per month, I'm assuming 12.5M anonymous events and

12.5M user-identified events, which combine for the highly competitive price of $1,721/mo. All-anonymous data would make the price very low. Your particular split will be different, though—it might be 100% anonymous, 100% identified, or anywhere in between.

This discussion of anonymous vs. identified users is very relevant to PostHog and the product analytics category in general. In Chapter 5 - Types of Tools, we said that *identified users* were more emblematic of product analytics, and *anonymous sessions* aligned more closely with web analytics. PostHog follows the product analytics paradigm, and working with identified users and their actions across multiple PostHog apps is the best way to fully utilize the product.

In PostHog, "identified users" means that a user has a profile saved within the tool that has things like events, recordings, or feature flags associated with that profile. It doesn't mean PostHog knows who they are or that the user has an email or login associated with them (though it could and usually should); it just means there's a PostHog user id profile to attach data to across all the different things PostHog can track.

The downside of all these features is that the platform can feel overwhelming. If all you want is web analytics, then navigating through everything PostHog offers is a lot. It's like trying to find and set up BigQuery within the sprawling Google Cloud Platform, or using Amazon Web Services and its dozens of options when all you want to do is host your website. For example, while PostHog's "Web Analytics" app is itself quite basic, its integration with the wider platform makes it much more complex than the tools in our simplified category.

While I do find PostHog's user interface to be usable, intelligently designed, and pretty snappy, it also sometimes piles on complexity by trying to be too novel or clever. For instance, it recently launched a new home page that mimics the look of a desktop operating system. As PostHog itself is designed to be a "Product OS," this new design is in alignment with its marketing goals in a meta sort of way (which is presumably the intent).

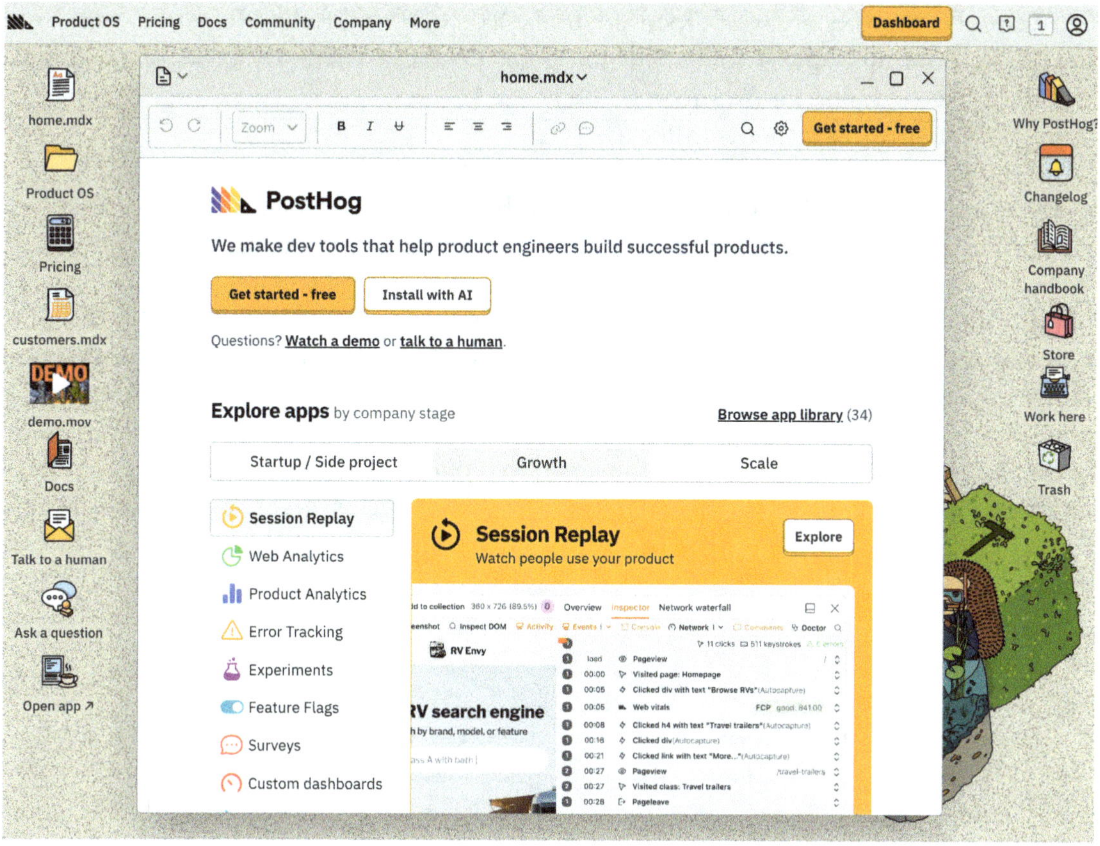

It's fun, it's fully interactive, and it is an impressive technical achievement. For someone trying to figure out how to use the product, it can be confusing and add to cognitive load. It's easy to end up with a lot of overlapping windows, have scrolling issues, or simply lose track of where you are. The app interface of the tool itself is thankfully more utilitarian, but still has some OS-mimicking elements. This kind of technical geekery highlights how PostHog targets its product towards developers. PostHog is, in fact, very clear that developers are its target market!

That's great if you are a developer, but what if you're an analyst or marketer? Being geared towards developers has led to some potential gaps in marketing analytics functionality. For example, the tool may have 34 different apps, but that list does not include a tag manager or a consent management platform (though those are both requested features).

PostHog is designed to be an all-inclusive product data platform, with everything that a product engineering team could possibly want. It is also highly customizable, right down to the ability to edit the SQL behind any particular insights report.

Compared to web analytics-focused tools like GA or Piwik PRO, you may find PostHog's offerings not as robust in that area. PostHog currently lacks some typical web analytics features, for example:

- No saving of segments (filters)
- No easy IP address exclusion (has to be done with data pipelines)
- No Google Search console integration (has to be done via BigQuery export)
- No multi-touch attribution reporting (assuming you want such a thing)

With the speed of change in the platform, those gaps may all be filled by the time you read this. PostHog iterates quickly, as illustrated in its Changelog. The most recent month as I write this (October 2025) had over 50 changes shipped, or roughly the same amount GA4 shipped in its first two years as a product. That's an unfair comparison since that includes all aspects of the PostHog platform, not just web and product analytics, but it's still impressive. That speed of change is great if you have a new feature you've been looking for it to add, but it can also add to complexity due to changing functionality.

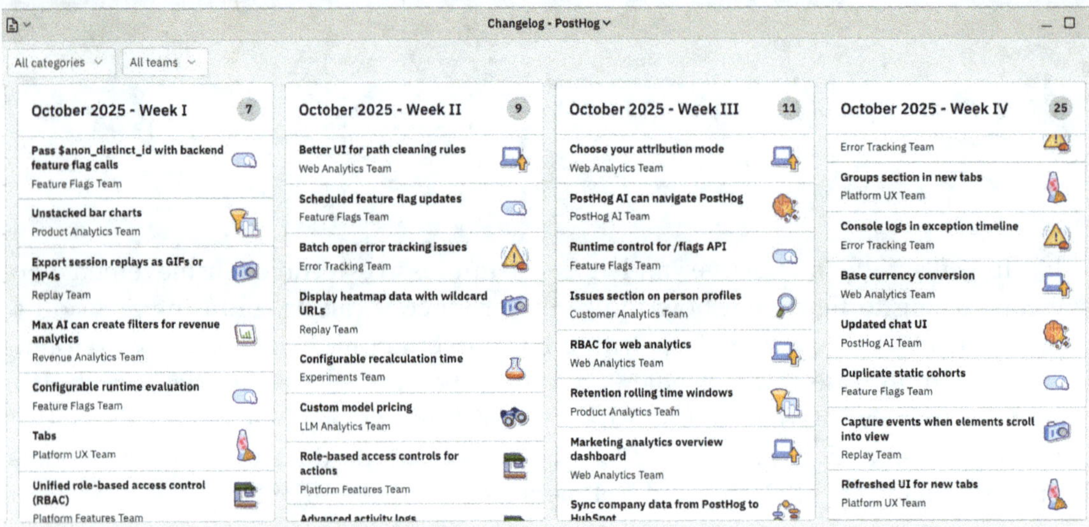

As we talked about in the GA4 chapter (Chapter 19), "changes" don't necessarily mean the changes you want—but when looking at what PostHog has launched, it seems like it includes many good features and requests from the community.

A lot of change is not what we expect to see from an "enterprise" product, which are typically very stable. Is PostHog ready for the enterprise level? While the reporting and dashboarding features are solid and richly featured, they are not quite as deep or bulletproof as the top-tier report-building options like Adobe Analytics Workspace. The data for large reports also sometimes returned a bit slowly in comparison to its enterprise competitors like Adobe, Piano, and Amplitude. This may be due to architectural differences, or could simply be growing pains within PostHog.

In investigating uptime, I found that PostHog had the weakest numbers measured over the last 90 days vs. similar competitors (among those that disclosed uptime percentages on public status pages).

90-Day Publicly Reported Uptime

	Reporting Interface	Data Collection	Data Processing
PostHog (US cloud)	99.83%	99.98%	99.52%
Amplitude	99.96%	100%	n/a
Mixpanel	99.99%	100%	n/a
Piano	99.96%	100%	99.94%
Piwik PRO Core	100%	100%	100%

"Data collection" is by far the worst kind of downtime, and all tools did well here, though PostHog did have a little downtime. Reporting interface downtime means you can't pull your numbers. Certainly frustrating, but you can come back later. When data collection is down, it means you are missing events that likely can't be recovered. "Data processing" being down means the data is just delayed, but you will eventually be able to see it. Not all platforms report on these delays.

If 99%, 99.9%, and 99.99% all seem basically the same, consider this table:

Availability	Downtime per Month
99%	7.3 hours
99.9%	44 minutes
99.99%	4.4 minutes

In PostHog's case, that 99.83% of reporting uptime meant that during those 90 days, the reporting interface was unavailable for around 3.5 hours. In case this amount of downtime makes you start to think about self-hosting, I would not recommend that path in most cases.

While PostHog is open source, not all features are released as open, and it does not, in general, promote self-hosting. It publishes a decision tree about self-hosting (https://posthog.com/docs/self-host) where nearly all decision paths end up with its cloud-hosted version. PostHog is a very large and complex piece of software that you shouldn't jump into self-hosting without understanding what you are getting into. While a Dockerized version of PostHog certainly makes installation much easier, consider that the container includes powerful back-end applications like Kafka, ZooKeeper, ClickHouse, Redis, and Postgres. By self-hosting, you are also committing to maintaining those. Compare that to Matomo, which is intended to be easily used with existing shared hosting that likely already has PHP and MySQL.

Finally, those of us coming from the "measure" marketing analytics community will also not find much discussion or activity about PostHog in the community to date. No community-developed GTM templates, few mentions at analytics conferences, no dedicated events, etc. It is more popular in the open source developer community, but even there, PostHog has shied away from running events.

If you have a team with significant technical aptitude and are looking for user analytics across a whole application, you are going to love PostHog. If you are looking for *just* web and marketing analytics and are focused on acquisition or attribution, look elsewhere. If you enjoy working within a highly flexible and quickly evolving platform, and reading some detailed (and quirky) documentation sounds like fun, then PostHog! If you work within an enterprise organization where your boss wants to have a sales rep walk them through your onboarding and meet up at the yearly conference, then perhaps not.

CHAPTER 33 - CROWD-SOURCED OPINIONS

You've read my opinions on 15 different tools, but what does the rest of the internet commentariat think? In addition to my own testing and discussions with experts, for this edition of this book, I'm including aggregated crowd-sourced opinions.

These opinions were sourced from a set of posts and comments from Reddit and Y Combinator's Hacker News. I searched both of those sites for any mention of tools on our list, including GA. From a dataset of approximately 450,000 posts and comments, I narrowed that down to 3,500 that were discussions of the tools, not just passing mentions or low-relevance matches.

From that smaller list, I... :

- counted the mentions of each tool.
- assigned a 1–4 rating via OpenAI GPT for each comment that expressed an opinion. 1 was the lowest, 4 was the highest. 3 was the modal rating and represents an "acceptable" or "ok" rating from the user.
- also used AI for an aggregate opinion summary from the raw posts.

Volume-wise, it should be no surprise that GA is the most discussed. It was actually surprising to me that it wasn't out further in front.

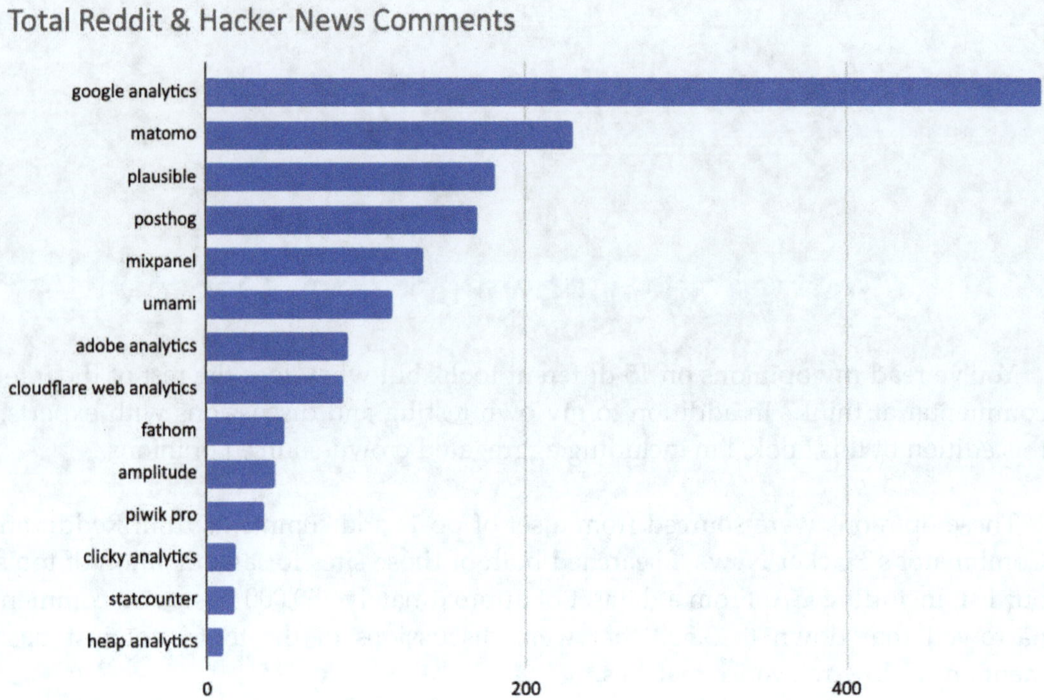

Beyond GA, we saw a lot of talk about Matomo, Plausible, and PostHog—all of which are open source. As the dataset was composed of comments from the developer-oriented Hacker News and Reddit, it shouldn't be surprising to see open source tools among the most discussed. We should also keep in mind that highly searchable terms like "matomo" and "posthog" could also lead to over-representation in the dataset. If someone had mentioned just "adobe" or "CJA," we might not have captured that user's comments. Piano Analytics didn't have enough mentions to be included (possibly because of its historical EU focus, or the tool's renaming from AT Internet).

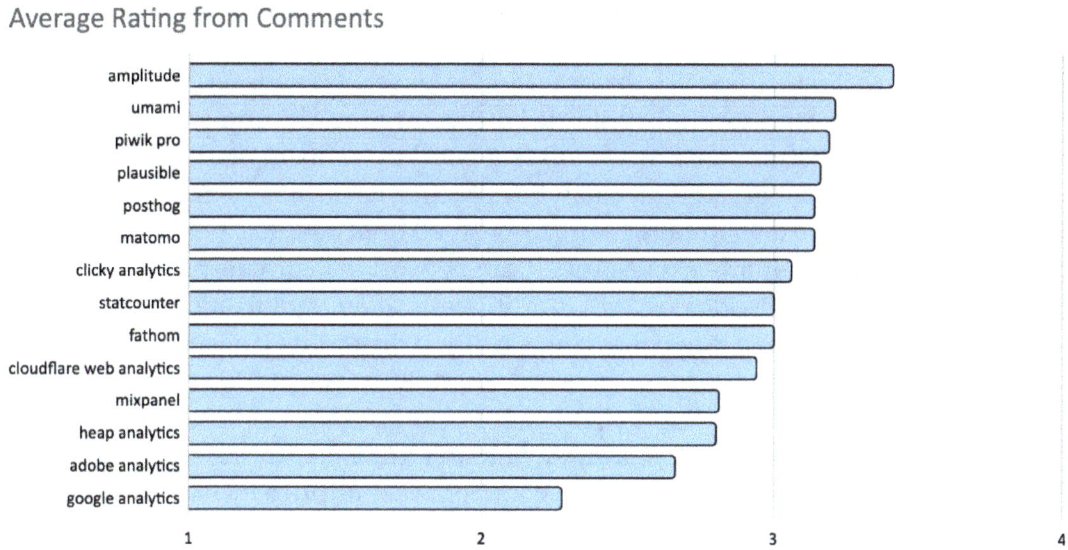

Folks... you read it here first, people don't like GA4!

But seriously, this analysis does show that most tools had averages approaching an "ok" rating overall from users, which is great news. As much as we all might gripe about tools, there are more people giving positive reviews than negative (aside from GA4 and WordPress Jetpack—which people hated even more than GA4). Adobe also did not receive strong marks from the crowd, though it was significantly ahead of GA4.

Who did well? Other than Umami (which I did not previously review), the crowd's top picks match my own from the first edition of this book: Amplitude, Piwik PRO, Plausible, and PostHog.

Since the point of this crowd analysis is to provide a diversity of opinions beyond my own, let me call out some of the cases where the crowd and I differed.

The crowd focused on self-hosting. They preferred self-hosted solutions and reviewed them based on the ease, cost, and efficiency of hosting. As discussed in Chapter 10 - Self-Hosting, I argue that self-hosting is a relatively niche solution, and in most cases, cloud-hosting should be the choice. The crowd did not agree with me here (though again, the consider the dataset source).

The crowd highlighted positive customer support experiences from many of the vendors. Matomo, Plausible, and Fathom were mentioned very positively, whereas only Google was given an overall negative rating for support. Community-based support, such as that offered by many of the open source tools, was given mixed reviews. For example, PostHog was given good reviews for its responsiveness to the community and the depth of its documentation, but also, some users found the community-based questions to be a confusing method.

The crowd was highly price-sensitive. I'd love to proclaim something like, "$9/mo. for Plausible or $40/mo. for Piwik PRO is a good investment, and if you undervalue the tool, you may undervalue the analytics practice itself." It's clear the crowd doesn't agree, and they have a valid point. For many small organizations with limited budgets, any new recurring monthly expense at all can be hard to justify (especially considering how GA normalized the idea of free). Additionally, if an organization isn't utilizing its analytics, how much is a pageview count really worth to it? Collecting analytics data without doing any analysis doesn't provide good ROI, even at $40/mo.

People love to get free stuff, and they hate to struggle with their stakeholders over budget. There were also many negative comments about price increases and big jumps in cost from free tiers to paid ones. That's understandable as well; if a tool has a free plan to 100k MTU and the next step is a $500/mo., when you hit user number 100,001, that can be very frustrating. Especially if you've invested a lot of time and effort into a platform that you may all of a sudden struggle to afford.

The crowd was not keen on "functional but outdated" UIs. I don't mind if a tool (e.g., Matomo, Clicky) doesn't have the prettiest or most modern UI, but I can find the stuff I need. Not all users agree with me, and maybe you don't either. In particular, the Hacker News crowd was keen to jump on newer products.

How should you consider these opinions? Or more broadly, how should you interpret any commentary you read about a particular tool? It can be hard to find commentary online that is both unbiased and well-informed.

The answer is, of course, to put on the same analytical thinking hat that we use when we normally look at numbers:

- Consider the source and quality of the data.
- Consider the statistical power of the dataset.
- Look at in-depth samples of the raw data.
- Be wary of your own biases.

CONCLUSION

There's a very old adage in tech: "Nobody ever got fired for buying IBM." This dates to the early days of computing, when IBM held a seemingly unassailable stranglehold on the industry. In the 1960s and 1970s, IBM dominated IT much more thoroughly than any of today's giants like Facebook, Apple, Microsoft, Google, etc. In 1975, IBM had over 288,000 employees—more than any of the aforementioned giants have now—in an era when the overall size of the industry was much smaller (Amazon has many more employees for obvious reasons). IBM was all of FAANG rolled into one monolith, at least in regard to the tech sides of those companies.

One meaning behind that IBM quote is that the market dominator is always the safe pick. However, it can also be read that the opposite may be true. It warns that, although following the crowd and conventional wisdom can keep you out of trouble with your bosses, it's also a narrow view that puts self-interest ahead of deep thought and investigation.

IBM is still a huge and successful company, but it now has to compete on more equal terms with everyone else, and the same should be true of Google. GA could still be the best choice for you, but I hope I've given you useful insight into how to evaluate alternative products beyond simply picking the default choice for no other reason than convention or "best practice."

The tech industry has a tendency to believe that paradigmatic change will happen faster than it actually does. Small changes do occur rapidly, but the underlying fundamentals stay relatively consistent and shift slowly. Even with the explosion of generative AI, a generational-level change in tech, organizations aren't moving nearly as quickly as tech leaders have suggested.

Evaluating and discussing tools can be fun, and the choice of tool is important. Ultimately, how you implement and use a tool is the more important part. Having a clear tracking plan, a robust reporting methodology, and a strong data culture will take you much further than the marginal benefits of tool A vs. tool B.

We spent the first half of this book going over a wide range of technical and strategic topics, from how to pick a pricing model to the basics of server-side tracking and bot filtering. While I'm sure that many readers will go straight to my reviews of the individual tools they are most interested in (a totally valid way to use this book!), I hope that it's also clear how the topics covered in the first half are what drive the content of the reviews in the second half.

Analytics will continue to change, but the analyst's role as someone who carefully applies critical thinking skills to create clear and well-considered communications will not.

Ultimately, when selecting a tool, I'd like you to be thinking first and foremost about how to turn your business requirements and constraints into a decision-making process. This process isn't about becoming an expert in a bunch of different tools or picking the tool with the most impressive feature set and technology. It's about understanding what's needed now, what might be needed in the future, and what solution best fits.

Thanks and Acknowledgments

Writing a book is, somehow, both a highly solitary endeavor and one that requires a lot of support from others. I'm very grateful for the support I received from the first edition, and would like to thank everyone who read that version, as without your support, I wouldn't have produced this second edition.

Specifically for the second edition, I'd also like to thank:

Andrew Packer, my wife Andrea, my parents, Mac Liaw, Tim Wilson, Jenn Kunz, Josh Silverbauer, Juliana Jackson, as well as my reviewers: Bogdan Nazaruk, Mehdi Oudjida, and Fosca Fimiani.

www.ingramcontent.com/pod-product-compliance
Lightning Source LLC
LaVergne TN
LVHW080047210926
848481LV00011B/3296